Our Jimi

Our Jimi

An Intimate Portrait of Jimi Hendrix through
Interviews with Friends and Colleagues

AIDAN PREWETT

political animal
PRESS

Political Animal Press
Toronto • Chicago
www.politicalanimalpress.com

Distributed by the University of Toronto Press
www.utpdistribution.com

Cataloguing data available from Library and Archives Canada
ISBN 978-1895131-53-6 (paperback)
ISBN 978-1895131-54-3 (ebook)

Typeset in Garamond, Bookmania, and Futura
Cover image © Bruce Fleming

Table of Contents

FOR QUINCY – MY LITTLEST WING

Intro

"HE DESERVES TO BE HONORED," Bob Kulick said in his interview regarding his time with Jimi Hendrix. In our interview of September 2019, Bob Kulick provided one of the most intriguing perspectives on the life of Jimi Hendrix that I had ever heard. Back in 1966, Kulik was a sixteen-year-old kid playing guitar for teeny-boppers during daytime sessions at the Café Wha? in New York City when Jimi Hendrix walked in and changed his life forever.

The friendship that Bob formed with Jimi meant a lot to him. *Means* a lot. His sentiment – that Jimi should be honored and celebrated – was echoed by every voice in this book. This is a collection of entirely new interviews with the people who knew Jimi best – his friends, colleagues, and family. Through their words we are able to catch a glimpse of the world Jimi lived in, the way he lived, the people he chose to surround himself with, and some fascinating highlights of the time he spent with them. The enclosed interviews offer detailed, intimate insight into *moments* with Jimi. These specific incidents and anecdotes are recalled with great clarity, because – let's face it – a moment spent with Jimi Hendrix is likely to be a memorable one. Fifty years after Jimi's passing, we are treated to a collection of intimate, personal stories of his life, music, career, and character. It is this last item, Jimi's character, that will receive our special attention.

In terms of interview subjects, this book features the voice of nearly every presently living person who enjoyed a close relationship with Jimi. Kathy Etchingham, Roger Mayer, Keith Altham, Eddie Kramer, and Jimi's brother Leon are all featured within. These are the people who spent the most time with Jimi. Their stories are full of rich detail and insightful observations and, by virtue of the interview format, we're able to hear their distinctive voices as they bring to life a realistic picture of what time spent with Jimi was like.

We also hear other voices – those who provide completely new perspectives on the Hendrix story. These are people who spent less time with Jimi, but who often recall very specific anecdotes involving him. As their time with him was briefer, their moments with Jimi Hendrix have stayed with them as treasured memories. A happy and unexpected turn in my research occurred when *Rolling Stone* journalist Anthony DeCurtis provided a hot tip: "You should speak to Janis Ian – she's got some great Hendrix stories." With Anthony's recommendation, I quickly found myself speaking with Janis Ian, who provided some wonderful recollections indeed, which are of course recorded herein. Another great story was revealed when photographer Bruce Fleming told me about shooting the cover for *Are You Experienced?* and then later hosting Jimi for Christmas dinner. And still another when I learned that Jimi gifted Al Kooper one of his Fender Stratocasters. Many of these interviews feature moments that made the hair on the back of my neck stand on end. At times, it felt almost like being there with Jimi himself.

Several major figures in Jimi's life have passed away in the last decades, including managers Chas Chandler and Mike Jeffery, and bandmates Noel Redding and Mitch

Mitchell. Here, we recognize and explore their important contributions to Jimi's story through recollections of them by Jimi's other friends and colleagues.

Each interview in the book is presented according to the timeline of Jimi's career. That is, interview subjects are introduced approximately in the order in which they first met Jimi. Our focus is on Jimi's close relationships as he came into his own as an artist. We explore Jimi's life from his first moments in Greenwich Village through to his final jam at Ronnie Scott's Jazz Club in September 1970. The only exception to this general plan is an interview with Jimi's brother, Leon Hendrix, which is more contemplative in nature. That interview has been saved for the final chapter. It is, in general, a characteristic of the interview format that we are invited to share in the *feeling* of what it was like to be there. We are invited to spend time with friends of Jimi. We accordingly gain a sense of what it was like to *know* him.

Ultimately, this book is not just a portrait of Jimi. It is also a portrait of the people who he chose to spend time with, the people he cared about, and it is a collection of their stories. Many of these stories have never been written about or published before. Some of these stories have been touched on but glossed over in the narratives of more traditional biographies. This book is not a traditional biography. There are many books available that can set you straight on where Jimi was at any given moment in the course of his lifetime. Here, on the other hand, we are trying to capture a living portrait of Jimi's world, from the people who shared it with him. These are the people he called friends – people who can, in their own words, provide a sense of what it was like to be regarded that way by Jimi and to call him a friend in return.

I was surprised by how willing and open Jimi's friends are to talk about him. It was clear that several were relieved to read the proposal that I sent in the hope of securing their participation, and to learn that this project is a celebration; this book takes no interest in rumor, nor does it seek scandal. The proposal's sample chapter, which included Bob Kulick's interview, provided a sense of the angle I was going for. *He deserves to be honored.* Here we honor Jimi by speaking frankly and honestly, drawing out an accurate portrayal. One by one, Jimi's friends let down their walls and allowed me in to ask more questions. I soon found myself speaking with people that I had previously only dreamed of meeting. I had been trying to get through to Eddie Kramer's people for almost ten years. He is someone I have wanted to speak with for every music documentary I have ever been involved with. So, I was thrilled to finally speak to him – and even more thrilled when he gave me significantly more time than I was initially told I would be granted. This was a common occurrence; people could see that they were speaking to a deeply interested, slightly nervous fan. By way of encouragement, they gave me their best stories. And for that, I am profoundly grateful.

The people interviewed here loved Jimi. The stories they have chosen and been encouraged to share are stories of enjoyment, mischief, humor, melancholia, and the rock 'n' roll lifestyle. Jimi is painted as a real person – not a god. Here we honor Jimi through accurate portrayal from primary sources: his friends. *He deserves to be honored.* That phrase has remained with me ever since my conversation with Bob Kulick – one of the first interviews conducted for this project.

As mentioned previously, back in 1966, Kulick had struck up a friendship with a then-unknown Jimi Hendrix, and he watched in awe as his new friend and guitar hero was snapped up by the record business. Bob Kulick is a unique voice in this book. He was there right at the start – as a friend of Jimi's – and he can illustrate that period in Jimi's life with great clarity. With Bob, we get to *be* the sixteen-year-old guitar nut who suddenly gets to hang out with Jimi Hendrix, both before and after he made it. Those four years of Jimi's life, from the period at the Café Wha? to his last days in London, are central to this portrait of him. Here, we learn who Jimi was through his relationships at the time of his greatest creative peak. The years from 1966-1970 cover the time from his discovery as an artist through his ascent within the music business. These are the years where he reached maturity and achieved his most important work.

Beyond all the remarkable insights into Jimi's character that were gained by interviewing his friends and colleagues, there was still another wonderful part of putting this book together: the research. That consisted in trawling through the ever-expanding body of Hendrix literature to piece together some parts of the story that I have always found confusing – like the timeline of events for the Band of Gypsys/Gypsy Sun and Rainbows. I have tried to condense my findings into the introductory and closing paragraphs for each chapter. There are still gaps, of course; by its very nature, this book unfolds as a collection of stories, sometimes connected, sometimes not. My hope is that this book will encourage you to check out some of the great linear Hendrix books. My personal favorite is *Jimi Hendrix: Electric Gypsy* by Harry Shapiro and Caesar Glebbeek. I have included several other recommendations as an appendix.

On a personal note, I first heard Jimi Hendrix when I was a fourteen-year-old kid, a young guitarist myself. As it has been for many guitarists, that first listening was like an explosion in my mind. I spent many hours trying to emulate his playing. I never got anywhere near it. But since that time, I have wanted to know: *what was it like to kick back and share stories with Jimi Hendrix?* Through conducting these interviews with the people who spent time with Jimi, I feel like I now have some idea. Through this book, I hope that you will, too.

But first – before the interviews – a quick account of the journey Jimi took before he showed up in the lives of our subjects.

Some Background

JIMI WAS BORN JOHNNY ALLEN HENDRIX in Seattle on November 27, 1942. His father Al was overseas serving in the Second World War at the time and was unable to return home until his son was three years old. When Al got back, he talked things over with his wife Lucille and they changed little Johnny Allen's name. He became James Marshall Hendrix, after Al's brother Leon Marshall Hendrix who had died in 1932. Lucille and Al's relationship was a passionate one; it was often marked by heated arguments. They struggled with money and with alcohol, and they separated in 1951. Jimi and his brother Leon stayed with Al.

Jimi had four siblings, three of whom were adopted shortly after their births. Throughout his childhood, Jimi lived with his brother Leon in difficult circumstances and the Welfare Department was frequently called in. Al was forced to move around a lot, through boarding houses and short-term accommodations. Leon was placed in foster care on seven occasions, and the boys often found themselves "tippy-toeing over the border" to stay with their grandmother in Vancouver.

Jimi was a quiet, well-behaved child, but he never took much interest in school. He used to carry a broom around with him and strum it as if it were a guitar. Later, Al would find pieces of straw scattered around Jimi's bedroom. He was supposed to have been sweeping the house.

Al took on many odd jobs during Jimi's childhood. He went from a steel mill to pumping gas, then to cleaning and to general handyman work. At one stage he was employed to clean out the estate of a recently deceased person, whereupon he found a one-stringed ukulele. He brought it home to Jimi. Jimi forgot about the broom handle.

In 1958, when Jimi was 15 years old, his mother died of cirrhosis of the liver. Jimi and Leon were unable to attend the funeral. The loss hit Jimi very hard. He was fond of his mother's outgoing, carefree nature, and the freedom afforded him on the occasional visits to her, away from his usual residence with Al.

At this time, Al thought it appropriate to buy Jimi a guitar. It was a cheap acoustic, but Jimi loved it and started a band called The Velvetones. He soon realized the importance of volume in live performances and convinced Al to trade in the acoustic for a Supro Ozark solid body electric guitar. He spent hours practicing and found his first paid gig with a band called the Rocking Kings at nightclubs around Seattle.

In early 1961 Jimi found himself in trouble with the law. It's often been reported that he took a ride in a car with a friend in a stolen car, and the pair were later arrested. Joy-riding in cars may well have happened, but the actual police report from the incident includes a written confession from Jimi. He and a friend had used a coat-hanger to purloin clothing through the broken back window of a Seattle garment store. In any case, eighteen-year-old Jimi was offered a common choice for young offenders: the army or prison. In May 1961, Jimi started eight weeks of basic training and was assigned to the 101st Airborne Division. The 101st was a celebrated unit which had parachuted behind enemy lines on D-Day in 1944.

But Jimi's career as a paratrooper was short-lived. While jamming at a servicemen's club, Jimi met bassist Billy Cox. Together they formed the King Kasuals and decided they'd had enough of the army. The army also decided that it had had enough of Jimi. He was granted a Discharge Under Honorable Conditions in June 1962, after which he headed for Nashville.

Billy soon joined him, and as the King Kasuals they followed the Chitlin' Circuit throughout the Eastern states. The circuit was a well-established tour route for black performers and audiences, covering Boston to Tampa, Chicago to Houston. The name "chitlin'" refers to stewed pig intestine – the only food that the performers were likely to afford. Performance venues on the circuit were well-known for their exploitative practices, and Jimi and Billy joined the long tradition of artists who struggled to feed themselves between gigs, as had Robert Johnson, Son House, and Charlie Patton before them.

It was a difficult life, and the band soon broke up to pursue other ventures. But by this stage, Jimi had developed into an excellent guitarist. He secured further work on the circuit backing the Isley Brothers, Ike & Tina Turner, and Little Richard. In competition with these big names, performers on the circuit often employed flashy stage antics. Jimi took note of this and began refining his own unique stage presence. Little Richard soon fired Jimi – he didn't want to be upstaged. But he hadn't been paying Jimi properly anyway. By early 1966, aged 23, Jimi was still barely making enough money to eat. He decided that he might fare a little better in New York. So he formed a new band called Jimmy James and the Blue Flames and headed for Greenwich Village.

Bob Kulick
Café Wha?

JIMI'S NEW BAND soon found themselves auditioning at the Café Wha? near Washington Square Park. This was the same venue Bob Dylan first appeared at when he arrived in New York in 1961. The band took up a residency and was soon making minor ripples in the New York music scene. The whole area was a happening place for the counterculture at the time. Keith Richards' girlfriend, Linda Keith, met Jimi and was particularly enamored with him. In July, she convinced Chas Chandler, bass player for the Animals, to go down and see Jimmy James perform. The Animals were winding down and Chandler was on the lookout for an act to manage. He found one – and along with his business partner Mike Jeffery, he took Jimi Hendrix on the next step of his journey.

As a sixteen-year-old guitarist for the afternoon house band at Café Wha?, Bob Kulick witnessed Jimi's audition, his pre-fame performances, Chas Chandler's entry into the picture, and even some later interplay between Hendrix and Eric Clapton. Kulick was taken under Jimi's wing – the dream of every rock guitarist of the last half-century.

Some years later, in 1973, Bob would audition for an emerging New York band called Kiss. He went on just before Ace Frehley. And while Ace would get the gig at that time, Bob would maintain a friendship with the band and collaborate with them in years to come. His guitar playing is featured on four Kiss albums, as well as other gold and platinum records with Paul Stanley, Lou Reed, Meatloaf, Diana Ross, and others. Between 1996 and 2004, Kulick co-produced Motörhead, with whom he won a Grammy in 2005 for Best Metal Performance with *Whiplash*.

Bob's time with Jimi has barely been touched on in the Hendrix literature, as their time together was perhaps not as lengthy as some of Jimi's other relationships. But in Bob I found the touching story of a young musician captivated by the talent of a generous and prodigious player. Bob's story holds many enlightening details about Jimi.

BOB KULICK: It was a really great scene in Greenwich Village in the mid-sixties. It was much like Haight-Ashbury and the Sunset Strip – you know, anywhere on a Friday or Saturday night, all the kids would come down there. They were mainly hippies. People who went to the coffee houses went to the Café Au Go Go, went to the Café Wha?, went to the Night Owl – the Lovin' Spoonful was playing at the Night Owl. James Taylor was playing at the Night Owl. There was tremendous talent being showcased. At the Café Wha? where I met Jimi, Richie Havens and Richard Pryor were the two main headline acts that they had. Richie Havens went on to Woodstock as a star songwriter and singer, and sang on hit commercials. One of the greatest singers I ever met. The guy played an open-tuned guitar, and his hands were so big that he would just use his thumb to fret the whole fingerboard. And his attack was so heavy that he would break strings all the time.

So my band – the Random Blues Band – we played Saturday and Sunday afternoons for teeny-bopper kids. Fifteen-year-olds. The place did not have alcohol. It was a tuna salad sandwich and a soda pop – one of those kind of places. Ice cream sodas. You walked downstairs into this club with a stage in the middle. It held about 200.

So one day my band is playing. It was a Saturday afternoon, and this other band was loading stuff in to audition. They start bringing their gear on stage, and I notice this black guy – he's asking, "How do I hook up two of these amp bottoms?" I'm standing there and I'm like – "How do you do *that*?" We couldn't play at that volume. We were using small amps – tiny club. They had those amps that had reverb on them.

I do remember when Jimi got up there to play, it was a life-changing moment. Because he was *so far* above anyone's talent level on the guitar than I had ever seen. *Seen*. So the guy gets up there, and he's playing 'Hey Joe' with his teeth. Playing the solo with his teeth. People are freaking out. He did a version of 'Third Stone from the Sun'. His use of the whammy bar – back in the day, there was no device that would keep a guitar in tune when you did *what he did* to it. He would literally be able to bend the strings into tune, or if the low strings were out, he'd play the high strings only. If the high strings were out, he'd play the low strings only. And then after the song, he'd quickly tune up – *bom bom bom bom bom bom* – an E chord. It never bothered him at all. I never saw him show any frustration at tuning.

So he got hired after the audition at the Café Wha?. And there he was opening up for Richie Havens and Richard Pryor. We were the last band on that day. He was the first band up at night. He's tuning up in the dressing room, standing there. I'm like, *I can't believe I'm standing here with this guy*, you know. And he busts a string. So I was like, "Excuse me," – 'cos I could see he was panicked – *I don't have any other strings!* You know, he wasn't rich. He was a musician. So I said, "Look – here's a set of strings. What do you need? An E or a B…" And he was just like "Hey, thanks – oh, what's your name?" I said Bob. And he shook my hand, and I said, "Keep the whole set, just in case". He was just like, *"Great, thanks."* So I provided service to him. So he remembered me. And from then on, we had sort of an ongoing thing. He taught me a lot of things. Me specifically. I was very lucky. He came out one night to watch us play and sat down right in front of me. I finished the song, and I looked down, and I said, "Please don't sit here – it's totally intimidating." He said to me, "I learn something from every band I see – good, bad or indifferent." That's what he said to me. So he sat there and watched us – I'm sure it was the *bad*. But the fact that the guy – he saw me play. We played 'Hey Joe' right in front him. *"Is it okay if we play 'Hey Joe'?" "Sure, why not?".* So yeah, my band, the Random Blues Band, that I had at this place – it was a life-changing event.

aidan prewett: Is there one particular moment of time that you spent with Jimi that really stuck with you over the years?

BK: There were several. All of it was kind of surreal. Hanging out there one night – I loved seeing Jimi play. It was just – it was like seeing somebody from another planet. Nobody used the whammy bar like that before him. And he had pedals, and two amps together. It was a *wall of sound* unlike anything anybody had ever heard. The band was like – nobody paid any attention to the rest of the band, *yet.* The other guitar player was Randy California from Spirit. And there were a couple of guys from the Raggamuffins. That was the name of the band – the Raggamuffins. So Chas Chandler showed up that night. I'm not sure if it was

Mike Jeffery that was with him or not. I did not know what Mike Jeffery looked like at the time. So I'm not clear on that. But I clearly saw Chas Chandler's malt – his whatever it was – egg cream, or soda pop, or some kind of concoction there. *"Uh, the ice cream soda please, thank you..."* He dropped it right in his lap when Hendrix played. I saw it. He dropped it *right in his lap*. Well, cut to the chase here – three weeks later, *"Bye everybody."* *"We'll see you when you get back, Jimi..."* So Jimi James went off to England, played in front of Paul McCartney, John Lennon, Jeff Beck, Eric Clapton, Pete Townshend, and all the rest. They all threw the towel in, and he became a huge star. And then he came back, and they stuffed him on the bill with the Monkees.

So after the Monkees thing – he was fired after a few concerts with them – I got a phone call from one of the guys from the Café Wha?. He's like, "I just got off the phone with Jimi. He's inviting five or six guys up to the hotel tonight, and he wanted to know if you wanted to come." I said, "Are you kidding me?" So we went up to the Warwick Hotel, five or six of us. And Noel Redding was there, he introduced me to Noel and Mitch Mitchell. They were very pasty-faced English guys. Like they never saw the sun. I was just like – it was close to when I worked with Lou Reed. He kinda looked dead. Pasty-faced – you know, white! People say, you know – *you're pale*. But pale is one thing. *White* is something else. And they were smoking some DMT or DET, which is like, grass or hash loaded up with some other stuff. As I recall. I have to say that now because people – *"That's not true. He said an untruth."* *"He said As I Recall".* So I'll give you the *as I recall.*

So Jimi came back, and we went up to the Warwick Hotel. I think that was the night he got fired – he was in a great mood, 'cos he didn't want to play in front of twelve-year-olds and their parents who were mortified at the guy who was putting the guitar between his legs and sticking his tongue out at them. You know, I'm sure it was like, *ahhhhhhh!* You know – twelve-year-olds waiting for the Monkees.

He had rented a turntable – a 45 turntable. He had a stack of 45's that he brought back from England. So he was just like, "This thing isn't really loud, let's just sit on the floor and gather round. I'll play some of the stuff that I heard – I think you guys will get a kick out of hearing this." So we're sitting there and he's playing this, that and the other thing. We're smoking a joint. I'm sitting right next to him. We're passing the joint around. Noel's over *there*, they're hanging out. Everybody's having some wine. He pulls the song that he was playing off and puts on 'Tales of Brave Ulysses'. Halfway through the song, he sees me smiling and he's like, "You know who this is?" and I'm like, "Yeah, it's Eric Clapton." So after the song he looked at me and said, "You *know* who this is?" I'm like, "Yeah. Yeah – exactly. Uh, Eric Clapton played with Yardbirds, and Eric Clapton played with John Mayall, and he is a phenomenal blues guitar player. And Hendrix said, "He's a better guitar player than me." I said, "I wouldn't look at it that way – you play totally different. He's a *blues* player. But – there it was. 'Tales of Brave Ulysses', that wah-wah pedal thing. The look on his face. I'll never forget. That ending solo – *diddly diddly diddly* – that fast torrent of notes at the end of 'Tales of Brave Ulysses'.

They jammed once at my loft – Jimi Hendrix and Eric Clapton. Hendrix played bass. Eric Clapton played guitar. It was four o'clock on a weekday night. They couldn't get a taxi. So my friend who lived in New York played drums, he opened the door and said, "I met them in a club, they were hanging out..." And he brought them back to my loft, and they played. Clapton played my Epiphone Riviera. So it's a walk down memory lane for me.

I met Eric Clapton at one of his gigs, backstage. This is when Clapton had his really really *really* long hair – '67, '68 – with the moustache. And he was playing that painted Gibson SG. One that belonged to Jackie Lomax. We shook hands – my friend, his name was Hash. Hash Howard. He introduced me to Clapton and he said, "That was Bob's guitar that you played that night when you jammed with Jimi Hendrix." "Oh, hey mate, I really liked that guitar. It's a lovely guitar. Nice to meet you." And he shook my hand – his fingers were so long, they passed by the palm of my hand. His fingers are tremendously long. Which is part of the reason he's such a good guitar player. Here's an example: on the cover of the John Mayall record *Bluesbreakers*, you see his fingers. He's holding a cartoon magazine called *Beano* – as I recall. And you can see how long his fingers are.

aP: Are we talking like Robert Johnson long? Are we talking that length?

BK: Thinner. Like I'm saying about Richie Havens. I remember getting the programme for the Muhammed Ali/Joe Frazier fight. And they had the size of their hands there, so you could put your hand on it to see how much bigger their hands were. Well, Clapton's hands were definitely bigger than mine. His fingers were long, that's the thing. That made it easier to play. Easier to reach some of those notes. Yeah – we think of it as only hand-eye coordination, but part of your hand is the length of your fingers.

You know, there are guitars that are made with – well, this is for a small-handed person. With a flatter neck, not as much of a baseball bat. And there are guys that preferred that – *"I prefer the frets closer together"*, close to their finger lines. Everybody's different.

That's why – with Jimi, let's put it this way – you could take Jimi Hendrix's setup, and plug a right-handed Stratocaster into it – you'd sound nothing like him. Period. And so it was all in his fingers, and all in his brain. And he was a tremendously nice guy, and taken from us way too soon.

aP: Can we go back to Café Wha? for a second, 'cos it's completely blown my mind that you knew him both before and after – so let's say, we're at the Café Wha? 1966 – Jimi hasn't even met Chas Chandler yet. I can't believe you saw them meet. But let's say this is before Chas is even on the scene – you're sitting back, you're smoking a joint with Jimi – what do you talk about?

BK: Music. Girls. The guy was a stud. You could play jump rope with that thing. He was a stud, he fucked everything in sight. Seriously, he lived the lifestyle. So it's not – he didn't put his stage clothes on, you know, like Billy Gibbons. He's not putting his stage clothes on. That's *him*. That's him. I mean, I feel so bad, that a whole generation of people might have never got to see him. I feel so lucky. That's what I always say, you know – when my time's up, I wouldn't trade my life for anybody's. I wouldn't. I mean that. To know Jimi Hendrix. To *know* – God – Holy shit – that he knew my name. That he knew who I was. That I provided service to him. He was my idol. That I saw, that I knew. You know – Jimmy Page, Jeff Beck, Eric Clapton, George Harrison, I didn't know them. I met Eric Clapton. That's it. Never met Jimmy Page, never met Jeff Beck. Never met George Harrison. So, at least two of the gods. But especially Jimi.

25

aP: To have him know who you are, and to invite you back after the Monkees thing – it's incredible.

BK: You know – being in the right place at the right time, New York – to be around the caliber of musicians… Cream played Café Au Go Go. Hendrix played the Café Wha?. The list of bands from the Night Owl… Blues Magoos – my friend and former bandmate Peppy Castro from the Blues Magoos. The Lovin' Spoonful. James Taylor in a band called the Flying Machine, with Danny Cooch. Danny Corchmarr on Guitar. I wish your audience could have seen these bands. Because these bands mopped the floor with anything anybody does today. No one needs to fix their recordings. No one needs to give them inner-ears. No one needs to fucking hold their hands. This was the real talent. The *real* talent. Like James Taylor. Like Jimmy James. Like Jimmy James and the Blue Flames. That was the name of his band then. And he'd played with Little Richard. And the guy could play guitar behind his head. And in between his legs. You know – so it wasn't just that he was a great guitar player. If he sat down, he'd probably totally blow your mind. But he was a *showman*.

aP: Would you say Jimi was a charming person? How would you describe his personality?

BK: Jimi was a happy guy – he was a shy guy. He was not a mopey guy. He took the music seriously. We smoked joints together, and we had drinks together, we smoked cigarettes together. We hung out together. He was a mellow cat. He took it out on the guitar. He was very mellow – and for women in a very reclusive, seductive way. Mysterious. Back then, there wasn't AIDS, he probably screwed four or five girls a night. *As I recall.* I mean, I think. Maybe not. But possibly.

aP: Would not surprise me at all.

BK: I mean, I'm not saying I saw him do it. But I saw what was going on there. He was a big fan of women. I mean, I was 16 – he was 23 or so. As I recall. So, you know – I was having some fun on my own way, but Jimi was just like… *who could compete with that?* And I will say this – a unique thing about him at Café Wha? – They were all white bands playing during the day. But at night, it was Richie Havens, and Jimi, and Richard Pryor. All black people, with a white audience. People were better about that stuff then, I think. They recognized what talent was. Just like Sammy Davis, Jr. He married a white woman, and all of a sudden there was something wrong with Sammy Davis, Jr. That's disgusting. The man was as good a singer as Frank Sinatra and Dean Martin and the people that he sang with. He should never have been disrespected in any way, shape, or form. Anyway, I'm glad that people respect Jimi Hendrix. Because he is and was a god.

aP: Is there anything I've missed – something we haven't touched on that people should know about Jimi Hendrix?

BK: He deserves to be honored. He deserves for people to be able to say, *I saw this person play.* I feel bad for you that you never got to see him. Like the Beatles. I will add this – Jimi had the *magic.* Paul McCartney said on Stephen Colbert's show the other night – Stephen Colbert asked him, "To me, being a singer and a musician is kinda mysterious, it's kinda, almost like magic. What do you think?" You know what Paul McCartney said? "It *is* magic. It is." Jimi had that magic. And when he played in front of those people, he scared all of them. 'Cos he was as good or better than all of them.

. . .

Chas Chandler dropped his malt soda *right in his (own) lap*. That turned out to be a defining moment for the music industry. Chas approached Jimi as he came off stage and offered to fly him to England. Jimi said he'd think about it. He'd been screwed around by enough would-be impresarios on the Chitlin' Circuit to know – now – that a deal needed to be worked out properly. Jimi had learnt that lesson the hard way. When Chas returned three weeks later with a firm offer, he discovered that he would need to buy out two – or maybe even three – other contracts. Jimi had forgotten just how many pieces of paper he had signed as an overenthusiastic youngster.

The possibility of legal wrangling was a concern; previous commitments turned into some major complications. But Chas wasn't worried. He saw big things for Jimi. *Big* things.

Kathy Etchingham
London

Jimi touched down in London at 9am on Saturday September 24, 1966. He stepped off the plane and was delivered straight to his first jam, courtesy of Chas Chandler. Not far from the airport lived Zoot Money. Zoot was a major figure in the London music scene – he provided an open house for musicians to gather and jam at any hour of the day or night. Coming back from a tour or setting out on tour, everybody stopped by Zoot Money's place. Chas knew that Zoot's was the first place Jimi should be seen. The buzz started immediately.

Kathy Etchingham was upstairs asleep when Jimi arrived. She didn't meet him that morning, but Kathy was out at the Scotch of St James that night. Jimi was immediately drawn to her. Kathy and Jimi quickly became an item. The couple moved in with Chas Chandler and his girlfriend Lotte Lexon, a Swedish model. Their flat was in Montagu Square, Marylebone; Chas had leased it from Ringo Starr and it was later occupied by John Lennon and Yoko Ono. Jimi, Kathy, Chas, and Lotte shared the flat while the Jimi Hendrix Experience was gaining a foothold in the music world. Eighteen months later Jimi and Kathy moved out on their own to an apartment at 23 Brook Street in Mayfair, which became their base of operations.

Kathy Etchingham was the most stable element in Jimi's otherwise chaotic life, as several Hendrix biographers have put it. She was his most notable muse, providing inspiration for the songs 'The Wind Cries Mary', 'Foxy Lady', '1983… (A Merman I Should Turn to Be)', and 'Gypsy Eyes', among others. Kathy's memoir *Through Gypsy Eyes* provides an intimate portrait of her time with Jimi in Swinging London.

In 1997, Kathy organized for the installation of an English Heritage Blue Plaque for the Brook Street apartment in recognition of Jimi's contribution to the English music scene. In 2016 Jimi and Kathy's apartment opened as a museum called *Handel & Hendrix in London*. The baroque composer George Frideric Handel had actually lived in the adjoining apartment 200 years before Jimi and Kathy.

But as Jimi arrived at Zoot Money's house in September 1966, he had his whole career ahead of him. And he was about to meet the girl of his dreams.

KATHY ETCHINGHAM: I used to live in a flat above Zoot and Ronni Money – or George Money as I call him. I never call him Zoot – I spoke to him at Christmas and I still call him George. Jimi and Chas went down there and apparently Jimi tried to set up his guitar through some sort of speaker that Zoot had. They were making quite a din down there. But as a twenty-year-old, I slept through it. Anyway, Ronni came up because the bathroom was upstairs outside my room.

She came in and she said, "Are you awake? Are you awake?"

I said, "Oh…no…I didn't get in 'til four o'clock this morning."

And she said, "You should see this guy – he looks like the Wild Man of Borneo."

I said, "Oh, really…"

"Come downstairs!"

"No, no, no. I'm going back to sleep."

She said, "Oh well, we'll go down the Scotch later. Hopefully, he'll be playing down there."

"Fine – alright, Ron." And I went back to sleep. That was it.

And then later in the evening – 'cos we were always in and out of each other's places – we all went down to the Scotch together. When we walked in, the whole place was standing – basically silently – watching, all on the stairs going down, all in the bar and in the club area itself. Anyway, I worked my way down to the bottom – to where the club was – and he was just being brought off the stage by Chas.

The worry was that he didn't have a visa. He only had a seven-day entrance visa because they spun some story at immigration that he was coming to collect royalties. One of the roadies from the Animals carried Jimi's guitar through so that Jimi wasn't carrying a guitar. Chas was worried 'cos you're not supposed to work with or without pay.

So anyway, that's how we met, because I was already sitting around the table. There was Georgie Fame and his girlfriend of the time – Carmen. And there was Linda Keith, whom I didn't know at all. There was Ronni, me, George… Chas sat down, and then Jimi sat down next to Linda Keith. Anyway, we were all chatting and talking, and Chas was sort of explaining that this was a bit difficult because of the visa and everything. And at some point, Linda Keith got up and went to the loo, went upstairs.

And Jimi said, "Come over here a minute." So I went

over there and sat down where she'd been sitting, wondering what he had to say to me. And he said, "I think you're beautiful."

"Thank you," I said. And that was it.

I said, "I'd better go back to my seat."

"No." And he held onto my forearm.

So when Linda came back, she had no choice but to sit where I'd been sitting, because that was the only spare place. And that's when it all got a bit difficult, and she started speaking in a louder and louder voice. Chas tried to sort of intervene and say *look, keep it down; don't cause a fuss.* And then all of a sudden it occurred to Chas that *she's going to cause a problem and the police might be called. And Jimi's only here on a seven-day visa and she might spill the beans...*

So he said, "You! Jimi! Get back to the Hyde Park Towers Hotel!"

I said, "Well, where's that?"

And he said, "Bayswater! Lancaster Gate, Bayswater!"

I said, "Right, okay..."

And by this time, Linda was up on her feet smashing bottles and all sorts of things. And Ronni calling her a... well, Ronni came from Glasgow, tough-as-they-come. It was like coming from the Bronx; Hell's Kitchen or somewhere. They're very tough.

Anyway, we got out of there and we went up past Fortnum & Mason's, past Jermyn Street to Piccadilly. God, Jimi didn't know – or nobody'd schooled him that the traffic came from the opposite direction, and he stepped out into the road. A taxi was just going by and just winged him, just slightly. But I saw it – he had a coat on – and I pulled him back. So he just avoided being run over. That would have been the end of it.

I said, "No, you've got to look to your right – you've got to look to your right, not your left."

Anyway, eventually we got a taxi that wasn't engaged. I found one with its orange light on and hailed it and told them where to go. We went into the hotel and went into the sitting area – the guests' area. And then – I don't know – we got talking. We were probably on our own for about twenty minutes; twenty-five minutes, something like that. And then bit-by-bit they started filtering back…Eric Burdon was amongst it. We just sat there most of the night, 'cos we'd had to quit early, you see? We would have been in the club normally, but because Linda Keith caused such a fuss…

ap: And then the next morning – am I right? – she turned up again?

ke: She burst into the bedroom – and picked up the guitar that was on the floor. It was in its case, but the case was open. She raised it above her head, like – to come crashing down on us. I dived underneath Jimi. But she didn't. She just took the guitar. We looked out the window. We could see her – and I'll never forget it – and she doesn't deny that her dad had a blue Jaguar. That's what I saw. She threw it on the back seat, got in, and drove away.

Jimi was beside himself. It was like robbing a man of his music. Can you even imagine? He was absolutely – "*Oh God!*" You know. So the first thing we did; we had to tell Chas what had happened: It was *our* fault because either we didn't lock the bedroom door, or a maid opened it for her. We don't know which. And we couldn't remember. So anyway, Chas's plan was for me to go home to my place and wait for a call. And that's what I did.

And then I got a call at about seven o'clock that evening

that it'd all been resolved. Now, according to Chas, Jimi called Linda and romanced her. She gave it back and they made an arrangement to see each other the next night, and that Jimi would call. He never did. So, basically, she got dumped in a big way.

ap: During this whole bit – Linda was still kind of with Keith Richards?

ke: I'm not sure what their arrangement was. I didn't know her and I didn't know Keith. I think they'd split up, but I have no idea to be honest with you, whether they had or they hadn't. I didn't know them. I didn't know her – I'd never seen her before in my life; I'd never seen Keith Richards before in my life. They didn't mix in the same circles as us. I should imagine they were still together, because Jimi told me that he stayed at the Hilton Hotel in New York, which was the room that Keith Richards was staying in – but he was on tour; Linda was staying in the suite. So I should imagine that they were still together, or something like that. Who knows?

ap: I wonder – because this is pre-fame – when Jimi first found himself with a hit record, as a couple, what was your reaction?

ke: We were sitting on the sofa in Montagu Square when Chas came in waving the *New Musical Express*, shouting, "Ey! We got to number six!" So I do remember that. I can remember what I was wearing.

And we were, "Oh great!" But of course, it was all payola in those days. Mike Jeffery had paid people to play it. They banned that payola after a while, but it was still in operation then, and it got up the charts. And after that, things improved because once you get to number six the record companies are prepared to invest a bit more. But there was never a lot of money in those days. I mean, the managers took it all. It was only when he started having really big hits that the money started rolling in. But not as much as you would have expected, these days.

Mike Jeffery has been painted as a terrible villain, but they were all doing it. *All* the managers in those days. I mean, Marc Bolan's money completely disappeared. 'Cos Rolan Bolan said to me that they can't trace any of it. *Any* of Marc Bolan's money – they can't trace it, because accountants hid it. But that's happened to Michael Hutchence as well. Same thing there. His money's all disappeared.

They tell them that they need to be tax-efficient. They're usually young. *You've gotta be tax efficient. We'll do it like this – we'll put it in the Bahamas; Virgin Islands; Lichtenstein; one of these offshore tax havens.* And they usually put it in a company's name, of which *the accountant is the director*. And so if they die, nobody can get their hands on it. Anyway, all Jimi had when he died was something like $270,000 I believe.

ap: So at what point along the line did you and Jimi go *we've made it*.

ke: When Chas came in with the paper. That was the moment. And Chas said, "You and Kathy have won two weeks' holiday in South Africa. We'll be booking you a flight tomorrow."

That was in the depths of Apartheid. It was a joke. A white person and a black person couldn't go to South Africa in those days.

ap: At Montagu Square, you were sharing that flat with

Chas and Lotte – how was that dynamic between the two couples?

KE: Oh, it wasn't too bad because it was on two floors. Our bedroom was on the lower ground floor, with a bathroom, and their bedroom was on the floor above with their own ensuite. So we only met up in the living room occasionally, because our rooms were big enough to have everything we wanted in it. It was the width of the house; it was a big apartment. So there was never any... Oh, we met in the kitchen occasionally.

AP: Do you remember any particular moment, perhaps with Chas and Jimi that would sum up their dynamic?

KE: Well, Chas was very much the manager. He sort of evolved into the manager. Chas had quite a strong person-ality. He'd been a docker in the Newcastle docks, and was quite tough. He was a very big bloke; he was about six foot six. And he had it in his head how things should be. So it was all working well at that time. Everything was working well. Chas had a good sense of humor and everything. Lotte was a complete drip, you know? Swedish – she didn't have a sense of humor or anything. Didn't understand most of it, 'cos she was a Swedish speaker. So she never really got involved with anything; she just used to tag along with Chas. So things were quite good, yeah. And I think things started to fall apart later on in about 1968. Jimi was getting a bit self-indulgent in the studio, and instead of just going in and putting down the track, which was the sort of thing that Chas was used to – the four-minute record – Jimi was re-taking, re-taking, re-taking; re-mixing... this was cost-ing a fortune. And I think that's what started it all.

AP: There's a moment in your book where you said that at one point – was it Chas and Jimi who had to share a bed? Did I read that correctly?

KE: Oh yeah. When we went up to Chas's hometown, Newcastle. He came from a very working-class family where the toilet was down the end of the yard. A council flat. This house must have been built a hundred and twenty years before. It had no heating. They just had a coal fire in the sitting room. And when we got there, and 'cos we weren't married – and it was viewed as sort of, *you don't sleep in the same bedroom if you're not married,* Chas had to seep with Jimi and I had to sleep with Lotte. And it was so cold we slept with our clothes on. It was in the middle of winter – it must have been minus ten outside. Ice formed on the *inside* of the windows. Full of condensation. Oh God, I'll never forget that. I can still remember it – I had to sleep with Lotte, and he had to share a bed with Jimi.

I said, "I promise I won't tell anyone."

So they just slept with their clothes on. They were horrified, but it was the only thing that they could do. How things have changed, eh? We're talking about 1966-67 – if you weren't married, *ooooh.* We didn't know this – Jimi and I didn't know this.

Just before we were going to go to their house after the gig, Chas said, "I'll warn you – my parents are quite old fashioned. You'll have to sleep with Lotte and we'll have to share a bed."

She was like, "What?!"

But he was the butt of lots of jokes afterwards. I said, "Did he snore?"

But having to sleep with your clothes on – it was too cold to take your clothes off. I'll never forget that. I know you had to go up some steps to get to their door, and it was covered in ice. You had to be really careful not to slip. It was in the dead of winter. In Darlington, which is outside Newcastle, the van broke down and we had to push it. It was all through slosh and ice and I had little strappy shoes on and *oh my God.*

So we went through some rough times. But all in all, I was what – 20, 21? I could tolerate anything. You wouldn't get me to do it now!

ap: In your book, possibly my favorite moment is the one with you and Jimi and Little Richard.

ke: With his wigs – his wigs on stands all around the room. And his mother in the other room… Little Richard owed Jimi money from a gig somewhere in the American south. He hadn't paid him. So when he was in London, Jimi must have phoned the Rembrandt Hotel and spoken to him, and he must have invited Jimi 'round. So I went with him. He was very amenable, very American. He ordered a bottle of whiskey and we all drank whiskey and whatever mixers – coke, probably. He was quite amenable. The rumor is that he didn't give Jimi the money. But he did, and it was in dollars. I remember at the time – I vaguely, vaguely remember – that when he went to change the dollars, the bank charged him a big chunk of it to change it. I do remember that. That's when we were stopped by the police – we were leaving the Rembrandt Hotel, going to the Cromwellian club. That's when the police pulled up and stopped us, when Jimi was wearing that jacket.

ap: For the readers who haven't heard that story before, would you mind going into some detail on that?

ke: The police stopping us? They stopped him because he was wearing an army jacket, and it still had the insignia, the epaulettes and the badge buttons. In the UK you're not allowed to wear them unless you're part of that regiment. Even though, as Jimi argued, it was the Veterinary Corps from a hundred years ago. So he took it off, and then later he cut off the buttons – the little things on the stand-up collar of the jacket, the insignia of the Veterinary Corps. Indeed, I've still got one. He cut off two – I don't know what happened to the other one. And then he could wear it after that. Nobody said anything after that – he just carried on wearing it.

But they weren't rude and nasty as it's been portrayed in that dreadful film. They were firm, but not threatening or rude in any way. And it wasn't racist in any way. They saw the jacket. It was the early days of people wearing those. And everybody had to cut them off. That's not generally known. It gets out into the public that Jimi was being victimized in some way. Well, we didn't perceive it as that at the time. They had a genuine request that he shouldn't wear the insignia of a British Army officer that was probably dead. Well, would have been dead. And so Jimi cut them off. He understood.

AP: That's amazing – it certainly gets portrayed as being a racist thing.

KE: Rubbish. Absolute rubbish. They stopped and said, "Have you got any insignia on that jacket?" Or words to that effect.

Jimi said, "Oh, what – the Royal Veterinary Corps?"

And they said, "Yes, well you can't wear that." That's what they said.

So he took the jacket off. Later on, at home, he cut the two badges off. The jacket has a stick-up collar, like a lot of old army jackets have a stick-up collar. And he just cut those off. As I say, I've still got one in my jewelry box. I didn't see it for years and years. I only found it about twenty years ago. I was having a clear-out of an old chest of drawers that I've got – and there it was. Amazing. It'd moved house and never been found, and had been in the back of the drawer.

ap: Another note that I made on reading your book was this amazing moment of Jimi seeing a ghost in the Brook Street apartment.

ke: My friend Madeleine was around there at the time. Doing some – I don't know what she was doing; cooking or something. And Jimi must have smoked too much dope. He went up to the bathroom, and there was a mirror above the sink – above the hand basin.

When he came down, he said, "I swear I just saw a ghost with a grey wig on."

We didn't know that Handel had lived in the house. Well, he'd lived in the house next door, actually. But around that time, we got a knock on the door from a music student from America. The guy thought that it was the home of Handel, because he was a classic music scholar. That was the first we knew that it had some sort of history. It was only later that I discovered that in fact Handel's house was next door. The two houses have been knocked together now, and there's a museum. They've made our bedroom a museum.

ap: It's amazing.

ke: It was weird to go in. They didn't get it exactly right, of course. I was helping them from Australia and it was hard not being there. I couldn't keep popping backwards and forwards. I tried to guide them the best I could. I mean, they got it almost right. The carpets were exactly the same color, because they had remnants of the old carpets that we had put in that they could copy. They got the curtains slightly the wrong turquoise color, but – not bad.

ap: I wonder – in relation to Handel's ghost, it sounded as though Jimi really genuinely believed that he had seen it.

ke: He did. Ask Madeleine! She was with me when he came downstairs. She said, "Oh, you've had too much to smoke." He'd been smoking too much dope.

He said, "No, no, no – I saw it!" We all wonder now – did he have some sort of insight?

ap: Would you describe Jimi as being spiritual?

ke: Yes. Not too heavily – I mean, he didn't sit with his hands clasped or anything like that. It's hard to say. He was quite spiritual, just in his general thinking. But he wasn't deeply spiritual, that you could put your finger on. It was just a general part of his makeup, his persona. He was quite young, you know. He died age 27. His personality was evolving, like most men. They now know that a guy's personality doesn't actually settle until they're about 28 to 30. So it was evolving. But where his 'soul' – I say that with inverted commas – lay, was music. He thought about music all the time. He'd be sitting watching something on the TV, and suddenly jump up and go into the bedroom and start plucking on the guitar, because something had occurred to him, and he wanted to play it. Now – he didn't necessarily plug the guitar into an amplifier, 'cos he could hear it with just the strings. And he would do that. And then later on, maybe a day or maybe even at the time, he'd start scribbling things down. There were pieces of paper all over the place with lyrics on. They got thrown away at a rate of knots,

I can tell you. He'd write something; he'd throw it away. People who found bits of his writing thought they were meaningful and they were meant to be something. But he did thousands of them, and they weren't. They were things that he wrote and then discarded.

AP: Jimi's handwriting is quite phenomenal. The albums that come out and they've reproduced his handwriting quite well – do you have any insight into how he developed that? Or is that just what came out of him from school?

KE: It just came out of him from school. He did have interesting handwriting. He made terrible spelling mistakes – appalling spelling mistakes. And then he'd cross them out and spell it properly. He was in such a hurry, mentally, to write it down, that he would misspell it and then correct it later. But a lot of them he didn't correct, and they were wrong. But generally speaking, he wasn't too bad. Considering his upbringing, his writing wasn't too bad. It was quite good.

AP: In *Through Gypsy Eyes*, you mention that you spoke with Jimi about his upbringing. And you could relate on that level, I suppose.

KE: Absolutely. I mean, he used to try and play one string on a broomstick, and his dad would take the broomstick off him and hit him with it. I think his dad was a bit of a violent man. And Jimi was very sad about the loss of his mother. I think that hit him quite hard, 'cos he was only about 14 when she died. And I think a lot of it – he talked about some things, but I think a lot of it he kept to himself. I remember when he found out his brother Leon was in prison, he was annoyed. For *grand larceny*. I remember that word, because I'd never heard that word before. It's not something that the English use.

I said, "What's grand larceny?"

He said, "It's thieving."

So he was disappointed in his brother being in prison. He had morals, you know? But like anybody, blood's thicker than water. He wanted to speak to his dad. He didn't know his dad's wife – and he didn't know that his dad had married. So they obviously hadn't been in contact very much. His dad had adopted a six-year-old, Janie. He didn't know any of that.

AP: You first spoke to Al on the phone, is that right?

KE: In 1966. We did a reverse-charge call from the Hyde Park Towers Hotel. And Jimi told him that he was in England. First of all – Al didn't quite get where England was.

Jimi didn't say *I'm going to be famous* or anything, which has been reported. He said, "I'm in England and I'm going to get a recording contract," "We're getting a band together."

His dad told him about his new wife and everything and told him about what was going on in Seattle. And then all of a sudden it clicked that this was a long-distance phone call. And he said, "You write to me, son. I'm not paying for no long-distance call." And he basically put the phone down.

AP: I have to ask – 'The Wind Cries Mary' is such a beautiful piece. The story of where that came from is quite moving in itself – I wonder if you could tell me a little bit about that?

KE: Well, it was after a row – as you have rows with your partners. We had a row over mashed potatoes. Because my mashed potatoes are lumpy. They're *still* lumpy. It was only about two months ago I got a potato ricer to stop this. Anyway, as young people do, it all got completely out of hand.

I said, "Oh, right – if you don't want it…" And I threw it on the floor and stomped out. And he followed me out; grabbed my skirt. My skirt was held together with a new invention called Velcro. And it just came off. And there I stood. We didn't have tights in those days. Suspenders and stockings…

Anyway, I went down to a set of traffic lights on Gloucester Place, and I waited there to get a taxi and I went to my friend Angie's place. He wrote this song overnight. It must have been the traffic lights, my hair – at the time I had red hair, 'cos that was the fashion – and my name. Because in those days we used to call ourselves by our middle names. Angie was Gladys, I was Mary and he was Marshall. Silly kid stuff, isn't it? We used to say, "Hello Marshall!" and salute.

But the thing is, my name is Kathleenmary – as one. But everybody calls me Kathy.

ap: Just to clarify there – the Velcro skirt came off, were you waiting on the street corner in stockings and suspenders?

ke: No, no, no – I'd just got outside the building and he grabbed my skirt – it came off. I put it back on again and then went down to the traffic lights. He was shocked – *Oh!*

It was a pink linen skirt that had this new-fangled Velcro fastening – which probably wasn't as good as today's Velcro – and as he grabbed the back of my skirt, it just came off.

It wasn't funny at the time, I can tell you. Fortunately, there was no one around. This was in the dark, so I don't remember what time it was. I don't think it was particularly late at night, because I wouldn't have been cooking late at night. And then I went to the traffic lights, which were just meters away, to get a taxi to Angie's place.

Of course, everything was forgotten by the next morning. Young love, eh?

• • •

In his chaotic life, it was often the quiet moments that mattered to Jimi. Kathy told me in closing that some of the best music Jimi ever created was while he was sitting on the edge of their bed, plugged into a little practice amp. And Kathy was quite happy to stay at the flat in London and hang out with her friends while Jimi was out on tour. She wasn't naïve about what happened on the road – it was the sixties after all. But Jimi was always on his way back to Kathy, and their quiet moments together. In Montagu Square and Brook Street they would enjoy each other's company and spend time with friends like Chas, Eric Burdon, and Roger Mayer. Board games were popular – Twister, Risk and Monopoly were always a hit. And they were close to all the best London clubs. But Jimi's career – and his managers – kept pulling him back out onto the road.

Keith Altham
New Musical Express

JIMI WAS STILL ONLY 23 YEARS OLD when he arrived in London and all hell broke loose. Chas Chandler was well connected on his home soil and soon had the cream of the music scene lining up to see Jimi's act at the Scotch of St James, the Bag o' Nails, and Blaise's nightclub. Due to visa restrictions, Jimi was just 'sitting in' with the established acts, but this attracted an existing audience. In quick succession, Eric Clapton, Jeff Beck, Jimmy Page, and Pete Townshend showed up and were rendered speechless. Each has noted their amazement for the record: Hendrix had already changed the game. 'Killing Floor'; 'Wild Thing'; 'Hey Joe'... It wasn't just the playing-with-his-teeth, behind-the-neck, between-the-legs, humping-the-amps. The showmanship was fantastic, gleaned from the best of the Chitlin' Circuit. But it was Jimi's *sound* that knocked everybody out. The next step was to cause a buzz in the media. Chas knew where to start: Keith Altham.

Keith Altham was an old mate from Chas' days with the Animals. He was a feature writer for *New Musical Express* and had given the Animals a leg up in the music press. Now, Chas enlisted Keith to help launch Jimi upon an unwitting public.

Keith Altham worked in music journalism throughout the sixties, interviewing Beatles, Beach Boys, Rolling Stones,

Rod Stewart, Tom Jones, Frank Zappa, Dusty Spring-field, Jim Morrison, and the Who. In the seventies, Keith branched out into public relations – representing many of the groups he used to interview. The Who were major clients for sixteen years, along with the Rolling Stones, AC/DC, the Police, Slade, the Beach Boys, the Kinks, Van Morrison, Ozzy Osbourne, Marc Bolan, Carole King, and Genesis. Keith designed *image*. And for Jimi Hendrix, Keith's input was beyond influential; it proved to be career-defining.

AIDAN PREWETT: I love the idea of you backstage with Jimi – *what can we do to get a bit of traction in the press?* And then of course you come up with this incredible idea. I'd love it if you could paint for me what that room was like – how did it all sort of go down?

KEITH ALTHAM: I'd gone to review a show for the *NME*. This was in the days when I was still a journalist. He was on a tour with Engelbert Humperdinck, Cat Stevens and the Walker Brothers. We were in the dressing room back-stage, and I was there with Chas Chandler who was the manager and formerly the Animals' bass player. And Tony Garland, who was his personal assistant, and a chap called Gerry Stickells, who was a roadie at that time. He became a very successful tour manager later. Chas came up with the remark – I suppose because I was a journalist – he said, "We want to steal the headlines from everybody else on the tour." All the other guys at that time were more successful. "What can we do to grab the attention of the press?"

I said, "Well, you can't keep on smashing the guitar, 'cos people are just going to accuse you of copying the Who." Which he was. Again, Jimi saw something that he thought was an attraction and he adopted it to his act. Much to Pete Townshend's consternation. I said, "You can't smash a TV set or something crass like that, because the Move are doing that on stage." And I said, "It's a pity you can't set fire to the guitar." I don't know what made me say it, but when I said it, I knew that you couldn't set fire to a solid-state guitar. It's not going to burn. But I suppose in the back of my head I had this picture of Jerry Lee Lewis, who had once played a gig with Chuck Berry. And they didn't get on all that well. A Southern white guy and a black guy – they didn't gel too well. As Jerry Lewis walked off stage, he emptied some fuel or some paraffin into his piano and set fire to it. And as he passed Chuck Berry, he said, "Follow that."

So in the back of my mind was this flaming piano. After I said it, there was a kind of pregnant pause in the dressing room.

Gerry looked at Tony Garland and said, "Tony, go out and buy some lighter fuel." And that's what they used, of course. They spread lighter fuel across the guitar face, and then lit it – with a match, as it transpired that night. Because that didn't work. And then I think Tony Garland lent him his Varaflame cigarette lighter. And the guitar went up like a torch. Hendrix wound up whirling it around his head like an Olympic torch, much to the consternation of the fire chief at the time, who was not too enamored of the security risks that had been involved. And he was going to inform Jimi that he would never play the Circuit again, or something. But as they couldn't find the evidence... Amusingly, the agent for that tour was a man who rejoiced at it. A rather significant name, as it turned out – Tito Burns. Tito stole the guitar after Jimi had finished with it, and hid it in his raincoat. And then proceeded backstage to tip Jimi off as to what he'd done, and smuggled the guitar out of the backstage area so that the fire chief didn't have any evidence of the incident as it occurred. But it certainly grabbed all the attention that night; it was the first time that he did it. So I became the arsonist that had invented guitar flambé for Jimi Hendrix.

AP: That's fantastic.

KA: It did tend to cause attention. Especially if you're doing it in a theatre, with all the attendant fire risks. Jimi didn't do it that often, you know. I think I mentioned in those notes I gave you, I mean – he only did it about four or five times in his life. But everybody expected him to do it every time thereafter. So he wasn't all that pleased about it. It served its purpose. When he did do it, it created enormous attention – like it did in Monterey.

AP: Do you remember the very first time you met Jimi?

KA: Yeah – he came to England, and direct from the airport he went to Zoot Money's house. Zoot was a keyboard player, organist who worked with lots of people in England, including the Animals, Georgie Fame and a whole lot of other people. He's still out on the road; I still see him. So Jimi stopped at Zoot's house in Barnes, and I think Andy Summers of the Police was there. They had a chat and, in the evening, Chas rang me and said, "Look – we're going to do a jam tonight. Do you want to come down and see this amazing guitarist I found in New York?" 'Cos he'd already told me about him. I said, "Sure!"

They were playing the Scotch of St James, and I got there a bit late. Jimi was on stage jamming with, I think, Brian Auger. The Brian Auger Trinity were kind of big in the '60's, and they had a record out called *Wheels On Fire*, which became the theme tune for Jennifer Saunders and Dawn French in that *Ab Fab* TV Series. Brian Auger was the organist for that record. Anyway, Brian was there, and a couple of people from a Newcastle group called the VIPs. It was just a kind of made-up jam session, really. Jimi wasn't singing; he was just playing guitar. And he was amazing. There was no doubt the guy was a virtuoso guitarist. I only heard about three numbers 'cos I got there a bit late. He seemed to me at that time to be a jazz guitarist. From the limited amount I'd heard from the three numbers. It was like listening to somebody like Wes Montgomery. He's not going to become a pop star or a rock star. He's a jazz man.

Chas came up to me afterwards and said, "Well, what do you think?"

I said, "Well – he's amazing, Chas. What a musician. But you know – he's gonna go straight over the heads of the kids."

So Chas says, "Not if I can help it, he won't."

I said, "Oh, right…"

And of course, he ironed out the wrinkles. He knew what he was doing, Chas. Jimi hated singing. That was one thing. He'd spent his previous existence being a backing musician for people like Little Richard and the Isley Brothers and other American acts. So he regarded himself as a guitarist, pure and simple. And he didn't like his voice. He hated his voice. And Chas persuaded him to become a singer for his own stuff, virtually by making him sit down and listen to Bob Dylan – who was one of his heroes. "Your mate Bob Dylan can't sing, and look how well he does." And Jimi gradually came out of himself with that and became quite a good vocalist. At least, a good vocalist for his own work, and a couple of other people's songs. I mean, 'All Along the Watchtower', of course, which is a classic. And 'Wild Thing' by the Troggs, which he really, virtually made his own.

I really didn't latch on to Jimi again until there was

another press preview that Chas had organized a few months later. He'd taken Jimi out to France and worked him on a Johnny Hallyday tour. Johnny Hallyday was a kind of second-rate Elvis Presley in France, and became a kind of iconic figure over there – 'cos they didn't have much. Never have done.

He came back after that brief tour in France, and I think he'd found himself a bit more – soaked up some of the influences that were going down in so-called Swinging London at the time, and Jimi was a great one for pick 'n' mix. He found the best of what he could see in England. He met Eric Clapton. He picked up the vibe very quickly, with a bit of help and advice from Chas. He picked up the things that were attractive to the audience at the time, and then incorporated them into his own act. And so when I saw him a second time, when he came back to England, there was a press preview at a place called the Bag O'Nails in the basement. The press were invited to come down and listen to the Jimi Hendrix Experience. This was the first time the English press had heard the *band*, per se. They'd got Noel Redding and Mitch Mitchell together by that time. Mitch was a jazz drummer; Noel was a kind of rock 'n' roll guitarist. Not a bass player – but he had a feel for what Hendrix was doing, probably as a result of him being a guitarist. And they played this little club at lunchtime, for the press only. There were probably about fifty of us who'd come down to listen to him. And again, I thought that what he was doing was a bit too advanced to get popular acclaim. I thought he was going to appeal mainly to the art student audience, rather than the pop audience. Until, as I was leaving the club – and he was still playing – I was about to do an interview with somebody else – I got halfway up the stairs, and he struck into 'Wild Thing' by the Troggs.

And I thought *Jesus, that sounds amazing.* I walked back down and I thought *okay, I've got him now. Now I understand what Chas is talking about.* He could actually change the shape of rock music. Now he's got us down here – and he's singing as well. And he *looked* good. I thought *this is it – this is the next big thing.* So I hung on to his coat tails, and Chas's.

AP: Do you remember the first proper conversation with Jimi – or the vibe?

KA: I suppose the first conversation I had with him was at the Scotch of St James, but I can't really tell you much about what it was. It wasn't anything deep, it was just about *hey, how are you enjoying London; have you seen anybody?* He'd only been in England for a day. So there wasn't a lot to talk about at that stage.

So the first interview I did with him, which was probably after he got 'Hey Joe' into the charts, was again, fairly restrictive. He was desperate to meet Eric Clapton, I do remember that. It was something that Chas had promised him when he'd brought him to England. And he said to me a little enigmatic thing, "I want to be as good as he thinks I am."

I went down with Chas and Jimi to the London School of Economics – to see Clapton, who was playing with Cream. They were already creating quite a powerful following. Chas had asked Eric whether he could get Jimi on stage with him and do a jam. And Clapton said, "Yeah, sure – we'll put him on for the number before the encore." I wasn't privy to that conversation, but I was in the audience with Chas, and Jimi got up and chatted to Eric. Eric nodded and they started into 'Killing Floor'. After about four minutes, with Jimi into his solo, Clapton walked off stage. Chas turned to me and said, "Oh, Jesus. I think we've upset him. I'd better go back to see what's happened." So he disappeared backstage to see Clapton, and Jimi carried on and wiped the face of the stage with 'Killing Floor'. Just brilliant – playing with Ginger Baker and Jack Bruce. They were amazing; they got a rapturous reception.

And Chas came back. I said, "What happened?"

He said, "He was sitting on an amplifier, smoking a cigarette." He looked at Chas and said, "You didn't tell me he was *that* fucking good, did you?"

"Well, I told you he could play almost anything."

Eric said, "He's better than that, Chas – you know that. He's something very special."

Eric was alright after that. He got over it. But I think he thought he'd been deliberately upstaged or something. They became good mates after that.

ap: I was amazed to hear that Jimi and Chas had actually met roughly a year before all this.

ka: Chas went to see the Hollies, who were mates of his, on a TV show in New York. He was going to see Tony Hicks, who was a guitarist in the Hollies. They got into the lift, and Little Richard was in the lift. And so was Jimi. But Jimi was dressed in evening dress, with a bow tie; his hair pomaded back. Chas introduced himself prematurely in the lift. Little Richard was very agitated, because he was late for the call for this TV show they were doing on the top floor. And the lift attendant kept wanting to stop at every floor. And Little Richard was screaming at him to take it up. "Do you not realize who I am? I'm the Georgia Peach! They're waiting for me! There's only one Georgia Peach – get this lift up!" You know. He started to go into one of his tantrums. Chas and Jimi got out to leave them to it. They carried on their screaming match as the lift went up, and Chas and Jimi sat on a windowsill and had a cigarette. Then Jimi got back in the lift and went up and rejoined Little Richard.

Much later, when Jimi was in England with him... Chas was fond of telling the story that the first time he saw Jimi was at the Café Wha? in New York, where Linda Keith had tipped him off about this amazing guitarist. Linda was Keith Richards' girlfriend at the time. She'd already got Andrew Oldham, the Stones' manager, to go down and see him. He'd passed, because he didn't think – I mean, I would have passed too in a way. He must have felt, like I did – he was a great guitarist, but what do you do with a jazz guitarist? Linda had got Chas down there, and Chas said he saw Jimi play 'Hey Joe', which was a number that he'd always wanted to record. He had it in the back of his mind to do it with *somebody*. And Jimi played it on stage, not realizing that it was one of Chas's favorite songs. That kind of nailed it on with Chas, because he was a musician himself, and he saw the potential in Jimi. He wanted to take him back to England. Because he also saw, quite rightly, at that time England was a very sort of buzzy place. It was the center of rock 'n' roll with the Beatles and the Stones and everybody else. And people like P.J. Proby and the Walker Brothers had come to England with no success in America at all, but launched themselves on the platform of what England could do as the center of music interest at that time. He saw an opportunity to do the same thing with Jimi, to launch him from England back into America. And that was the plan.

ap: Is there a moment you had with Chas that might sum up his character?

KA: Oh god. I'd known Chas for years. The Animals were a band in England that I kind of latched onto very early, because they were the first *blokes'* band in England in that period. They were the first one where you went to the crowd and it wasn't just girls screaming. It was blokes who had taken their girlfriends along to see this semi-blues band. And although Eric Burdon had a following and lots of female interest, he wasn't that kind of feature attraction. He wasn't pretty. And neither, really, were the band themselves. But they were good. It was like a football team – you saw that kind of attraction in them, as a guy. I thought *at least you can hear this lot; they're not being screamed at.* And they sounded fun and I liked the stuff they were playing. So I did quite a lot of interviews on the road with the Animals in England. And Chas was somebody that you couldn't miss, 'cos he was the biggest bloke in the band. Built like John Wayne. And I just got friendly with him. It went from that to Hendrix.

They had a lot of hits, the Animals – 'House of the Rising Sun' being the biggest one. 'Don't Let Me Be Misunderstood', 'Bring It On Home To Me', 'I Put A Spell On You', all kinds of things. Eric loved Nina Simone, so there was a lot of Nina Simone-influenced stuff. That was the reason. And then Chas said at one point when the Animals were going through one of their kind of splinter-breakups – people were leaving – "I want to actually do something in management. And I think I might have found this guy in America who can play guitar, you know." And that was the first time I'd ever heard of Hendrix. And that was when Chas promised me that if he did get him off the ground, he'd take me to America. I'd always wanted to go to the States.

I remember – the first night in New York, we were

staying at the infamous Chelsea Hotel. Jimi said he'd take me to his haunts, where he used to play. We went to this club – I think it was the Café Wha?, or it might have been the Tin Star or something. Anyway, it was one of the places where Jimi did play before he came to England. We sat there – about 24 of us in this little club, and there was this guy sitting on a stool, a black guy, playing a guitar like he was playing a machinegun. And spitting out these incredibly good lyrics, with such fire and determination. I was thinking *Jesus, are they all that good in America? This guy's phenomenal!* And nobody's paying any attention to him but me. Everybody's talking around me, and I'm just *agog*. It transpired it was Richie Havens, who a couple of years later was playing to half-a-million people at Woodstock. I completely lost my sense of perspective. He was *that* good. That was my first night in New York City.

AP: Noel Redding and Mitch Mitchell – I'd love to hear something about those guys. They're very easily overshadowed, and I get little glimpses of those two guys. I'm looking for a moment that kind of sums up who those guys were.

KA: Mitch was a jazz drummer. He came from that background: his hero was Elvin Jones. And he played that kind of style that kind of worked with Jimi. When Jimi 'went off on one', as they used to say, they could hang on. Or at least Mitch could. Noel got a bit lost, and I think that was where he came to grief, musically, with them. But he fitted in – their personalities gelled. They got on with each other. And Noel was always a bit of a peacemaker.

It struck me as a band that was put together to do what it did: to get Jimi launched. And that he was going to look elsewhere, sooner or later, for Jimi Hendrix Mark II.

Which is what he was doing with the Band of Gypsys, of course, which didn't really work. But he would have found somebody where it did work, if he'd managed to stay the course and stay alive and say *no* to a few of these wrong people who were around him.

AP: You said that Noel was something of a peacemaker – that kind of surprises me, actually. Do you recall any specifics of that?

KA: Well, that was just his nature. He was a gentle soul, Noel. He got a bit fed up with it towards the end, because he was kinda getting – as he saw it – eased out. And I think he'd had enough by then. I stayed friendly with Noel for some time after Jimi died. I went across to Ireland to see him a few times. His house in Ireland was a shrine to the memory of Jimi Hendrix. He lived in Clonakilty.

AP: Did you see those guys getting up to mischief on the road, or elsewhere.

KA: There were childish things, really – just little pranks. Water pistols were quite a feature at one stage, backstage. Cat Stevens had a song on stage on that Walker Brothers-Humperdinck-Hendrix tour called 'Gonna Get Me A Gun'. And if you'd have seen Mitch and Noel backstage behind the curtains, shooting water at him while he was singing the song, you'd understand why Cat Stevens was none too amused by it. But they were silly little things, tour pranks and things. On a plane once, there was an announcement from Mitch over the intercom: "Will Keith Altham please report to the tip of the north wing, where he's urgently required." Things like that. Everybody had a sense of humor. Jimi was easy to get on with 'cos he was just such an easygoing guy. Too easygoing for his own good.

• • •

Soon after landing in London, Chas introduced Jimi to the Animals' manager, Mike Jeffery. There's no mistaking that Mike was instrumental in launching Jimi's career, as was Chas. Mike arranged many of the gigs – and absolutely grueling tour schedules. Chas would be the man on the ground, handling the band and staff on tour and in the studio.

Mike Jeffery is often cast as one of the villains in the Hendrix story, and not without reason. As well as arranging the tours, Mike also arranged the contracts. He took a huge piece of the pie for himself. Chas knew that Mike operated this way, but he needed capital and big-picture connections to get Jimi started. His old manager was his – and Jimi's – ticket.

Roger Mayer
The Tone

A WORK PERMIT WAS SORTED OUT QUICKLY. The next step was to recruit band members to complement Jimi. It was, of course, *his* experience, but both Chas and Jimi were clear that they didn't just want session guys. They wanted a tight, committed band. Casual auditions commenced for what would become the Jimi Hendrix Experience. The first cat through the door was 21-year-old Noel Redding, who had come looking for a shot at playing guitar for Eric Burdon's New Animals. Instead he met up with Chas, who liked his curly 'fro haircut – matching Jimi's. There was no room for a second guitar in the Experience, so Chas asked Noel if he'd give bass a crack. He and Jimi jammed on a few numbers with some other session guys and the next day Noel was offered the gig.

Jimi liked Noel. His basic approach to the bass provided an uncomplicated platform from which Jimi could propel himself and circle back to. Jimi also liked Noel's hair. The perfect counterpoint was Mitch Mitchell on drums. A cherubic jazz kid, nineteen years old. He could *play*. His influences were of the old-guard – Elvin Jones, Max Roach, Buddy Rich. His style was busy, showy. With staid Noel sandwiched between them, Mitch balanced the group perfectly. They proved a formidable trio.

Amid the chaos of the early gigs, Jimi was quickly befriended by Roger Mayer. Mayer was already highly regarded as an electronics whiz among the guitar cognoscenti, designing significant improvements to the distinctive guitar 'fuzz' tone used by the Rolling Stones on 'Satisfaction' and working closely with Jeff Beck and Jimmy Page in their session work and Yardbirds days. Together with Jimi, Eddie Kramer, and Chas Chandler, Roger Mayer helped to design the soundscapes of the Hendrix oeuvre. The guitar tones, heavily affected by Mayer's chains of effects boxes and pedals, came to redefine the sound of the electric guitar. Mayer and Hendrix also became regulars at the Speakeasy club off Regent Street, and they hung out at Jimi's various London flats whenever Jimi was in town.

Fifty years later, Mayer is still in the business of *tone*. Other companies were quick to attempt emulation of his sounds; many are still chasing them. Never resting on his laurels, Mayer continues to design original effects for the cream of the music industry. There is only one Roger Mayer.

ROGER MAYER: I think it's important if you're going to talk about Jimi – let's not talk about him completely retrospectively, you know what I mean? He's left a legacy that has endured for fifty years, and it's still going very strong. I suppose – I'm still flying the flag for him and everything that we did. Because we are producing today some very interesting studio effects that have been used by some of the top people on records today.

We can talk about some of the stuff that Jimi and I talked about, and the fact that you can experience the difference between good and bad very easily. Which was really part of the philosophy behind Jimi.

AIDAN PREWETT: That sounds perfect. What I've been starting with is – is there a moment, a single moment that you had with Jimi that has really stuck with you over all these years?

RM: Yeah – I guess, this might seem strange. After we finished recording the solo to 'Bold as Love', the title cut of the album – that moment sticks in my mind because we had left Chas' flat in London and gone to Olympic Studios. The whole point with Jimi was that solos should be a freeform expression of the moment, you know what I mean? It's not something you practice, per se. So that was part of the philosophy that we grew up to understand. Beginning by listening to Coltrane, and jazz; where people are interested in the freeform element of the playing – which really was what Jimi was about. He was a free spirit. He didn't practice anything, really. He played a lot, but that's different. He was really about creating a moment, creating a soundscape.

Anyway, let me fast-forward a little bit. In the studio, the backing tracks had been laid down. And now came the time in the evening for Jimi to start putting the solo down. So Jimi and I left the control room and went out into the studio. I'm standing with Jimi, and we plug in a few boxes; one of my special boxes. We got a sound that was pretty well what we thought was appropriate for the track. There's so many ways you can tune the sound. It's infinite, you know? Especially in the recording studio.

Imagine this: we've both got our headphones on and we're listening to the track and Jimi's playing a bit, and then we're adjusting the signal chain – or the various signal chains – until we would get the sound and go *yeah – that sounds pretty good. I think we can start from there.* So the track is played back, and Jimi smiles at me and he's laughing. And he says, "Alright, let's try one, Roger."

And I said "Yeah, sure – no problem." Part of my relationship with Jimi was to be like insurance cover to him. If I'm in the studio, there isn't much that technically could get by the both of us. Almost nothing. So Jimi lays down a solo for 'Bold as Love'. Then he looks at me.

He says, "What do you think, Roger?"

I said, "Hmm, I dunno."

So Jimi says, "Go into the control room and have a listen." So Jimi remained in the studio, and I walked into the control room. And I had a listen to it. All the guys in the control room were jumping around – *oh, that's fantastic, that's the one – that's the one!* So I went back to Jimi and he said, "What do you think, Roger?"

And I said, "That wasn't the one."

He said, "Yeah, I don't think so either." So all the guys in the control room are going *oh no. You mean you're not going to keep that one?* Because we didn't have unlimited tracks with the recording systems we were using.

So I said, "No – Jimi said don't worry." So then Jimi – I was still standing next to him in the studio. We were just sitting there looking at one another, and then Jimi put the solo down.

Then Jimi said, "What do you think, Roger?"

"Now let's go into the control room." So then both of us went into the control room.

The people in the control room said, "I would never have believed you." They were all – to a man – gobsmacked.

And Jimi said, "Yeah, I told you so. I told you that one wasn't the right one." Because other people have no idea – unless you were really close to Jimi, you didn't really have a good idea of what he *could* do. You know what I mean? So basically, Jimi didn't really want to be around people that would *yes* him to death and didn't push him and didn't have an idea of what his actual capabilities were.

That really stood out in my mind, because it was a personal thing with Jimi and me. He trusted me to go into the studio and give him the right feedback. And in a little way, it was a little game. Because he was testing me to see whether I'd be honest. *No no, that's not the one.* So that was a bit of fun. Then after that solo, I think we pretty much packed up and drove down to the Speakeasy and had some fun.

The thing about Jimi, when you're working with him on his music – and helping him, really – you've got to appreciate what the guy's looking for and try to help him attain it. It's a quest in a way. It's not a job, it's a good old-fashioned quest. *Let's get this done.* It was a lot of fun. And the thing with Jimi was, he wanted to be around people who were honest with him, and also brought something to the table, rather than just brown-nosing. He didn't like that at all.

aP: I'm going to go listen to 'Bold as Love' once we're done and appreciate that solo in a new light. That's beautiful. So from there, you guys went down to the Speakeasy – do you have any memories of anything specific that happened there?

rM: Oh no, I can't remember because we used to go to the Speakeasy all the time. If we were in London and a bit bored, or after we were hanging out in the flat just listening to records or playing board games or something – just to be really chilled, we would go down the Speakeasy. Quite late I suppose – twelve o'clock, one o'clock in the morning – and see if there was anyone 'round there. Because Jimi loved to jam. Basically – well, I say jam – he liked to play the guitar. So if there was anybody down there, he would get up on stage. Many times, we'd put a guitar in my car with a couple of pedals, and leave them in the car. And then go into the club and if there was anyone he fancied playing with, or the situation arose, I'd just go upstairs and get a guitar and a few pedals so he could have some fun. 'Cos it's all about having fun, really. Jimi really liked to have fun and play music with people. But a lot of people were intimidated by his playing. They couldn't relax and have fun and jam with him.

I mean, I used to jam with him in the flat. I had to play one of his guitars upside down. "Yeah, don't worry about that, Roger. Let's have fun. Just do something that fits in. Do what you can." You know what I mean? So it was all about having fun. And interfacing with someone who loved to play the guitar. That's the main thing about Jimi. He loved to play the guitar. He didn't really care who he was playing with, what he was playing – if he was playing the bass, or he was playing upside down. It didn't matter as long as he was interfacing with people and they were having fun – and they weren't uptight. After all, the mantra goes behind it, doesn't it? Music is a mission. It's not a competition. So many people, when they play, get very very competitive. And that stops them having fun, you know.

We had that discussion – we used to say, "Listen, the musician is the same as an artist. Most people say *oh, what do you do?* 'I'm a musician, I play the guitar.' You must never forget that word, *play*. Because play infers that you're having fun". It's not a job, you know? It's not a professional occupation. You're playing music. If you're blessed to be talented enough to play music, and you enjoy it, great. And if you're playing music that's freeform, or you wrote yourself, it's even better. That's why Jimi, when he performed, he never played exactly the same thing twice. There would be no fun in that. And it's the same thing with soloing. A solo by definition is not something you've practiced or remembered. It's not.

If you go to a jazz nightclub, which I did with Jimi many times, to hear all kinds of people like Roland Kirk – whoever was in town at the time. *Let's go to a jazz club where it's chilled out.* It would be away from the rock 'n' roll crowd. It's a different crowd. You get to sit down and hear somebody blow, or play the piano, or whatever. Which is great, because those people then, in that small intimate atmosphere, get the opportunity to interface with the audience. Jimi loved that. That's when I think Jimi was at his best, you know – really – was if he could actually interface with a small audience in a way. If it was in the studio, maybe a nightclub, maybe at home. But that's Jimi being quiet, you know what I mean?

I think when people talk about Jimi being quiet – he *was*, basically. Most people who play, who perform. I've worked with a lot of great people – Bob Marley, Stevie Wonder – they are not the same people was when they're on stage, are they? The thing about having somebody around you who knows you – he's a friend, really. He has to be a friend. You can't be an employee of the band. I was never employed by the band. I refused to be. I said, "I'll help *you*, Jimi, but I'll have nothing at all to do with your management." Because at the time I was working for the British Royal Navy Scientific Service. I'm a scientist, by profession, who is interested in the science of sound and vibrational acoustical analysis, you know? So it's an interesting alternative understanding of what's going on – or it's another way to look at it. The whole thing about playing and performing is different.

Imagine this: We didn't have a huge staff then. We had

a driver, a tour manager, Jimi and the band, maybe one roadie who drove the truck. And if I was helping Jimi, I'd have my arms filled up with guitars. We might have had five guitars. But Jimi would have to take at least two of them, 'cos I can't carry more than three. And the other fact of the matter is, in the dressing room, Jimi and I would be busy changing strings and doing that. We had no roadies to do that – we had to do it ourselves!

The other thing I think you've got to realize – in those days, there was no such thing as an electronic tuner. So you didn't have an electronic tuner to tune the guitar up. So while Jimi's going live on stage, he's going to break a string. Maybe four or five in a half hour. So it's like a Formula One pit stop giving him another guitar. What you had to do was to tune the guitar up to the last song.

AP: Oh my god. Yeah!

RM: So I'd have the guitar. Obviously, it's quite loud on stage. You had to put the head of the guitar behind your ear. Things were a lot different. So I think the actual intimacy of the performance then was very much more – it was more real. It wasn't like people nowadays. When you go to some of these shows and the guys rock up and they've got a whole bunch of people around them with fuckin' clipboards and doing this and that and just basic flunkies who are doing everything to destroy the atmosphere, if you know what I mean? You don't need those type of people around you if you're a performer.

What the hell are they doing there? Ticking boxes and shuffling passes and all that. What a load of crap. So the atmosphere behind stage is not conducive or helpful to the performer performing. Or, what can happen today – the other side of the coin – people nowadays, without a backing track, without this, without that – they just can't perform. They can't perform without auto-tuning the vocal... you're not seeing a performance that is freeform, are you? You're seeing some kind of mixture of a contrived performance that could be backed up with electronic means. However the playback is. I think a lot of things have changed. The thing is about someone who can play, and who *loves* to play, and is basically a very quiet man. That's his passion – to play. He picks a guitar up and he starts smiling. That says it all, doesn't it?

AP: Absolutely. You've just earlier described a situation that has run through my head a million times while I've been practicing guitar and going *wouldn't it be amazing if Jimi Hendrix was here, and we're just playing through some old blues tunes...* Let's say you're on guitar, Jimi's on guitar, it's just the two of you: What songs did you do?

RM: We didn't play a song, you see. That's the conception that people get wrong. The first thing is, if you're going to jam, you're not going to play someone else's song, right? That's not jamming, really. Almost by definition, that is not jamming. If jazz guys sit down and they're going to have some fun, the drummer might play a particular beat, or the bass guy might start off with a riff, or do this and do that. That's how they play. They don't go *let's play a blues in A minor or B flat* or whatever the fuck it is. I mean, how boring is that? Because it's totally out of context. It's not freeform. It's not reacting to how you feel at this moment in time with the people who are around you, and you have no reaction to the Chinese meal you might have eaten, or the joint or the wine or whatever. It's non-organic because it's preconceived. And that's what Jimi – Jimi never did that.

I mean, he didn't consider himself a bluesman at all because he didn't see it that way – *I was born in Seattle of mixed race, I'm no Mississippi bluesman from the cotton field, from the Delta. I know plenty of people who are, but I don't have the credentials or the upbringing to call myself a bluesman.* 'Cos you're not. It would be like white men playing the blues. They've got no fuckin' reason to play the blues, really. Because they become hobbyists, you know what I mean? It's just like hijacking a genre and trying to make it your own. You're not playing from your heart. And *soul* blues is about playing from the heart. If you don't feel what you're singing about or playing about, what does it mean? I don't know. I have no answer for that, because I get bored to death with a lot of white people trying to play the blues. It's just absolute crap, you know what I mean?

Buddy Guy, Albert King, all these people. They're the real deal, man. How can you compare those with… Clapton for instance – no one knows how difficult it was for him to play like that. Or how much practice it took. But I know from seeing him – speaking with Jeff Beck and Jimmy Page – we *know* that it doesn't come *that* naturally to him. So that's why, basically, his best work came out when he was playing with Cream and he wasn't playing the blues and he was stoned out of his head. So, I mean, I think people have got to be true to themselves and have fun.

How can you jam, and everybody knows what's coming next? How fucking boring is that? You know what I mean? It's ridiculous. Jimi – his idea of jamming was to sit down and play a riff. All you'd say was, "Oh, what key's it in, Jimi?" That's all you need to know – *F sharp, fine.* Because once you know the key…they don't call it they *key* for nothing. That will tell you basically that there's a few notes you can't play, and that's it. What else do you need to know? You don't need to know anything else. All you need to do is use your bloody ears, for goodness sake. And then interact with the people you're playing with and try to anticipate the changes. Not force the changes, but guide the changes by what you're playing. That's called jamming to me.

AP: To me, that's a beautiful lesson in music. I'm hoping that some musicians will be reading this book and going *wow – I need to re-think my approach.*

RM: You really should. Because, I mean, first of all – if you don't have the correct approach and you're not having fun, how will you come up with something new? You tell me. You won't. People ask me all the time, "How do you go about designing new sounds?"

With Jimi, when we used to sit down together and we were being quiet or we're hanging out at the pub, he might talk about a song, but he'd say, "Look – this is the story for the song." And that gave you the vision. If you've got the vision for the song, like *oh yeah, 'Little Wing' is about this,* and at the end it's a little story. Once you've got the beginning and the end, or you've got a synopsis of the script of the song in broad brush strokes, then you get an idea of what sounds you might want to use during the song to take people on what would be a sonic journey. That's what Jimi and I tried to create in the studio – a sonic soundscape that transported people into a musical journey from the beginning to the end of the song. Much in the same way that an orchestral philharmonic piece would be. The actual composer has got a broad palette of different sounds to create incredible music.

Of course, as you go slightly forward, more to the jazz and the more experimental jazz, then they've got different horn parts, different sounds. Much more complicated rhythms. That's why if you went to see Miles or Coltrane or somebody like that, he'd never play the same thing twice. I don't know anyone who plays the same thing twice. Albert King never did. Buddy Guy – any of these people. Why would they? They don't have to remember *exactly* what they played last time. Because that would require too much brain power. If you're playing continuously, you've got so many different ways of moving from one sequence to another, right? It's virtually unlimited. You can't practice that – you won't have any fun doing it – because you're trying to pre-conceive something that hasn't already happened. It would be like a tennis player trying to choreograph a particular set play. They don't do that. They play so that their mind gets into the game, and they've got all the muscle memory and the experience so that they can anticipate what's going to happen. That's how it's done on a professional level; much the same as the way Jimi played. He never mentioned to me *oh, that's a hard song to play – it's tricky, I've got to remember this.* Never! I mean, you'd never talk about it. The thing you ever might talk about in the studio is the type of sounds we were going to use. And you can't talk too much about it because you've got to create them. And that takes two people, normally. It's very interesting.

So if someone wanted an insight into Jimi – he played guitar an awful lot. On his own, or around people. Better around people – it was more fun playing in front of some-one. It doesn't matter if it's three or four people in a small room. It's too paradoxical playing on your own. You're going to have more fun playing with people and reacting to them. Just playing a riff and just having fun, basically. That's what Jimi did.

I saw him play live maybe eighty, ninety times. It was

a lot. But I mean, I know what the guy's capable of. If I'm standing beside the stage, Jimi's only got to smile at me, and you give him a smile, and that's reassuring – that your mate's over there and we're going to have a good time. Because there's only six feet between you. If you look at it from another standpoint: Jimi's in the spotlight, he's playing the guitar, he's got all the pressure on him. But he's only got to look sideways six feet and that brings him down to earth and grounds him, you see. Because being in the spotlight's one thing, but if you're playing a thirty-minute concert, in a whole day that's only thirty minutes out of twenty-four hours. It's a small percentage. Two or three percent of the day.

AP: I'm really interested to hear a little bit more about Jimi's flat. Could you paint sort of an image of the scene there?

RM: If you go online and you look at the Handel House museum, they've got pictures of Jimi's bedroom and flat that we used to hang out at in Brook Street. That was one of the later flats. The earlier flat was in Upper Berkeley Street. Just a regular two-bedroom flat, really, with a living room in the middle and a bedroom at each end. And a kitchen. Jimi used to hang out there, and we'd all meet up there. If Chas was around there, we'd listen to records and just play cards, play games, whatever. You know, you didn't have much TV then, and videos didn't exist. No internet, no distractions. So you just had music and the nightclub, and that was it. And the recording studio. Or going over – Jimi might just want to play some ideas for you. *Have a listen to this*. And he'd gauge your reaction.

You'd say, "Oh, yeah – that's a nice riff, Jimi."

"Yeah, yeah – we can use that later." His songs were put together over a period of time by all different segments of him playing. Not tricks – but riffs put together and so forth.

ap: Do you remember a riff that you heard, Jimi just saying, "What do you think of this?" And then that went on to become one of the iconic songs?

rm: Oh yeah. That happened quite a lot. We were both into science fiction – it's an escapism, as you begin to realize that someone's imagination has painted a wonderful picture and described it in an alien world. What it came down to – and that came down to the music as well – if you could imagine it, it's probably possible. In your mind – maybe not in reality – but in your mind, or in the music.

And we're programmed to recognize all kinds of different sounds. Danger sounds; all kinds of different stuff. The sound of the mother, baby crying, all these things are programmed into us. You don't learn those. It comes with the package when the baby's born. The fact of the matter is that when you listen to a record, or a sound, you've got about eight seconds, and the brain makes up its mind if it likes it or it doesn't like it. Almost instantaneously. If you hear someone play the guitar, it doesn't take you more than, maybe, maximum ten, twenty seconds. If they're sensible, you can work out if they can play or not. Doesn't matter what they play, but something comes across in their playing that would either be attractive to you or won't be attractive to you. With different sounds that you're going to make – like I put together the Octavia for 'Purple Haze' – people loved that sound instantaneously. It had almost an electric reaction with the crowd, because it's so alien – yet it's so exciting.

AP: Let's say you're with Jimi, just kicking back – what would you talk about?

RM: What would we talk about? We'd talk about the possibilities of recording, and the soundscapes that you can create. I mean, you've got to realize stereo was brand new, then. 1967-1968, there weren't many records that were in stereo. *Sgt. Pepper's* was in stereo, but up to that point in time, most of the records were in mono. But stereo was just coming out, so the actual techniques of moving the guitar around, and using other techniques, various echo techniques. The concept of – you can have a concept, basically – what I call a 'brick wall' concept of mixing a record. That means that you decide where the drums are, the bass and the vocals and this and that. You position them and you add a little bit of echo and you mix the record. But nothing much changes from the beginning of the record to the end of the record. So you have created just one fixed soundscape that gets imprinted in someone's mind. And that's just the fixed, brick wall, simple technique. Not to be denigrated, but that's what it is. Now, when stereo came in, and a few people experimented by moving the image around, you then began to realize that – *ahh, that's painting a completely different soundscape, because it's moving.*

Knowing that, you can also add into the other equation which Jimi and I worked out. That by carefully crafting the equalization, and also the echo and the reverberation that you're using, then you're really getting into science fiction territory, because it could be perceived as being far away. And then, by manipulating the parameters, you can make it appear to zoom towards you or zoom away, like a spaceship might do – or a racing car or something like that. But you have to first have a vision – an understanding of what you can do, and when it would be appropriate. And that comes down to the person who's writing the song and also somebody like me, who's explaining to Jimi what can be done and what can't be done. Or what we can do – just injecting different ideas, you know. In a way it's a bit like being chief engineer to a racing car driver. To get there, you come up with a fast lap.

AP: In terms of this science fiction stuff, and the sound-scapes, the first thing that pops into mind for me is 'Third Stone from the Sun'. Were you in the studio when that was being put together?

RM: Oh yeah. I can't remember a lot of it. That was early on, it was on *Are You Experienced?* I was there for an awful lot of the sessions. I was definitely there for pretty much all of *Axis: Bold as Love*. And obviously 'Purple Haze', 'Fire', and a lot of sessions leading up to the summer of '67, when Jimi went to Monterey. We actually considered – making a record is completely different than playing live. Nothing at all to do with one another.

AP: In terms of his interaction with Noel and Mitch, do you remember any specific moments of their interaction – I imagine early on especially, they would have been having some laughs and enjoying themselves quite a bit in the studio.

RM: Oh yeah – that was the point. Jimi, for instance – you've got to realise, Jimi chose Noel to be his bass player. Noel wasn't a bass player, he was a guitar player. So Jimi chose him to play the bass. And many times, Jimi told Noel roughly what he imagined the bass part would sound like. He'd just show him. Or Jimi might go over to Mitch and play the guitar and say *oh yeah, the beat's this…* and hum the beat out, right? And they'd get some synergy happening between him and the drummer, and allow Mitch enough freedom to take it further, if he could. I mean, Jimi was the captain of the ship. He was in charge, for sure – of inspiring and also helping the people to produce the musical part that he imagined.

It was all very exciting, because it happened quite quickly. Recording time back then was very expensive. As a matter of interest, Olympic Studio then was about thirty quid-an-hour, thirty-eight quid-an-hour. Now, that worked out in those days as 250 pints of beer. *An hour.*

aP: Wow. That's amazing.

Rm: I mean, guitars were expensive back then too. To buy a new Stratocaster in London in 1968 was about 40% of the price of a Mini. You could buy a new Mini for about £400-500. A Stratocaster would cost you about £150.

aP: I had no idea.

Rm: Oh yeah. Guitars were expensive, you see. Recording was expensive. I mean, you had to be serious in the studio, and you had to have your chops down. It's not like today, where – everybody thinks: *oh, isn't it wonderful, we can record everything…* What all these people forget when they produce 290 tracks on Pro-Tools and they have to give it to one of my mates to mix it, is that it takes him three days at £1000 a day to mix the tune, and then it still sounds like shit because it's been recorded badly – it's been recorded without any vision, not everyone was present… It's just ridiculous. In the old days, the idea for that song would have been rejected in about three minutes. *No, it's not good enough.* Why are they wasting that much fucking time in the bedroom on something that has no chance of ever being any good. Wouldn't they be better off going down the pub and relaxing and hanging out with some mates and writing four more tunes – they've got a better chance doing that, of being successful, than there are pissing around with one tune and producing 290 tracks on Pro-Tools.

aP: How did you come to meet Jimi, the very first time?

RM: Oh, I met him after a show at the Bag O' Nails club in London. I just introduced myself and told him what I was into, and the people I'd been working with. It was an evening where it was a who's who of people at the club – the Beatles and other people were there. He invited me down to a gig in a couple of weeks' time and I showed him one of the prototypes for the Octavia and he said *wow, wow*. Then we made a date for another show in about a week's time, and after the show we went to Olympic Studios, and that's when we recorded the two solos – one for 'Purple Haze' and one for 'Fire'. And that, as they say – that was the beginning of the end. Or the end of the beginning.

aP: At the start of the conversation, you spoke about the philosophy that Jimi had in terms of music – I'm wondering if you could expand that a little – did Jimi have a particular philosophy toward life?

RM: To a degree we talked about life, but music was – the actual creation of the music and playing – that was the inspiration for him. I think he probably enjoyed that more than anything. Being around the right people in the studio, creating the music. Because that gave him access to all the tools in the recording studio to paint the picture. The actual playing *live*, and getting from A to B in playing live can be very stressful, because you're not in control. Every day you can rock up to a different venue, and you're saddled with the acoustics of that venue – the reverberation and all the

76

pitfalls of that. Plus, you've been travelling and so on and so forth. That wouldn't coax the best out of you, 'cos you're under a lot of pressure. Travelling is tiring, and there isn't enough time. Jimi never came off a show and said *oh yeah, I really enjoyed myself – that was fantastic.* You know what I mean? That really wasn't brought up. Everyone else would say *oh yeah, you played great, Jimi – fantastic* and this and that. But Jimi would just say *let's go down to the Speakeasy and hang out.*

Many times, when we went off stage, the first thing we did was to pack up and get in a car and piss off out of there. We didn't want to hang around backstage particularly, because it's not very conducive to having a good time, is it? The last thing that I would want to do is be at an after party, really. The best after party would be down at your favorite pub. Not in the back of a theatre.

AP: Do you remember any moments where Jimi's humor really came to the fore, or if there was a mischievous quality…

RM: He liked to joke. He was very funny. If he was making a joke, you might see him – he kind of laughs behind his hand. So that was cute. And if you were playing and he came up with a little riff that he hadn't played before, that made him laugh. You could see that he hadn't played that before. So that was always amusing; by playing a lot and having fun, you're going to come up with fresh stuff. That's where the sense of humor comes. If you can make yourself laugh while you're playing guitar, *wow – that was fun* – you know what I mean? Then you're doing something right.

And obviously, playing cards or messing around and having fun, you would do that. His idea of fun might be: at the Saville theatre, *Sgt. Pepper's* had just come out, right?

The record had dropped not long before. So what does he do? Walk out on stage – opens up with 'Sgt. Pepper's Lonely Hearts Club Band'. Only about thirty seconds – but the Beatles were in the audience, and that must have been like firing a shell right across their bow. *This is how it could sound.* He used to like doing things like that – or he'd play 'Sunshine of Your Love' if Eric Clapton was about. Not to piss him off – it's like paying homage. *Here's one of your songs. I dig it.* He's not going to play the whole song; he's just going to play enough so anyone listening will go *Jesus Christ.*

AP: Did you ever see him jamming with Clapton or Page or Beck or any of those names?

RM: Jimmy Page didn't used to go and hang out at clubs much, anyway. I certainly saw Jimi play with Buddy Guy and Albert King and lot of other people – John Mayall, Mike Bloomfield. Whoever was in town: Billy Gibbons, Randy California, all kinds of people. Basically – if anybody wanted to get up and play – *come on.* You know what I mean? Someone had to kick off a rhythm or something. Jimi's not stupid, he's not going to play one of his songs and expect someone to play it, is he?

His general demeanor – the way he was with people. He wasn't arrogant in any way at all. As I said, he really enjoyed playing the guitar, you know. And he was very generous when he actually played with people. He would encourage them. He wasn't playing over the top of them. He was quite happy to sit back, because he had many years of experience of playing in R&B bands, with the guys out front in their shiny suits – everyone was discouraged to do anything in the backline to take away from that.

If you can get to the stage where you can virtually

play anything you hear in your head – *then*, the problem becomes *how do I think of new ideas*, you see? That's the difference. If you play a lot, you want to get to the stage where you can play things that you never played before, see? And how do you do that? *Just keep playing.*

• • •

Chas Chandler changed Jimmy to Jimi. Mike Jeffery provided the group name: The Jimi Hendrix Experience. The boys were treated to all the showbiz hype and presented with a contract. It was a rip off, but they readily signed. They knew this was their shot. If the band took off, they could renegotiate later. And so it was – they would receive 2.5% of royalties from record sales: split between them. They set off for their first tour the next day – four shows as the support act for Johnny Hallyday in France. As soon as they got back to London, they headed for De Lane Lea Studios to record their first single.

For this recording, Chas and Jimi selected 'Hey Joe', a solid Billy Roberts cover that was a staple in Jimi's stage act. The B-side was a Hendrix original, 'Stone Free', as a demonstration of his songwriting ability and some more elaborate guitar work. Seed money was spent in an effort to push the single up the charts. This process was also known as 'chart-hyping'; a combination of buying bulk copies from stores known to be used as data collection points for the charts, and bribery of various retail and radio personnel. Seed money would often get a single into the Top 40, at which point any further success would rest on the tastes of the buying public. The strategy worked. Within a month of its release in December 1966, 'Hey Joe/Stone Free' hit number six in the UK top ten. Jimi Hendrix had arrived.

Gered Mankowitz
The Experience

As RECORDING COMMENCED on *Are You Experienced?*, Chas Chandler and Mike Jeffery started the ball rolling with publicity. It was an exciting time for the group. Although the pressures on them were considerable, they could already taste the payoff. They were the new rising stars on fertile soil, accepted and applauded by the musical establishment. They were on the cusp of their own musical revolution, and they knew it.

And so, on March 9, 1967, the Experience piled into a van to be dropped off at the studio of Gered Mankowitz, official photographer for the Rolling Stones. Mankowitz was already a top name in photography and went on to shoot the cover images for albums and singles by the Stones, the Yardbirds, Marianne Faithfull, John Mayall, George Harrison, Slade, Traffic, Suzi Quattro, America, AC/DC, Eric Clapton, Cliff Richard, Donovan, Elton John, Bing Crosby, Kate Bush, The Who, Kim Wilde, Duran Duran, Genesis, and the Eurythmics, among many others. Images from these shoots have, of course, been exhibited all over the world.

Gered Mankowitz's photos of the Jimi Hendrix Experience were originally intended as cover imagery for *Are You Experienced?*. Mankowitz's choice of style for the shoot was distinctly black-and-white, and was later shelved in favor of color images shot by Bruce Fleming. The now-famous Mankowitz shoot remained unseen by the public until 1992. These images now grace posthumous album covers, official Hendrix marketing materials, t-shirts, posters… you name it.

GERED MANKOWITZ: Jimi struck me immediately as being the most extraordinary looking musician that I'd ever seen at that moment. He just had a wildness to him; a naturalness to him. He was an extraordinary performer, and yet off stage he was very quiet and very modest – very humble, very gentle. He seemed sweet-natured, funny, and yet on the stage was this sort of wild, sexual rock 'n' roll icon. And I was much more interested in the man, in the person. At that moment in time, it seemed to be very important that I treat Jimi with respect and dignity. So I made the decision to photograph him only in black-and-white. Because I related what I suppose one would call studio portraits as being black-and-white. But color was a bit trivial, a bit poppy. So I made that decision, and it was very stupid commercially. But I think it was very genuine, and very sincere, and I really did think that it was important to treat him as a really important musician, and not as a sort of potential pop star. That seemed important to me.

I don't know whether I even discussed it with him, because in early '67 we weren't using Polaroids. So as a subject, you had to trust the photographer completely. If you're not very experienced in having your photograph taken, you really can't know what the photographer is doing. You really do have to put your trust in him. It's not as though Jimi has had endless studio portraits and had a strong idea about how he should be portrayed. He didn't have *any*; he had no idea whatsoever. And so in that sense, what you establish very quickly is some sort of bond based on trust. That you're there to do the very best you can for him, and he's there to let you do it. And that's the key, because most people don't like having their photographs taken. *Most* people. Some love it. But generally, they're narcissists and the results generally aren't necessarily very good. The majority of people don't really like it very much. So you have to somehow draw it out of them. And he was very responsive – not in as much as I was directing him very specifically – 'cos I never did that, that always felt uncomfortable and wrong. It was more a question of making him feel comfortable and at ease in front of the camera, and to try and encourage him to communicate with me through the lens, and therefore with the viewer.

aidan prewett: How would you go about doing that? Especially with someone like Jimi Hendrix – how do you go about drawing out a persona or a performance in that setting?

GM: I think that what you do – I don't like thinking too hard about my technique, because then you become too conscious of it. But what I think you do, really, is you behave towards them in the way that you would like them to behave towards you. I think you have to strip any of your own ego completely, really. You have to focus on them, and you have to make it clear that you are on their side. That you are trying to communicate something about them – sometimes something about them that they're not even particularly sure of themselves. And you do it, I think, by being a friend. Just for that moment. It's a sort of – there is a sort of psychological aspect to it. But it's a professional thing. It's difficult to explain in too much depth, because as I say, I don't want to be that conscious about it. It's just in something that you try and draw out of people for that period of time, being a friend.

AP: In terms of that – in being a friend – specifically with Jimi – do you break the ice, was there some kind of a joke, was there humor involved?

GM: There's always humor, and there's always food. I discovered very early on that most musicians are hungry. And poor. And often have only just got up, rolled out of their pit into the van, and the roadie's dropped them off at the studio at sort of 12-ish. And they probably haven't eaten. And they're probably a bit hung over, and they're probably not crazy about being in your studio. And I found that food was a great icebreaker. And so I usually fed them. And that gave everybody an opportunity to just sit down; take a breath. Eat something, and chat. So the whole thing is, you try from the outset to turn the whole thing into a really friendly, close, intimate event. And that the photography is almost an incidental.

AP: The idea of someone like Jimi Hendrix coming into *your* space... what was that like? Did he sort of come through the door, was there a hubbub? Could you just talk me through the very first time he came to have his picture taken?

GM: There was no hubbub – there was no assistant, there was no stylist or security, there was no manager. His driver – his roadie – dropped him, with Mitch and Noel, off in Mason's Yard, which is where my studio was. And they just bustled in. There was probably a girl called Julia on the desk, she was very prim and proper – twin-set and tweeds – and she would have known they were coming, and they would have been hustled up the stairs and Jimi would have emerged in my studio on the second floor. And that would have been it. You've got to remember; he hadn't had a hit. He wasn't Jimi Hendrix the huge star. He was Jimi Hendrix: this enormously talented, this extraordinary looking, very nice, gentle, humble man. With his band – as far as they were concerned – early in the morning, coming to have their photographs taken. Which was part of their job as musicians. So it wasn't – there was no hubbub, there was no real expectation. I mean, I was shooting bands – let's see, '67. So I'd been shooting bands consistently since '63. And they'd been coming to my studio. The Stones had been there in '65. So for some people who were aware of my background, my history and my experience, coming to my studio was quite an experience in itself, for them. Because it was the studio where the Stones had been. It was the studio where Traffic, and Spencer Davis, and Free and a lot of others had been there. So it was part of the scene, if you like.

AP: Wow. So Chas Chandler wasn't there. That to me is really interesting.

GM: He never came. He never came to the sessions. He and I might have talked, but he completely trusted me. I don't think he gave me a brief. He knew that I would get something. I think he was disappointed that I didn't shoot color, but he respected me enough to know what I was trying to do. And I think that up to a point, he supported it. But the record company insisted on having color for the sleeve. So I didn't get the first album cover, which was a big disappointment. But the pictures were always great pictures, but they were limited commercially from the record company's point of view because they were black-and-white and not color. Nobody really shared my sort of

Irving Penn, Richard Avedon, Arnold Newman-type vision for photographing Jimi Hendrix.

AP: But I think the fact that they're black-and-white that they perhaps have stood the test of time more so than a lot of the color ones that are out there. I mean, yours – they're everywhere.

GM: They are everywhere – but everything is different after 50 years. After 25 years everything is different. I mean, the fact that Jimi passed so early and so young – you know, his career, his primary solo career is compressed into three extremely rapid, fast-paced years. And the fact is that he never really looked the same again. I mean, that moment – when he put on the military jacket and just stood there, he looked exactly as you would want Jimi Hendrix to look, and he looks like that forever. That's the power of a really strong portrait – it doesn't have anything added to it. It doesn't have anything hanging on it that ages it, or puts any sort of time frame on it. The purity and the simplicity of it is what makes it a timeless photograph. But, you know – I was trying to take *everybody* like that. I didn't know Jimi was going to become the star that he was, and I had no idea that the poor chap was going to pass in three years' time and become this great iconic symbol of rock 'n' roll insanity.

AP: You mentioned the military jacket – did he bring that with him? Was that his idea, do you think?

GM: Oh, completely. Again, you see – it's interesting, the way you phrase that. You're coming from a time where people were styled. He wasn't styled, not at this moment. He wasn't styled at all. He'd been introduced to the Kensington Antiques Market, and to a place called Granny Takes a Trip, and to a place called Lord Kitchener's Valet, which was up in Portobello Road, Notting Hill Gate. And Lord Kitchener's Valet sold ex-military, ex-services uniforms. And he found this jacket. He brought two military jackets, actually. And bits and pieces, and shirts, and velvet stuff and silk and satin that he bought at the Kensington Antiques Market, because people were beginning to wear frilly Victorian bed jackets. Fashion was going through a strange period where men and women were changing clothes, exchanging clothes, sharing clothes. And he brought everything with him in a couple of little canvas bags. There was no one else. There was no stylist, there was no makeup, there was no art director, there was no designer, there was no manager. Nobody. Just the three guys and me.

aP: Given that this was fairly early on, he was obviously getting along fairly well with Noel and Mitch at the time – I guess?

GM: Well, they were just – basically they'd only been together for about five months, I think. So it was full of energy and excitement, and I sensed that they were enjoying themselves hugely. He – at this point in time, when I worked with him, he had everything to look forward to. He was excited, he was positive, he was thrilled by the response to him, that the English music industry and the English press had had. He loved being in London, he loved the complete lack of any sort of racial tension, as far as he was concerned. He loved the acceptance. He was absolutely on the verge of this fantastic career. 'Hey Joe' had been out, maybe three or four weeks. Things tended to take longer to chart in those days than they do now. But he was right at the beginning, and it was exciting to be with him. He got on – he and the boys were in great shape. The atmosphere was extremely good – giggly and relaxed.

AP: Do you have any recollection of what any of the laughs and giggling would have been about?

GM: A lot of the giggling was about Mitch's pathetic attempts to look mean, moody, and sexy. The general feeling was that, you know, you wanted to be mean, moody, and sexy. And Mitch was a year younger than me. I was twenty, and I think Mitch was only nineteen. And he had this little baby face, and when he tried to look into the camera and give us the *mean, moody and sexy*, he just didn't – he couldn't. And Jimi thought it was funny. And a lot of the pictures have Mitch looking sort of cute and sweet, and Jimi giggling. Not that they were used or seen at the time.

AP: Was there any particular thing that Jimi said or a piece of a conversation like that that you can recall?

GM: Not really, and I don't really want to sort of be in a position where I try to make up a quote. But one of the things we talked about – a bit – was, we did talk a little bit about when he was doing the Chitlin' Circuit with the Isley Brothers or Little Richard. I'd been to America at the end of 1965 with the Stones. And being a very naïve and completely innocent North London kid, I was just completely blown away by the racism in the South and the segregation that I saw. That really made an impression on me, and I was completely taken aback. I wasn't prepared for it; I wasn't aware of it. The Stones were aware of it, because this was their fourth tour. They always insisted on playing the South, and they always had black acts on their bill. So they were, in a sense, being confrontational from the beginning. And I was very taken aback by the black artists having to stay in different hotels, and couldn't eat in the same restaurants and such. So all of that made a huge impression and we did talk a little bit about that. But I can't tell you specifically what Jimi said, it was just something that I felt that I could talk to him a little bit about, and we did.

AP: Do you remember any specifics of his view?

GM: I think, like most Americans, they just accepted it as being the norm, and that was what you dealt with, and that was how it was. And it was wrong, clearly, and it was a problem, but we didn't go beyond that.

AP: So Jimi visited the studio twice – was there a different feeling the second time?

GM: It's funny about the second session. The second session was only about five or six weeks afterwards and Chas rang me. He said, "You're going to have to do another session with the band."

And I said, "Why? What's happened? What's gone wrong?" Because in those days, to be honest with you, I would expect one of my sessions to last three to six months. That was always the idea because the artists in those days were working so hard, that to get an opportunity to do a proper session was rare. So I would try to make sure that I delivered a range of photographs that would keep everybody going for the next five or six months. To get a call back after only a few weeks was a bit of a shock, and I was a bit worried that maybe something was wrong with the pictures.

He said, "No, don't worry about it. I only want you doing pictures of the band – I don't need any more solos of Jimi." Because the guys had had their hair permed, to look more like Jimi. So Mitch and Noel had permed their hair into a sort of stylized afro, and to give the band a little bit more of a uniformed look. And, of course, the pictures that I'd done from the original session, they just had their own regular messed-up hair. And so they arrived with the intention of just doing a series a new group pictures. The guys with their funny afros. And Jimi had begun to style his hair a little bit and was already looking quite different to how he had been looking five or six weeks previously.

ap: Is there anything that strikes you as being different – between this icon and the real man?

gm: All I can ever do is to pass on my own personal feeling. He was very charming, he was humble and modest, he was quietly spoken. He looked absolutely sensational. He wore the fashion of the day. You know – he wasn't the only person dressing up in these Lord Kitchener's Valet ex-uniforms. I've got pictures of Keith Richards in the same type of thing. But he wore them perfectly. It was as though this whole moment in fashion history was designed specifically for Jimi Hendrix. And I sensed a sensitive, absolutely fundamentally nice chap. But none of the frustrations of success had entered into it. Which is why I said earlier – everything was before him. And it was an optimistic moment in his life, and he was excited and thrilled to be looking forward. But I don't think it took very long for the rigors of his work schedule and the frustration began that he experienced as an artist. He was clearly a genius musician, and an artist who needed to evolve and develop – and I think he found playing the same songs over and over again difficult. But I only knew him briefly, for a few moments. I didn't hang out with him; I wasn't a mate of his. I bumped into him a couple of times at clubs afterwards and we'd have a drink and eye up the girls. But that was as far as it went.

AP: Well, on that note – if you're eying up girls with Jimi Hendrix – how does that go? What happens there?

GM: Well, they're all looking at him and not at me, I can tell you that. He was certainly a sexual magnet. He had fantastic sexual charisma. And he loved it – I mean, he appeared to love women, and they seemed to love him. He certainly was never short of female company, as far as I can work out.

AP: And you were about twenty at this point – is that right?

GM: I was twenty, yeah.

AP: How does one, at the age of twenty – what was the journey that got you to become the photographer for – I mean, were you with the Stones at eighteen? How did that come about?

GM: I started with the Stones at the beginning of '65 – when I was eighteen. I went to America with them when I was nineteen. I started my own studio when I was just seventeen, and I think I did my first album cover when I was sixteen or seventeen. The thing is that you have to understand that things happen in a strange way. I was very lucky. I started photographing young actors, shooting their 10x8 glossies. And a couple of them announced at the session that they were folk singers and that they played in a coffee bar in Mayfair, and would I come down and take some photographs of them. And of course I did. They started to have a bit of success and they were signed to a record company, and that record company took my photographs, and then asked me to photograph them again, and gave me other artists of theirs to photograph. So my focus was always on music, and I just got picked up very quickly.

Andrew Loog Oldham, who managed and produced the Rolling Stones – he saw pictures that I'd taken of Marianne Faithfull at the time, with 'As Tears Go By' and he liked them. It was a time when you'd meet somebody at a dinner party and you'd say *oh, what do you do?* And they'd say *oh, I'm a singer.* And you'd say, *well, what's your name?*

"Marianne Faithfull."

"Well, I'd love to photograph you."

"Okay, well why don't you pick me up at ten o'clock tomorrow morning?"

"Okay, I'll see you then."

It sounds ridiculous, but that's how it happened. I met Marianne socially, I photographed her, I took some great photographs of her. She was managed by Andrew Oldham, he asked me to photograph the Stones… And Andrew understood that fifty percent of it was chemistry. He was very good at putting people together. So he put me together with the Stones, and that seemed to click. And then suddenly you had little old me popping up, who was this kid with a Hasselblad, who just seemed to fit in. And obviously had a vision, without knowing what that was. I just did what I thought would be a good idea – like photographing Jimi in black-and-white.

• • •

Gered's photographs were shelved – for the time being. But the photographs from the two Mankowitz shoots have since taken on a life of their own, providing a visual insight into the humor and enjoyment of the early days of the Experience. Jimi was already impressing those around him with his 'fundamentally nice' personality. Meanwhile, Mitch Mitchell was trying his best to look mean, moody, and sexy. Chas Chandler and Mike Jeffery decided to use color imagery for the cover of *Are You Experienced?*. Nobody was going to argue with them – Jimi's business partners were no joke.

Mike Jeffery had managed Chas in the Animals. They'd had serious hits before. The entire track for 'House of the Rising Sun' was recorded in less than fifteen minutes and hit number one on both sides of the Atlantic. And Chas was quick to prove the benefits his experience in other ways. One night after a gig, Jimi, Chas, and Kathy were followed by two guys who were hassling them, looking for a fight. Chas had dealt with this scenario many times on tour with the Animals. He told Jimi to keep walking with Kathy, and promptly decked one of their assailants. The other one scarpered.

Meanwhile, Mike Jeffery's past was riddled with innuendo and rumor. He liked it that way. He had served in the British Army and then the Secret Intelligence Service during the 1950's, where he had worked largely in anti-communist operations and become fluent in Russian. He was involved in significant operations during the Suez Crisis and had been on the Italian border with Yugoslavia during Tito's dictatorship. One story Mike told his close friends: he had to kill a Yugoslavian guard in order to get out of a tricky situation. He then found a photo of the guard's family while looting the body. He kept the photo. True? Who knows.

Mike later told his secretary he wished he'd done all his bookkeeping in Russian. He was very fond of the tax-dodge and perfected his method while managing the Animals: investing the band's funds into offshore businesses in the Bahamas. Of course, Mike was the only one with account access. He took more than a healthy cut for himself. But the band members were initially happy – they were 'accruing massive interest'.

Mike Jeffery was a charismatic, alluring figure. He came dressed in standard counterculture attire – and he was pushing drugs. *If the artists aren't thinking straight, they aren't thinking about money.* And Mike knew how to charm them – until the breaking point. The Animals underwent several lineup changes and walk-outs prior to their eventual disbandment when Eric Burdon formed War.

But as the year 1967 clocked in, Chas Chandler was still paying the bills. He sold some of the bass guitars he'd used with the Animals. In this way, he cobbled together enough cash to book a top studio – Olympic. And with Olympic Studios came recording and mixing engineer Eddie Kramer.

Eddie Kramer
The Studio

THE EXPERIENCE LAUNCHED THEIR ASSAULT on the English scene, touring constantly and jamming at clubs and recording in between. Mike Jeffery secured them back-to-back gigs supporting acts like the Walker Brothers and Engelbert Humperdinck. Even at this early stage, Jimi was a hard act to follow. Amid the hectic schedule, sessions for *Are You Experienced?* had to be squeezed between an increasing number of performance bookings. The venues were getting bigger, and Jimi's price was going up.

These early tours established a kind of group dynamic within the band. Jimi was happy to hang out quietly backstage, Mitch was the prankster, and Noel was along for the ride. Fire extinguishers were set off in hotel corridors, smoke bombs on the tour bus, and water pistols were frequently employed to stave off the tedium between performances. Mitch once placed stink bombs under a rival drummer's bass drum and hi-hat pedals, rigged to explode on impact.

The fans were getting more intense, too. Jimi lost some hair to a young girl with scissors, and one poor bloke fell over a theatre balcony trying to get closer to the music. Imitating Jimi's wild stage act, the fans responded in kind, tearing up theatre seating and getting into brawls. At a show in Germany, Jimi was pulled off stage by fans. When he got back up, the neck of his guitar had cracked. Jimi decided to smash it. And some amps. And some mic stands. The crowd went apeshit.

The entire album *Are You Experienced?* was completed in sixteen sessions, while the Experience flitted in and out of De Lane Lea and Olympic Studios. Chas Chandler had serious recording discipline, and he liked to work quickly. Chas took charge and schooled the band – at that time, studio novices – in how to translate their raw live sound into studio finesse. Jimi was happy to take direction, for now. A small team set to arranging microphones and setting gear *just so*. They knew they were recording something special. Instrumental in this process was Eddie Kramer. Kramer was seated behind the mixing desk for much of *Are You Experienced?,* and his involvement grew with each subsequent Hendrix release.

Kramer himself is responsible for recording some of the most iconic aural experiences of the 20th Century: Nearly the whole of the Hendrix catalogue, the Woodstock recordings, five albums with Led Zeppelin, six albums with Kiss, further work with the Beatles, the Rolling Stones, David Bowie, and so many more. His contribution to the wider music industry continues to this day, so it's not surprising that Kramer has been recognized with a plethora of honors, including five Grammy awards.

EDDIE KRAMER: I think it's worthwhile expressing the thought that he made such an impact on the scene in London in '66 when he first arrived, it was like a meteor had hit the town. All of the famous musicians then are now superstars. We're talking about Clapton and Townshend and of course all the Beatles. Particularly Paul McCartney. Anyway, I went to see Jimi, and he was the star attraction. There's no surprise there. But what was surprising was the level of astonishment and amazement at this shining light of *blues magic*, I guess you would call it – who just turned the world on its ear.

And of course, the stories have been told many times about how Clapton said *oh my God, what are we going to do now?* Having seen what he did. And Townshend saying *Jesus, wait 'til you see him, mate – you're going to have a big shock.* So having that all go down, I had not met him yet. This was now, I guess, late Fall of '66. People in the music business were all sort of aware of Jimi Hendrix. I mean, you can't avoid it. He's in *Melody Maker* and *NME* and all of those magazines. You know how the British press are – they can be quite tough. But they were just over the moon about Mr. Hendrix. I'd heard about him, heard the singles, and went *Wow, this is really quite something.*

The first actual face-to-face meeting was I think late January of '67, when Chas managed to have enough money to come to Olympic to record. And just meeting him for the first time, he was very shy. Incredibly shy – sometimes painfully so, I think. And once he picked up the guitar, there was an instantaneous transition into *the man who's in charge.* The guitar – sort of – was this magical wand, I guess. He would just wave and *wham* – there was just this incredible sound.

Having heard about him; heard the records; heard all the stories; and then meeting him for the first time was like – *wow, who is this guy?* Sitting in the corner there, looking very introspective, wrapped in a sort of funky white raincoat. It was bloody cold as you can imagine at the beginning of the year in London. He didn't say much until the amps got switched on, and then he strolled – or rather ambled – over to the amp and plugged in and all of a sudden there's this sound that I'd never quite heard anything like.

It just overwhelmed me. It was not something I'd ever heard before, nor will I ever hear again quite in that way. You know – that impact. That initial impact of just being in the room with him playing was just mind-blowing. And then the other part of my brain kicked in, which was *shit – I'd better get my act together and record this man properly, somehow.* I just was running around like a blue-arsed fly, trying to figure it out, which I did. And he kept surprising me. He kept doing things that would make me go *wow, okay – so now what do I do? I really have to get to my next bit of gear...* And it was a race to the finish, to see who could top the other person.

He was showing off, and so was I, and it was brilliant. And we got on incredibly well. We sort of bonded because he kept giving me these sly winks and nods that meant *well okay – you could do that. Let me just try something else over here.* It went brilliantly. And that was the very beginning. There were many, many other instances in the studio, but that one always stands out in my mind.

AP: Do you remember what it was that he played?

EK: No, I don't. My memory's not *quite* that good. But I would hazard a guess – it was obviously one of the tunes that we had to cut. Whether it was 'Purple Haze', or one of the newer ones. We were working on *Are You Experienced?*, so it could have been any number of songs from that album that had not been cut yet. They'd cut 'Hey Joe' and 'The Wind Cries Mary' and maybe one or two others that were in basic form, but whatever had been cut before, other than the two singles, we overdubbed and tweaked and made better – whatever we needed to do. That first record was done at a very quick pace, as one can imagine. You had to remember that Chas Chandler came from the school of *we've got three hours, chaps – and I'm paying for this. Get your arses in gear!* And generally speaking, between the hours of seven PM and ten or eleven o'clock at night, he would cut a couple of tracks. Done. He wasn't buggering around.

AP: When everything clicked with Jimi, what was it about *you* that he was drawn to?

EK: I don't know. I guess I was lucky that I had a really broad musical education. I studied classical piano from the age of about four until I left high school. And my parents gave me a very wonderful musical education at home too. I listened to everything from Bach to Shostakovich. And beyond. So nothing really scared me, musically. My mind was open all the time. And the jazz thing that I got into. I got into jazz and rock 'n' roll as a teenager, much to the chagrin of my dad. But I experimented a lot at Olympic with very avant-garde jazz guys. So my musical tastes were very broad. So nothing he did surprised – well, I wouldn't say it didn't surprise me – but nothing really shocked me. The only thing that shocked me was the power of how he was presenting it. And the fact that my brain was open to all kinds of things. Experimentation was the name of the game.

AP: In terms of all that – is there a moment with Jimi that might illustrate something about his approach to making music – or his philosophy of music?

EK: It's interesting you use the word philosophy. I'm not sure that – I don't think Jimi was conscious of doing it in a philosophical way. But I think the question would be – where did he come from? You have to go back to his roots.

I think because of the nature of the human being, he was presented with a very strict set of rules from an early age. His dad was a strict disciplinarian, and as a teenager later on he gets into the army. There's another set of disciplinary rules and regulations. And somehow, he manages to work within that. And then he leaves the army and he's further into the discipline of the music business, which was the Chitlin' Circuit. And you couldn't get more tough training than – if you're standing on stage with, say, Little Richard or the Isley Brothers, and you put one foot out of place, you'd get fined five dollars, which was a lot of money in those days.

So think about his background, and how he was raised, and how he came up through the ranks – no pun intended – and then apply that to his discipline on himself and how tough he could be on himself. I think he was very open – this is the conundrum. If you put that on one side of the equation, and then you look at the mind of Jimi Hendrix, which was always open. His ears and his mind and his heart were always open. I think if a garbage truck went by a window he could pick up that sound and put it into the guitar, do you know what I mean?

AP: Oh yeah.

EK: So that's the best way I can think of describing his philosophy. It was just *all encompassing*.

AP: Is there anything that would illustrate something of Jimi's humor?

EK: Oh God, there's so many. Jimi loved to hang out with his friends. One in particular was Buddy Miles who always made Jimi laugh. But if one ever met Jimi – because he was so shy, very circumspect, very contained within himself

– his laughter was wonderful. He had a sort of sly, slick sense of humor. Very self-deprecating. And he also used to take the piss out of me and Mitch and Noel, and anybody who was in his immediate circle. But more importantly was how he laughed. He was so shy that when he laughed he put his hand in front of his mouth and laughed like a girl sometimes. *He he he* – that style of laughter. So he had a wicked sense of humor, absolutely cutting at points. But it was done in such a way that it would make the session go very well.

And he would break into riffs – let's say he's in the middle of a take, and the song is going downhill – rapidly he would break into a *Batman* theme, or *Peter Gunn*, or any one of those crazy shows. He loved TV; he loved television soundtracks. Theme songs from various television shows would creep into his music all the time. And that was just generally meant to keep things loose. And that was his *modus operandi*.

AP: You mentioned that he might take the piss out of people in the studio – do you remember a time that he might have taken the piss out of you?

EK: Oh, all the time – it was constant. Nobody escaped. But it was done in fun – it was in good form. *Don't get ahead of yourself* kind of thing, which is great. He knew – imagine all the egos in the room. There's only one Jimi Hendrix, and I was not going to battle that.

AP: With Mitch and Noel, could you tell me a little bit about how he worked in the studio with them? It's a really interesting musical dynamic that they had going.

EK: Well, just look at the two individuals. You've got Mitch, who is hyperactive like the energizer bunny. And absolutely brilliant, as a jazz drummer initially. Elvin Jones being his inspiration. And managing to take that jazz-influenced feel into his playing with R&B bands in the early sixties. And then meeting Hendrix, winning out against a bunch of drummers. His sense of timing was so crazy, in the sense that he could play a drum fill and we're all looking around going *holy shit, he's never going to land on the 'one'*, but he does. And then Jimi would look around at him with a jaundiced eye like, *I can't believe you just did that*. And break out laughing. So he was the perfect foil for Jimi's music, because he would do these outlandish, outrageous drum fills and then still keep the groove going. And I think intellectually he was on a par with Jimi. He knew what Jimi wanted. And Noel was grounded – even though he started off life as a rhythm guitar player, all of a sudden he's plunged into this world of playing bass. I thought he was perfect for Jimi.

AP: And of course, Electric Lady Studios – you obviously had a hell of a lot to do with that.

EK: Yeah, it was my idea – Jimi was going to have a nightclub, which you probably are aware of, and he bought this place called the Generation nightclub with his manager, with the thought that this would be a great place to jam. He was jamming there all the time anyway. The place went bust and was sitting there for six months. He and Michael Jeffery decided to buy it. And the word came down – the architect John Storyk has designed this beautiful nightclub for us, and we'd better get Kramer in to see if we can put a little 8-track studio in the corner someplace.

I walked down the stairs of this empty shell of a building underground, and looked at it and I said, "You want to do *what*? Build a *nightclub*? Are you out of your frickin' minds? Jimi spends over two hundred thousand dollars a year in studio time – why don't we just build him the best studio in the world, and you won't have that problem." And everybody looked at each other and said, "Oh yeah, that's a good idea – let's do that." And that started it all. Of course, Storyk pulled his hair out because he had the club all designed – but it started him off on his career.

ap: Specifically, in terms of recording needs, or desires that you had for that space – could you talk me through a couple of those?

ek: Well, up until this point, nobody had ever built a studio specifically for the artist. Most of these studios – or I would say *all* of them – were just bloody great big, uninspired boxes. But because of John's genius in design, we came up with something that looked cool, sounded great – which was a bit of luck and a lot of hard work. And we came up with a magical place that was owned by the artist, and made specifically for the artist. It was a place where you would feel immediately – *oh, I could make a record here.* Because it had a great vibe. And the vibe is part of the history. It's in the walls, this vibe. Yes, of course it had to look great, and sounds great. But it became this wonderful home away from home, that people would feel incredibly comfortable in.

ap: And of course I have to ask about Woodstock.

ek: I've never heard of it.

ap: My understanding is that you spent something like four days locked in a caravan just mixing everything – is that right?

EK: I wouldn't say a caravan – it was the tail end of a tractor-trailer, in a space about eight foot by eight foot. Basically, like being in prison, but with the door open occasionally.

AP: When Jimi came on – I'm guessing that of all the artists, you knew him the best – when he came on, what was going through your mind? What was your thought process, let's say when he launched into 'The Star-Spangled Banner'?

EK: It was well into the show by that point. Oh, it was magnificent. You cannot believe the searing quality of it – the fact that it had so much emotional impact. Think of the times – we're at war in Vietnam. And within a few months of Woodstock, he's formed a new band called the Band of Gypsies, and that's another wonderful part of Jimi's life. But just imagine, even though there were only a hundred thousand, or a little bit more than that in the audience, they were stunned with the power and the delivery. That's probably the greatest performance he did of 'The Star-Spangled Banner'. It certainly had the most emotional wallop and bang for the buck.

AP: Is there a specific conversation, or something that Jimi said to you, that you remember very clearly?

EK: Yeah, many. Every time we were in the studio, there was a conversation between the two of us when I'd kept the tapes rolling. Generally speaking, it would be at the end of each song, or just before. *Rolling, Jimi* – that kind of thing. He would say *take the headphones out* – as usual. What else is new? But at the end, I would always give a comment. In the later years as we started working closer together, when Chas wasn't involved anymore, he would look to me for an opinion. Which really was the beginning of my career as a producer as well. So I thank him for that.

And the word would be, "Yeah, that was a good take – but, you know – maybe *blah blah blah*..."

And he would go, "Yeah, let's do that." Or he would ask "How was the take?"

I'd say, "It was great!"

He'd say, "Yeah, but we've gotta do another one."

Of course, Jimi. Naturally. I wouldn't expect anything less.

ap: Is there anything that you wish people knew about Jimi that doesn't get brought up as much as you would like it to?

ek: He was a very kind and generous soul. He would never let a friend down. And a great example of that is: At Woodstock, when he was putting the band together for Woodstock, Larry Lee had just got back from Vietnam. I think he was pretty banged up. Now, music is a great healer, as we all know. And Jimi encouraged Larry to join him on stage. You see that row of beads that was hanging down in front of Larry's face, if you look at the Woodstock footage. I think he was kinda shy, and I think that gave him a feeling of *okay, there may be half a million people out there, but I don't have to look at them.* But Larry Lee was a dear friend. He may not have been the greatest guitar player in the world, but Jimi *wanted him to be on stage with him at Woodstock.* Not that anybody knew what Woodstock was ever going to turn out to be. But he was a good friend. And that, I think, is very admirable.

• • •

Are You Experienced? was launched in the UK on May

12, 1967. Within a month it climbed to Number 2. Only *Sergeant Pepper's Lonely Hearts Club Band* kept it out of the top spot. These were the two albums everybody was talking about that summer. Both became major hits across Europe and North America – and later, the world. *Are You Experienced?* is still held as a benchmark for groundbreaking musical innovation, not only by *Rolling Stone* and its contemporaries, but also by national institutions such as the Library of Congress. It only takes one listen to realize why.

In the US, however, the album was released a few months after its English success – and after Jimi's performance at the Monterey International Pop Music Festival.

D.A. Pennebaker &
Chris Hegedus
Monterey Pop

FOR THE AMERICAN MUSIC INDUSTRY, Monterey Pop was the perfect introduction to the Jimi Hendrix Experience. The festival was held from June 16 to 18, 1967, at the beginning of the Summer of Love. The scene was set: *Sgt Pepper's*, Timothy Leary, *Are You Experienced?*, Monterey.

D.A. Pennebaker, the acclaimed filmmaker behind the Bob Dylan film, *Dont Look Back* (1967), was there to make his next documentary feature. The film, *Monterey Pop!* (1968), became one of the most enduring motion picture documents of the era. Hendrix's performance is a clear highlight, among now-classic performances by Otis Redding, The Who, Jefferson Airplane, Janis Joplin, Country Joe & the Fish, Ravi Shankar, the Grateful Dead, the Mamas & the Papas, Simon & Garfunkel, and Laura Nyro, among others. Pennebaker's film provided a blueprint for audiences, who now had a motion picture demonstration of what *peace & love* looked like. The creators of Woodstock were paying close attention.

Hendrix and Pete Townshend famously flipped a coin to see who would follow who. Jimi lost and had to go on after the Who destroyed their instruments amid rudimentary smoke bomb effects. Hendrix, in the wings, saw this as a challenge. It was here that he closed the show with 'Wild Thing', then poured lighter fluid onto his painted Stratocaster and dropped a match.

Pennebaker – Penny to his friends – passed away in August 2019. He is survived by his wife and filmmaking partner, Chris Hegedus, and his eight children. I had the honor of meeting Penny and Chris at their New York offices in 2012, when this interview was conducted for the documentary, *A Venue for the End of the World*.

D.a. PenneBaKeR: Monterey was like a big party. I think 10 or 15 thousand people filled the place. And they were all kind of mixed between San Francisco types and Los Angeles types. And between them, there was not a lot of love lost. Between them, they each had their own kind of singers. And the singers were now going to sing for *everybody*. I mean, Janis – a lot of people had not heard Janis before. Or Hendrix. We just watched. The chemistry that took place was in place before we even got there. So we just watched what happened, and filmed it. Filmed everything we could film.

aIDan PReweTT: With Hendrix, most of the audience at Monterey had not seen him…

Da: Well I'd never heard Hendrix either – John Lennon had told me about him. He said there's this guy – a blues player – and he sets himself on fire. And I thought, *well that's blues like I had never thought about it*. I don't know what to make of that.

When I heard Jimi in the beginning, he was chewing on his – he had a pick, a flat pick that he was sometimes using, but he was chewing on it – I thought he was chewing gum, and I thought, this is really laid back. *He's chewing gum and he's going to set himself on fire?* What kind of blues is this…? And then, as you listened – at the beginning I just thought it was a racket. I didn't know what I was listening to, I had never heard him before, I didn't – couldn't make sense out of it. And about ten minutes into it, he just – it just stopped. As everybody in that audience did. It was just such an amazing kind of sound that he could conjure up out of that. I don't know – it was like he was going beyond music, in a way that nobody understood. So that really, he was trying to understand how it worked.

CHRIS HEGEDUS: We made a kind of a longer film using all of Jimi Hendrix's performance, which I edited. It was just – it's an incredible performance. Each song kind of somehow builds in excitement to the next song to the next song. You can tell the crowd – 'cos he wasn't really well known at that point – has all of a sudden *woken up* to what this guy is doing. I mean, Jimi's such an amazing creature to look at – he has this pink boa on and he's just fabulously wild looking. And how he's playing is amazing. It gets to the point where he gets down and lights his guitar, and you can just see everybody's faces in the front, like *oh my God, what is he doing?*

Before that, they had already seen The Who destroy their drum set and do all that – but this was like, *what is going on?* He's crashing the guitar and feedbacking erotically against the speaker with it. He kind of starts to throw pieces of this flaming guitar into the audience – although it wasn't really flaming by the time it reached them – but still, big chunks of his guitar are coming at them. In the audience, you can see fear in people's eyes – *woah…what's happening?* But I'm sure that performance, for that audience – I'm sure they never forgot it for the rest of their lives.

Da: The audience was watching a once-in-a-lifetime scene, through the whole thing. And that was such an amazing kind of aspect that for those three days, all the musicians – it wasn't like Woodstock. The musicians in a sense had agreed to throw the money away. Lou Adler was probably responsible for that – they were just playing for whatever the minimum music wage was at that point – which is amazing when you consider that these are the best musicians you could get together in North America. And that audience had such a feeling of *depth*.

I've since met people who were there – for instance, I got a traffic ticket out in East Hampton, for parking my car near a street that I shouldn't have. And I had to go to court in South Hampton, and I went in there dreading it because I thought it was going to be like a hundred dollar fine or something. And this woman, who was the judge, said, "Is there a D.A. Pennebaker out there?" And I thought *here's where the shit hits the fan.* And I said yeah, and I raised my hand. She said, "You made Monterey Pop?" And I said yeah, and she said, "I was there, and you're free." And I met her again recently, and she still remembers it – she's such a terrific person. She said, "You changed my life." She was young, sleeping out on this football field – it was such a collection of people, that you would never expect to spend time with. It was kind of an amazing moment in music, for everybody. Everybody in that film – it changed their lives in some way that they hadn't expected.

CH: I think it was a different kind of era then, because you weren't competing with so many things when you released a concert film. The exposure of the bands wasn't that widespread. At the time most of these bands were seen as too outrageous for family television. Monterey was really an intimate view of a performer. And I think one of the challenges, when you make a concert film, is to give the audience something that they can't get from being there in the audience. And that is that kind of close-up view or backstage view of a performer. And I think that's why we're as interested in following a performer off the stage as we are kind of seeing the performance as well.

• • •

After Pennebaker's passing I heard a wonderful story about Jimi Hendrix working as a sound recordist for Penny. I was able to ask Chris about it in March 2020.

CH: A few days after Martin Luther King, Jr. died in April 1968, a small group of musicians gathered together in grief to perform an impromptu concert in tribute to King at a small venue called The Generation Club in Greenwich Village. Pennebaker came downtown with a few rolls of film to record some of the evening. Hendrix performed, as well as one of his idols, Buddy Guy, plus Joni Mitchell and Janis Joplin with Big Brother.

According to Penny, at one point he needed someone to run the Nagra tape recorder while he was filming Janis. Hendrix volunteered and came down to the front of the stage and held the mic and recorded the audio. The footage is part of a yet to be released film that Penny called *Wake at Generation*.

Penny was very fond of Jimi and always thought of him as a gentle soul.

• • •

Shotgun microphones – as used in film and television – are precision instruments in their own right. They capture sound in a very direct line – focusing in on the exact area toward which they are pointed. The rule of thumb is to aim the mic directly at the subject's lips.

Jimi wanted to help. He took the tubular shotgun microphone and pointed it at Janis – or the band – or the speakers. He put on the headphones and listened to the highly focused sounds being delivered direct to his ears. The pure clarity of directional sound can induce an otherworldly, ethereal experience. For Jimi, recording Janis would have been magical.

And for that moment, on that night, Jimi Hendrix was an unpaid documentary filmmaking intern.

Keith Altham
Fire

THE MONTEREY POP FESTIVAL came into being at the behest of entrepreneur Alan Pariser, the Mamas & the Papas, and their record producer Lou Adler. They saw the three-day festival as an opportunity to promote rock music as an art form in the vein of the popular jazz & folk festivals. They recruited Derek Taylor, publicist for the Beatles, in the hope of a live performance from the band. The Beatles had no wish to face the seething throngs again.

This was the first festival to include big acts from each major city music hub: San Francisco, Los Angeles, New York, Memphis, and Chicago. This was the first time many of these performers were to meet each other in person; in many cases, they would enjoy each other's company.

Paul McCartney attended and was involved in the planning as a kind of talent scout. He had seen Jimi Hendrix perform in London and insisted that Monterey was the place to debut the Jimi Hendrix Experience in the States. He also suggested that The Who could use a re-introduction to the American public.

Chas Chandler and Jimi invited their journalist friend Keith Altham to accompany them to Monterey. After Keith's suggestion of the guitar flambé, it was more than appropriate for Keith to be the man to cover the incendiary

Monterey performance for *Melody Maker*. With his ticket to the States paid for by the Jimi Hendrix Experience and his return flight covered by the Who, Keith Altham found himself at the center of another critical moment – for both bands.

AIDAN PREWETT: Is there a moment with Jimi or around Jimi that summed up what Monterey was?

KEITH ALTHAM: It's difficult to explain. It was that kind of hippie dream; the flower power period that was at its zenith at that time. We stopped off in New York on the way over – to give you an indication of the reaction of the establishment. I used to try to hail a cab for Jimi in Greenwich Village. You had three chances of not getting a cab to stop for you: One, if you were a hippie; Two, if you'd got long hair; and Three, if you were black. And in Jimi's case, he made it on all three counts. So not only wouldn't they stop – they'd try to run him over. I had to hide him in shop doorways, hail the cab and then we'd pile into the back of the cab. And even then, we were forced to get out the back of a couple of cabs because of his appearance. He was wearing these pink boa scarves and a black hat, and long frizzy afro hair, of course. And the cab drivers all seemed to come from Brooklyn: everything sounded like *toity toid and toid street*. Except when they wanted Jimi to get out the back of their cab. Then it would be like, "Get that piece of shit out the back of my cab."

And on one occasion I took the guy to task and I said, "Why don't you just drive to the nearest police precinct and we'll have a little chat about civil rights." And Jimi is pulling me out of the cab by my collar. I said, "What are you doing?" The cab sped off.

Jimi said, "Look, Keith – I thank you, but don't do me any favors. Did you see his gun?"

I said, "No, I didn't see his gun, Jimi."

He said, "I did. Don't worry about it. I've been handling this shit all my life. And the next time we come here, they'll be asking for my autograph." And of course he was right. That's exactly what happened. But it was difficult, and sometimes just because of the disappearance and the fact that... He took little risks, and he knew what he was doing. He had a military jacket that he loved. He got it from Lord Kitchener's Valet in Carnaby Street. And the police even stopped him at one point for wearing this military jacket and degrading the armed services. This was a jacket that was worn in the Boer war. And it so transpired that it turned out to be – not an active service jacket, but a vet's jacket. The guys who looked after the donkeys that pulled the cannons, in the Boer war. And Jimi said, "Oh, that figures. I've always got the shit end of everything."

Monterey was a foot in the door for him. It didn't break him – Woodstock broke him, like it did for a lot of other acts. But it gave him a foot in the door, and people were aware of who Jimi Hendrix was. And there was an argument backstage at one point at Monterey, which I was privy to, where Townshend and Chas Chandler, basically – Jimi was in the background, pretending he didn't know what was going on. Jimi hated confrontation. Townshend was saying, "Look – there's no way I'm following Jimi Hendrix. I've seen what he does in England." I mean, Pete was a great admirer, but he wasn't having the Who follow Jimi, and having Jimi rip off his stage act – which was Demolition Derby. He said, "We'll toss for it." He tossed the coin and won, so the story goes – although I never saw that happen. And the Who went on stage and did their act before Jimi did his. So Jimi followed the Who – and he pulled out all the stops when he did it. Including smashing the guitar, burning the guitar and generally trashing the area. So it was a kind of repeat performance, in a way, of what the Who had done. But because he's such an extraordinary musician, I don't think anybody really noticed that. I think Chas was quoted as saying that somebody said to Townshend, "He's stealing your act."

Townshend said, "He's not stealing my act. He's *doing* my act."

ap: And Townshend was upset with you because he was paying for your return flight?

ka: Yeah – that's been a bone of contention over the years. I think Pete's memory kind of fails him. 'Cos I was the Who's PR for nearly 16 years. But that stage, when I was at Monterey, I was still working as a journalist. For the first 12 years I was a working journalist. Primarily for the *NME*, and then after that I became a PR for 23 years, looking after most of the people I'd written about in the first 12. And I think Pete's got it into his head that I was working for him, rather than working for the *NME*. My responsibility was to the paper, even though I was being paid for one-way by Jimi, via Chas Chandler. Chas had always said to me, "When I go to America, I'll take you with me – if we can get Jimi off the ground." So I said *great*. And that's what happened. But Townshend got a little bit irked about the fact that I was spending a lot of time with Jimi. I mean, I'd flown out with Jimi from London. That wasn't my fault; the Who were already out there doing gigs. Anyway, I gave them as good a write-up and as much space as I gave Jimi in the *NME*. So it all fizzled out. But it was just Pete fighting his corner for the Who. And this is what you expect from the man, you know. Good on him.

In fact, when we went to Monterey, one of the people who was introducing all the acts on stage was a guy from the Monkees called Peter Tork, who was a folkie. And this guy Richie Havens had a folk influence in the stuff that he did. I said to Peter at one point, as we were chatting in the bar backstage, "Have you ever seen Richie Havens?"

"Richie Havens is a god!"

Oh really? Okay – I'm not completely deaf.

ᴀᴘ: So it's not your fault that Jimi went off and toured with the Monkees shortly thereafter?

ᴋᴀ: No, no. They had formed some kind of contact. But that was a funny situation. Chas always inferred that it was some kind of master plan that he had, that they were going to play to lots of kids and create a lot of publicity because the kids wouldn't understand Jimi. It was the teenybopper audience that would come out for the Monkees, from the TV show. And what was Jimi Hendrix doing on there? But I think Chas knew that they would create a lot of publicity for it, and he'd just do a few opening gigs and then they'd scarper.

He arranged this –what would you say? Well, it was a *lie.* He and I together concocted a story when they got thrown off the American tour – well, he wasn't exactly thrown off, he left. 'Cos it wasn't working, and the kids *didn't* understand Jimi Hendrix, of course, at that age – nine or ten – coming to see the Monkees. We concocted a story that there was this group called the Daughters of the American Revolution, who objected to Jimi Hendrix's erotic performance, and that the minds of the youth were being corrupted, and so he'd been sacked from the tour.

That made quite a nice little publicity story in the papers back in England, in the *NME*, of course. But actually it was a complete fabrication.

AP: Fantastic.

KA: The Daughters of the American Revolution – or whatever they were called – had nothing to do with it. So you can see why I got my ticket to America, can't you?

AP: It's brilliant to see this stuff behind the curtain – the ingenuity that goes on. Speaking of which – Mike Jeffery. Did you come across him at any point?

KA: Oh sure, I came across Mike quite a bit. He was a kind of cloak-and-dagger figure, as you can probably gather from what you've read about him. There's some truth in that, and some exaggeration. He was an entrepreneur in Newcastle on the club scene, and quite a tough character. He was quite clever; he spoke a few languages. He wore dark glasses wherever he went, and a camelhair coat over his shoulders. He looked more like a boxing promoter than a rock group manager. I always found him to be okay. But there were stories about him manipulating Jimi. And arranging a kidnap in one instance, which he rescued Jimi from, having organized the kidnap in the first place. I don't know whether that was true or not.

You're not going to survive in the rock 'n' roll business, and certainly in the sixties, either as an artist or a manager or an agent, unless you have an element of ruthlessness. Because it's a ruthless business. Unless you have that quality, you're not going to be there at the end of the day. You're going to get eaten alive by the business. So some of these guys who had a reputation for being hard men, like Don Arden, who was Ozzy Osbourne's manager, amongst others. There were some more mafia-like figures in America. They were kind of tough guys, but they weren't *spies*, you know? That was an exaggeration, in those terms. They weren't Reg and Ronnie Kray. But there were a lot of the criminal element on the fringes of the rock business. You required security, you required minders, you required bouncers. And some of those guys, when they learnt the ropes, if they had a bit of a brain – like Peter Grant of Led Zeppelin – came through and managed major stars. Because you had to be tough. Otherwise you're going to get eaten alive. And your artists would get eaten alive with you. So I think that's where Mike fitted in. He wasn't as bad as people say he was, but he wasn't a pussycat either.

AP: Did you have a personal moment with him that might illustrate something of his character?

KA: Not really. I mean, I didn't know him that well. I was much more friendly with Chas than I was with Mike. Chas got written out in the end, by Mike. 'Cos Mike was more ruthless than Chas was. And in point of fact, I've always maintained that if Jimi had stayed with Chas – who had his heart in the right place – he'd probably still be alive today. But Jimi was one of those people who could never say *no* to anybody. He was a nice guy in many respects, but he just wanted everybody to be happy. So he signed this, he signed that; he said *yes* to everything so everybody went away with a smile on their face, having ripped him off a bit. A bit more; a bit more. That's where he came to grief, really – he just wasn't tough enough.

AP: Is there one particular moment that you had with Jimi that sticks with you more than anything else?

KA: Well I suppose, probably the last interview I did with

him. I did the last interview five days before his death, at
the Cumberland Hotel. I didn't realize it was going to be
the last time I ever spoke to him. But it was. And he was
in pretty good shape then, talking about the Isle of Wight
experience that he'd just had – that he wasn't all that happy
with. And even considering getting back with Chas Chandler, not as a manager, but as a producer. Because I think
he recognized that he needed somebody to be in the studio
to curtail his more extravagant excesses. And Chas certainly
would do that – I mean, he was a Geordie lad and straight-
as-a-die. And it was because of him that I got involved with
Jimi to begin with.

But Jimi was in a room in the Cumberland Hotel with
a bottle of Mateus Rosé which was a filthy, sweet wine that
he loved. And a couple of girls, I think. Alvina Jones and
somebody else. It wasn't Monika Dannemann. There were
two of them twittering away in the background, serving
drinks. Jimi's handmaidens. He was talking animatedly
about maybe putting a small band together again. I think
he'd realized that the big band didn't work, the Band of
Gypsies. Or if it did, it didn't work as well as he'd hoped.
I think he was disappointed with that, and trying to find
some other way out, you know? So that would be the thing
that sticks most in my mind, because it transpired to be
the last time I saw him, and the last time I spoke to him.
I remember about five years ago I was at the BBC studio
and they played the tapes back. Because it was recorded on
exceptionally good tapes for the BBC, of which they used
five minutes out of about half an hour, it brought back the
memories of that room and that time to such an extent that
it actually brought tears to my eyes. I thought *what a shame
he's gone.* Somebody that I loved. Not just for his brilliant
expertise on the guitar, he was a nice guy.

He was there when I made my first trip to America with him – my first trip to the States. We flew out for the Monterey festival together from Heathrow Airport, early in the morning. I sat next to him on the plane, and he found a blues channel on the headsets that were available in those days. And we talked about various blues artists that we liked. Jimi was a great magpie – he picked up on everybody else. He picked up on all these people like Elmore James and Son House and he knew a lot about the blues scene. His guitar style was really an amalgamation of all those people that he had listened to over the years. And to some extent, those people that he worked with, too. Like Little Richard and the Isley Brothers. If he saw something that he liked, he just stole it and put it into his act – into his guitar style. So what you got was an amalgamation of all those years of listening and soaking up music styles which turned out to be Jimi Hendrix.

I remember – one of the other things that comes to mind in that respect was that I remember one of the other acts I worked with afterward was the Police. Sting was a great Jimi Hendrix fan. This was long after Jimi had died. I went out to a jazz festival with him – in Perugia in France. It was a tribute to Gil Evans, who had died recently. He was Miles Davis' arranger and producer in certain respects. And I was sitting in the audience on this hot summer day, listening to the sound check. They were running through 'Little Wing'. I was sitting there thinking – *my God, they've actually found a guitarist who's almost as good as Jimi. He sounds wonderful.* Then I realized they had *two* guitarists on stage. Jimi had been doing on *one* guitar what they were managing to put together on two. That's how good he was. He would be playing bass guitar with his thumb, and lead with the rest of his hand. He had these incredibly long fingers and long arms. And he could make bridges on the guitar that were just extraordinary. I remember kneeling next to him once – there's a photograph of me kneeling on the stage with a few people behind me. I'm trying to work out how he actually… because I played a little guitar myself. *Badly*, I might say.

But I said, "How do you *do* that, Jimi?"

He said, "Well, put your hand on top of mine." Which I did. My hand finished roughly where his first knuckle was. I mean, he had these incredibly long fingers and long arms. It gave him that extra purchase on the guitar that ordinary guitarists couldn't get.

ap: Is there a moment of Jimi's humor that you recall?

ka: There was an occasion out in Majorca. I went on a trip to open a club called *Sergeant Pepper's Club*, which was owned by Chas and Mike Jeffery jointly. Jimi played the opening night there, and he managed to bring the ceiling down in the club with the neck of his guitar at one point. Which Chas and Mike had just paid a fortune to have stuck up, and he brought that down – that was quite funny in a way.

And the go-kart racing. Jimi loved go-karts. We went to this go-kart track in Majorca, and he beat everybody hands-down. We all got fed up with him 'cos he was far too good for us. But there was one little old lady on the track, who must have been 60 years old. And he could not beat her. And he stayed there, after we'd all left, because he was determined to beat this little old lady – who was a grandmother – on the go-kart track. He just stayed on and on until he could finally beat her on one circuit. I wasn't there when he did, but he said he did when he came back.

I thought that was quite funny. What are you calling the book, by the way?

ᴀᴘ: We're thinking about calling it *The Quiet Life of Jimi Hendrix*.

ᴋᴀ: That's great. I must have missed that one. Actually, there were elements of him that were gentle, and quiet. But everybody wants to know about the other one, of course. I think there was a bit of *Dr Jekyll & Mr Hyde* about him. You've seen what he did on stage – he was the wild man of rock when he was on stage. But when he was off-stage, he was quietly spoken, gentle and considerate. He talked in a very low, gentle voice. He'd tail off into et cetera et cetera et cetera a lot of the time; he wound himself down. And he liked his comics and his books. He read a lot of science fiction, which actually got into his lyrics. People thought they were LSD trips, but they weren't. They were usually Robert Heinlein or Asimov or somebody that he'd been reading at the time. I think he was a much gentler character and a much more fragile character than people realized. He would have his moments of rage, or anger, or whatever you want to call it, which usually came out on stage, or sometimes in his relationships. And that was the kind of *Jekyll & Hyde* thing, the stage side of it, and occasionally bursts of anger. But I think his primary character was one of softness and gentility. He was too nice for his own good.

• • •

"How do you do that, Jimi?"
"Well, put your hand on top of mine..."

Jimi's hands were part of the language of his music. Jimi connected with people in similar way. He didn't need to be a loud voice in the room. As reinforced here by his friends, a held gaze, a soft word, or a light touch might comprise Jimi's expressive nature. He enjoyed genuine connection with people.

Jimi's friendship with Keith Altham gave the Experience an excellent foothold in the music press. *Melody Maker* was one of the top music magazines in Britain, with a history stretching back to the dance bands of the 1920s. *Rolling Stone* didn't exist as a publication until November 1967 – it was founded in San Francisco shortly after Monterey Pop. So when *Melody Maker* carried a story, the international music press was paying close attention. And Keith Altham knew how to spin it: the Daughters of the American Revolution article was sure to turn some heads.

But Keith's personal recollections provide a genuine human context to what has become the Hendrix Legend. The Monterey coin toss with Pete Townshend and the guitar flambé now feel more visceral. And the story of the time that Jimi went go-karting with a Spanish grandmother. Priceless.

At Monterey, Peter Tork of the Monkees had been watching closely. He could see that Hendrix was getting some real cred from the music press and other artists. He decided that he'd like some of that for himself. I mean, the Monkees were killing it in every arena – save that of their own credibility. The Monkees put in a call to Mike Jeffery, inviting Jimi to support their upcoming tour. Mike started congratulating himself before he talked to Chas. Or Jimi.

In the US, the Monkees were outselling everyone bar the Beatles. A support slot with them would mean big, big exposure. But the Monkees were bubble gum pop. Their audience was made up of twelve-year-olds. Jimi thought it was ludicrous; Chas told Mike Jeffery he felt the same way, that Jimi's act would scare them. The tour went ahead anyway. Mike was tightening his grip.

Al Kooper
Like a Rolling Stone

THE MONKEES TOUR turned out to be the most farcical venture so far for the Jimi Hendrix Experience. Monkees fans were indeed too young for Hendrix, and most of them were accompanied by their parents. The kids tried to drown Jimi out, screaming that they just wanted to see Davy Jones. The parents were outraged by Jimi's imitation lovemaking with his guitar. Jimi left the tour after eight shows. He spent the next couple of weeks in New York, flitting in and out of clubs, jamming, and making connections with New York musicians. Jimi had his pick of the scene – and one musician he loved was Al Kooper.

Al is responsible for the improvised organ riff that leads Bob Dylan's 'Like A Rolling Stone'. That riff, and the song itself, marked a turning point for rock music in 1965: folkies could play, too – and they opened rock 'n' roll up to bigger concepts and arrangements. It is no secret that Jimi loved Bob Dylan, and the song became a live staple of Jimi's concerts and club jams. When Al and Jimi found themselves in the same city, Jimi would make sure to feature Al playing his original organ part. Al Kooper later worked in the studio with Jimi, providing organ for 'Long Hot Summer Night'.

Al Kooper plays a bunch of instruments. He is featured

in a variety of roles on albums by B.B. King, The Who, Bo Diddley, Alice Cooper, and Cream. He played French horn on the Rolling Stones' 'You Can't Always Get What You Want'. He produced the first three albums by Lynyrd Skynyrd. He founded Blood, Sweat & Tears.

Al and Jimi initially hit it off at Monterey Pop in 1967, where Lou Adler had recruited Al as the stage manager. The following year they saw a lot of each other in New York, where Jimi found himself in charge of production on *Electric Ladyland*. And he dug Al's organ sound.

aiDan PReweTT: Of all the time that you spent with Jimi, is there one moment that has stuck with you more than any other?

aL KOOPeR: There was a restaurant that we all hung out at. And I went in there by myself one night and he was sitting at a table with two women. He called over to me when I walked in. He said, "Hey, hey, Al – what're you doin'?"

I said, "Oh, I was just gonna get some dinner."

He says, "Well, come join us."

I said, "You sure it's okay?"

He said, "Yeah, yeah, yeah."

So I sat down and their food was just being delivered, and it looked fantastic. I said, "What is that? I've never seen anything like that on the menu."

He said, "Oh, they make this for me – I really like this."

I said, "Well, let's have one more order." And so I had this delicious meal, which he refused to let me pay for. And a lovely conversation. It was just great. He was so relaxed; it was great to spend time with him.

aP: Do you remember what it was that Jimi had ordered?

aK: Not anymore! I think that the reason I enjoyed that

meal with the two women was that he was the most relaxed I ever saw him. He was in a good mood; he was very relaxed. And the food was very good. It was just a really nice evening.

aP: What kinds of things would you talk about?

aK: I don't even remember. But because I met so many people and worked with so many people, I got unintimidated very early on. So it wasn't a problem. I recorded with Dylan, George Harrison, the Rolling Stones... So it wasn't a big deal. These are all – we're all human beings. So it's really more like that. But that meal that we had was the most comfortable I've ever seen him. We must have been in that restaurant for about two hours.

aP: You were one of the musicians on *Electric Ladyland*, is that right?

aK: Yes – I just played on one song. 'Long Hot Summer Nights'.

aP: Could you tell me a little bit about recording in the studio with Jimi?

aK: Well I had more experience playing with him in clubs. When neither of us were on the road, we would probably do that at least once a week. He lived half a block from me, so we would always bump into each other. But an interesting thing was that when I played on that song for his album, I got there early. And of course, this was after we already knew each other pretty well. So I went into the studio and I was trying to play one of his guitars. You know they're upside down, strung backwards. So I was curious to see if I could get anything out of that. And just as I was doing that, he walked in.

And he said, "Do you like that guitar?"

I said, "I can't tell because somebody strung it all fucked up and I can hardly play it."

He said, "No – do you like the guitar?"

I said, "Yeah, it's beautiful."

He said, "I'd like to give it to you, as a gift."

I said, "Oh no, no – no, I don't think so." We sort of dropped the subject. And the next day, his roadie brought it to my house. I said, "Well, okay." I moved around a lot, different cities in my life. And every place I went, my house got broken into, because people wanted that guitar. Finally, I got really sick of that and I sold the guitar. I can't remember what year, but it was a long time after I had gotten it. As I recall, it sold for about $100,000. At that point. If I had it now, it would easily sell for a million.

aP: What kind of guitar was it?

aK: It was a black-and-white Fender Stratocaster.

aP: Wow. So if you're jamming in a club with Jimi – how does that play out?

aK: The two of us will say, *well – let's play this, or let's play this,* and then we do. I wasn't interested in doing anything but playing *behind* him. It was his show, as far as I was concerned. Also, that was more comfortable for me.

aP: Was it jamming in the sense of *finding a riff* and going with it, or was it specific songs?

aK: Both.

AP: Is there a particular song that – when you're jamming with Jimi – just works every time?

AK: Probably 'Like a Rolling Stone'.

AP: Lots of people have said that he was very quiet back-stage, or that his persona in the wings was quite different from his stage personality.

AK: Well, yeah. I think probably every front man is like that. It's a different thing. When I used to play, over the years, I would talk between songs and I would just sort of ad lib and be funny. And that came to be known as my stage demeanor. So if you went to see me perform a lot, you could count on the fact that you were going to laugh.

AP: Do you remember the very first time you met Jimi?

AK: Yeah, that would have been – the first time we were able to speak to each other was at the Monterey Pop Festival. I was the stage manager. And so we had to talk. But he was – he was really nice, and he invited me to play with him on 'Like a Rolling Stone', but the person in charge wouldn't let me do it – Lou Adler. 'Cos I was technically working.

AP: So, as stage manager, did you know he was going to set fire to his guitar?

AK: Well, I believe the Who had already smashed up their instruments, in the chronology of the festival. But the question is – who got it from who?

AP: Is there a moment for you that would sum up what that festival was about?

AK: I would have to sit down and think about that. But

the management let me play a very short set with some of the musicians that I knew that were there. So that was kind of a high point. I think it was the drummer from Paul Butterfield's band – mostly the rhythm section from Paul Butterfield's band. Three or four of us.

AP: The Pennebaker footage of that festival is just mind-blowing.

AK: It's in the footage of that – just one song that we did. I think it was 'I Can't Keep from Crying Sometimes', which is a song I used to do with the Blues Project.

AP: In terms of being on the side of the stage while Jimi Hendrix is on stage at Monterey – and burning the guitar – what was going through your mind when he was doing that?

AK: I'd read about him doing that in England. And mostly I was enjoying it because Lou Adler was standing not far from me, and he was furious that that was happening. I enjoyed that as well.

• • •

Monterey Pop kicked off the Summer of Love and laid the foundations for musical collaborations to follow. Jimi was thrilled to meet his American contemporaries – Al Kooper and Jack Casady among them. Kooper and Casady later contributed to *Electric Ladyland* and jammed with Jimi at the clubs around Greenwich Village. Jimi was always looking to sit in with other musicians – to work with a new, fresh energy. And Jimi had a genuine appreciation and affection for his musical friends. The gifted Stratocaster is proof of this.

Monterey was a major career moment for Jimi. He had arrived in the States – heralded by the British rock establishment. But the impending Monkees tour would provide the impetus for the demise of the relationship between Jimi's managers. Mike Jeffery wasn't listening to Chas Chandler. Chas was on the ground with Jimi – he was at the gigs; he was *living* with Jimi. Shouldn't he be taken more seriously in his business partnership with largely absent Mike?

Chas was also growing frustrated with Jimi. After *Are You Experienced?*, Jimi started doing more of his own thing on the road and in the studio. He was listening to Chas less and less.

Anthony DeCurtis
'67 US Tour

By 1967, hippies were turning on, tuning in, and dropping out. They were centering around gathering places and hubs in cities across the US. There were epicenters on each coast. San Francisco had Haight-Ashbury and New York had Greenwich Village. The era was rich with possibility. Meaningful change seemed imminent. *Think for yourself, question authority.* Vietnam protests were ramping up and there was hopefulness and a sense of unity and fraternity among the people of the counterculture. Greenwich Village epitomized this feeling of togetherness with impromptu gatherings, music, dancing, and other performances throughout the day and night in the park beneath the Washington Square Arch. Bongos and caftans in the open air; slightly dazed people drifting in and out with long hair and acoustic guitars. This was the small Mecca in Lower Manhattan that had been Jimi's home in the Café Wha? days, and it would be again. But for now – July 1967 – Jimi was just passing through, a touring musician stopping in at his favorite haunts.

It's important to explore the nature of the Village, because this vibrant area formed so much of Jimi's world during his extensive time in New York City. The idealistic free love atmosphere provided the backdrop for the creation

of Jimi's music and his lifestyle – flitting between the clubs
and jamming with his musician friends. This area was his
home as much as London was.

Living in Greenwich Village at the time was a teenage
music fan by the name of Anthony DeCurtis. DeCurtis
grew up in the thick of the Village happenings – right
on Bleecker Street. His experiences in his formative years
created a deep connection with music. DeCurtis went on
to become a Contributing Editor at *Rolling Stone.* His writing has received some of the highest accolades: his essay
accompanying the Eric Clapton box set *Crossroads* won the
Grammy for Best Album Notes, and the book *Soundtrack
of My Life,* co-written with Clive Davis, is a *New York
Times* Best Seller, among ASCAP awards and many others.
DeCurtis is also a longtime member of the nominating
committee for the Rock & Roll Hall of Fame, and a frequent judge for the Independent Music Awards. While he
never met Jimi Hendrix himself, DeCurtis witnessed some
of the earliest Experience gigs in New York.

In July 1967, three days prior to joining the Monkees
tour, Jimi featured as the support act for the Young Rascals
for a concert in Central Park. This show foreshadowed the
coming weeks – the Jimi Hendrix Experience left the stage
with little room for anyone else to stir excitement. It was
clear to everyone present that Jimi would soon be the headliner. In the audience at Central Park that evening was an
impressionable teenager named Anthony DeCurtis.

ANTHONY DECURTIS: They used to have these concerts at
the skating rink in Central Park. They were sponsored by a
beer company called Shaefer Beer. They were either free, or
like a dollar – but you had to get tickets. I was going to see
the Young Rascals. This was in 1967 – it was right around

the time that *Are You Experienced?* came out. But I was a big Rascals fan, I really liked them.

I was fifteen. As I was walking to the show, I saw all of these hippies hanging around. I thought, like – *wow, these don't look like people that are going to come and see the Young Rascals. I wonder what's going on?* Because the Rascals – as great as they were – they wore matching outfits, there were a lot of moms bringing their kids to the show. It just didn't seem like something that these kind of hipsters would attend.

So we go in, and for the opening act they announce The Jimi Hendrix Experience. Hendrix came out – no one had seen anything like that. It's hard to really recover this, but nobody had hair like theirs. Even black people, for the most part did not have those massive afros – which the Experience had. Interestingly, Hendrix's hair was his version of Bob Dylan's hair.

So the audience was just stunned at the *sight* of them. It wasn't mean, but there was some laughter and things like that. But I knew who Jimi Hendrix was, 'cos I used to read this English magazine called *Rave*. They covered Hendrix in there. I'd seen photos of him, and obviously even at that early time a lot of English musicians were raving about him.

FM radio was just getting going; it became a serious alternative to AM radio. And one of the cool disc jockeys on the new FM station had played 'Hey Joe'. I said to my friends, "Look, this guy's going to be pretty good." 'Hey Joe' was *all* I had heard, but – you know – it's pretty impressive.

So the crowd is murmuring and laughing. Hendrix comes over to the microphone and just says, "We tune because we care." They were taking a long time with the tuning. Particularly for an opening act. They did seven songs, of which I can probably remember all of them. They opened with 'Purple Haze', they did 'Hey Joe'; 'I Don't Live Today'; 'The Wind Cries Mary'; 'Fire'; 'Like a Rolling Stone'; they closed with 'Wild Thing'.

aıDan prewett: What an incredible set to have seen.

aD: To just walk into it, too. I wasn't going there to see Jimi Hendrix. But it seemed very much the kind of thing that happened back then – you'd just kind of walk into something, and you're just gobsmacked. Because it was like a revelation. I couldn't believe it. It was just riveting. It was just spellbinding. It was just one of those evenings that completely tore my head open.

One thing that it did – I almost hate telling this story: It completely demoralized the Young Rascals. They just couldn't do what they do. They had a bunch of hits, and Felix Cavaliere was a great singer. They were a really good white R&B band. But they were just devastated. They were – at one point their guitarist Gene Cornish was trying to do some of the stuff Hendrix did. It was a disaster, and I felt bad about that. But Hendrix was a revelation.

aP: Was there a specific moment during that concert that has really stuck with you?

aD: The way they looked, just the way that they took the stage. Their sense of *command*. But then when they started playing 'Purple Haze', I have a very distinct memory of what that was like. It was just stunning. Hendrix was an extraordinary performer. At the same time that he was just an overwhelming presence, he seemed very genial. He seemed like he was in a good mood. So I was really floored. And I was way up front. You know – I was pretty close.

Very shortly after that, within a couple of weeks, the Experience did a run of shows at the Café Au Go Go, very close by to where I lived. I grew up in Greenwich Village, on Bleecker Street, so it was maybe a ten-minute walk. So I went to see one of those shows. That was – that was almost too much. It was such a small space; it was like a tiny club. And they were playing there for like, a week. On that show, I remember their version of 'Hey Joe'. I was sitting on Hendrix's side. And watching Hendrix and Noel Redding leaning over during that part in 'Hey Joe' where they do that *doo doo doo doo...* It was just – It was great. Then I bought the album, which was also a revelation. But seeing Hendrix in Central Park... I had a lot of great experiences in the sixties, even though I was a kid. But that was near the top.

When I think about evenings that epitomized whatever that era was – it was walking into Central Park on a beautiful Spring evening, thinking you were seeing the Young Rascals, and being exposed to Jimi Hendrix. It just seemed so much a part of what that era held. The possibility of revelation that existed during that period. When people say *the sixties*, to me, that's what they mean. And certainly, that's what it meant for me. I was just floored.

I saw them the following year at Hunter College – in '68. That also was great. It was a theatre, and Soft Machine opened, which was pretty interesting. So Hendrix came on, and they just started jamming. They kinda got loose – they just started playing, and that was kinda cool. I was diggin' it. At one point, Hendrix just lifted his hand in the air. He was holding a note – and it was the beginning of 'Foxy Lady'. That was their opening number. They were mostly doing stuff from the second album – *Axis*. I particularly remember they did 'Spanish Castle Magic'. Which was fucking amazing. I mean, it was incredible. So those three performances, all in a relatively short time. Each of those performances was breathtaking. There just was nobody like him. I saw everybody perform back then. And I often think of those Hendrix performances – he was just incredible. It was just *another level.*

AP: Can you think back to a specific moment, perhaps – that would sum up the scene or the atmosphere in Greenwich Village?

AD: I remember Allen Ginsberg was supposed to give a reading in Washington Square Park. There was a really good crowd there, but it started raining. So they moved it right across the street into this kind of student center at NYU. And so it was just jam-packed. And seeing Ginsberg read in an environment like that was thrilling. It was something that suggested *another world.*

I went to see Big Brother and the Holding Company – Janis Joplin's band – at the Fillmore East, with my older sister. We were walking home afterwards – it was four o'clock in the morning. It was Ten Years After opening, and the Staples Singers. And Janis brought the Staple Singers out, and they sang 'When the Saints Go Marching In' together. Benny Goodman was in the audience, as it happens. As we were walking home that night – it was a beautiful summer night – we were walking by Washington Square Park, and my sister found this great dress. Somebody had just left this dress on one of the fences – a metal fence that was about waist-high. And it was just gorgeous. It was this very rich colour. I can see it to this day – it was a maroon or dark red. She just picked it up and said, "Oh, this is actually a really nice dress." She took it home and washed it, and wore it for about two years afterward. It was just one of these things from that time. That was in 1968. The universe was just kind of giving you stuff. So not only do you get to see this astounding performance by Janis Joplin, but on your way home, your sister finds this beautiful dress. It was just amazing.

And there were demonstrations – all that stuff was going on, and I attended. I mean, that was part of it too. Things were *happening*. It really seemed like – it seems ridiculous, now, with everything that's going on here now. But it really seemed like revolution. Like things are just going to change in a big way. And for the better. It totally felt that way. Alas, that never really came to fruition. But for a minute there, it really seemed like everything was going to transform.

. . .

To try to get a sense of the feeling of the time – the possibility of revolution that existed during that period – is important in developing an understanding of Jimi's character. He enjoyed his time in the Village; he kept coming back to it – to the clubs, the hangouts; to the people and to his different living quarters over the years. It was easy to be swept up in the idealistic nature of the Greenwich Village scene. This was the scene that later fed directly into the spirit of Woodstock.

In July 1967, as Jimi and Chas had predicted, the Monkees tour turned out to be a disaster. But the publicity was gold: *Hendrix was kicked off the tour due to formal complaints from the Daughters of the American Revolution.* That was the message sent out by Keith Altham and Chas Chandler. *Lock up your daughters.* It was a total fabrication, but it added fuel to the wild-man-guitar-burning image. The outrage angle made great press, and the US launch of *Are You Experienced?* was only weeks away. A week before the launch, the Experience joined a tour headlined by the Mamas and The Papas. Again, it was the wrong audience.

But they were in front of crowds and they were being covered in the press. *Are You Experienced?* hit the American shelves in late August and exploded. It was now a major top-ten hit in both the UK and the US.

Bruce Fleming
Christmas '67

JIMI RETURNED TO ENGLAND AS A KING. *Everybody* was talking about the Jimi Hendrix Experience. They were whisked off to record television promos for 'The Burning of the Midnight Lamp', then straight back to the studio to complete album number two: *Axis: Bold as Love*. In September, Jimi received a major award from *Melody Maker* magazine: World Top Musician. Keith Altham was championing the Experience every chance he had. The magazine even gave Jimi a trophy. Radio performances and interviews followed. Then more publicity appearances in Germany and Sweden.

Meanwhile, Chas Chandler and Jimi were growing apart. The story goes that during production on *Axis*, the final stereo mixes were 'left in a taxi' by Jimi. Chas had been happy with the mixes as they were. Jimi was not. Whatever happened to them, they had to be mixed again.

The Experience then took off on their first UK tour as headliners. Also on the bill were Pink Floyd, the Move, and the Nice. A couple of concert dates in Sweden, France – and then back to London. December arrived. It was already time to release *Axis*. There was barely time to breathe.

As Christmas rolled around, Jimi found himself in his adoptive hometown with nowhere to go – that is, until his photographer friend Bruce Fleming worked out that Jimi might be a little lonesome in the holiday season. December 25 saw a brief respite for Jimi – the stampede of the outside world was calmed for a day, and Jimi enjoyed Christmas lunch and dinner with Bruce and some friends.

Bruce Fleming started his photography career with *Melody Maker* and the *Sunday Times*. His shots of Eartha Kitt brought him to the attention of the Rolling Stones, the Beatles and the Dave Clark Five. Bruce was soon shooting Jimi Hendrix with frequency and the two became close. Bruce was invited into the studio during recording sessions. Jimi would play him samples – 'What do you think of this?' To this day Bruce is one of London's top photographers in music, fashion, advertising, and the art world.

It is Bruce's classic shot of a cloaked Jimi towering over Noel and Mitch that adorns the cover of *Are You Experienced?*. One of the striking outtakes from this photo session features on the cover of this book. After a couple of sessions, Jimi and Chas took Bruce with them to shoot pictures at Monterey. Later, Bruce's studio was used for a classic filmed performance of Jimi playing 'Hear My Train A Comin'' on a twelve-string acoustic guitar. Amongst all this, Jimi and Bruce found time to attend some raucous parties and discuss their shared love of science fiction.

BRUCE FLEMING: In November I was photographing him; he was having his hair cut. He wasn't *really* having it cut. The PR man who was running his operation had two clients. One was a very fine hairdresser – they were very famous – called Sweeny Todd's, after the famous killer of the 1800's. And Jimi. And so they decided to cobble these two together. That was a funny day because Jimi was saying, "Please – for Christ's sake, don't really cut my hair, will you?" I've got photos of that. In some of them he's looking at me like *what the hell have I gotten into here?*

But anyway, on that day – this is November '67 – I said, "What are you doing at Christmas?"

And he said, "Not much – I can't go back home, I've got too many gigs coming up in the new year."

I said, "What will you do?"

He said, "I'll go to a hotel."

I said, "No you fucking well won't. You'll come and have dinner with my family and some friends."

He said, "Oh – great, man."

So come Christmas day, in the morning, I suppose about 11 or 12 he arrived. I had a flat in Gray's Inn Road, which is near Fleet Street – because I was doing a lot of Fleet Street photography then. And Fleet Street was our newspaper street. That's where all the newspapers were. So the nearer you were, the quicker you could get a picture in and make a buck. I was a kind of a paparazzi in a way.

Jimi arrived, and I had a guy staying with me called Jim. He'd fled the draft in America, which we all hated. And he said, "Can I come and stay with you?" He had a bag from America, and he'd run away from the draft. I don't blame him. And his girlfriend flew over. And she arrived and she was absolutely beautiful. Quite small, but she had a kaftan with mirrors in it and the whole thing. She came into the room and saw Jimi and collapsed. I mean, just fell on the floor in front of him, in worship. And he was terribly embarrassed. He was sitting in a big chair – we had these carved chairs, rather ostentatious chairs.

He said, "Please get up, please –"

She said, "Oh, I love your music." She's going mental. And he's very, very embarrassed. So he got her off her knees, and then we all sat down and talked a lot. And I think the party ended the next day, probably around about 9 or 10 in the morning the next day, boxing day. We were up all night. So we had a hell of a time.

The people who were there – Mike Smith from the Dave Clark Five, his girlfriend; my wife then, Laird – she was an American model; my dear friend who was a publicist who I shared the flat with, and also my studios with – David Block. Fantastic guy. And his girlfriend. There were about ten of us altogether, I think. And we had a *huge* turkey. We had a great time. And of course, we smoked a lot of dope, and we talked a lot and played music all the time and just had a thoroughly good time. And I remember Jimi always seemed to have a penchant for Mateus Rosé. It's a Portuguese drink – kind of a pale rosé from Portugal, in a funny-shaped bottle. He loved that wine, so we got some of that in for him. We just had a brilliant time 'til way into the morning, the next day.

AIDAN PREWETT: How fantastic. Do you remember a particular snippet of conversation, or anything that happened?

BF: No – not a hell of a lot. When you're stoned you tend not to remember very much!

AP: I did read that Jimi gave you some beads, is that right?

BF: Yes, yes he did. We were going somewhere, and I was a bit underdressed. He lent me some beads, and he couldn't get them over his head. So I had two sets – I had one set, little black beads. He took them off and put them over my head. But he had another set that he couldn't do much with, and I used to wrap them around my wrist. And they're hanging on the camera that I photographed him with – it was a Hasselblad – in the British Music Experience exhibition in Liverpool. Where I have my own – it's about twelve feet by twelve feet. A great glass case with all my work in, with Jimi. And the camera I shot him with.

aP: And you did several shoots with Jimi.

BF: There were quite a few. Some of the negatives I've lost, because obviously, Aidan – I was one of the young guys doing the town in those days, and I just used to throw all the negatives, once they were shot, into a box. And many of them were taken by different companies – borrowed – to make prints for publicity or for books, or for point-of-sale for the various events. And I never got them back, which was a shame. But the main one – I did a couple of sessions in the studio. Chas Chandler rang me. I met Jimi in '66, about September, I think. I got a call from Chas Chandler who I knew, because I was the first guy to photograph the Animals. You heard of that band?

aP: Have I.

BF: Right. I was the first guy to photograph them. A chap called Roland O'Reilly, who started a company called Radio Caroline – he rang me and said, "I'm bringing a band down from Newcastle. Could you do some photography?" So that's how I met Chas and all the boys in the band then. And became quite friendly with Chas.

He gave me a ring in September and said, "I've got a new black guy over from the States – a guitarist. Come and meet him, I need some photography done." So I went over and met him, and I just got on with Jimi right away. It's just so simple – the chemistry was right. We just got along. We both were very interested in space travel, and the possibility of creatures on other planets. He was reading Isaac Asimov, and I was reading John Lawrence and Dänekin, *We Are Not Alone,* all these books. We were very keen on that, and really did believe that there were beings out there, and had conversations about that. I tell you what – the stuff that we were smoking then was very good. You could honestly believe that there were creatures out there.

So we arranged the shoot – I think that was in the early part of '67. Could have been about January or February. He arrived with the boys, and he was wearing a bloody great cloak – a black cloak. I never seemed to prepare for a shoot – I seemed to hit it right off the cuff and try and do something I thought up on the spot, the spur of the moment. I just thought it would be kind of interesting or fun to do him as a kind of – not Dracula, but a *presence*. So I had him hold his cloak out and the boys were looking out from underneath. And that was the record cover.

One of my favorite pictures was – he didn't want to pose. He hated all this *da da da*, you know – razzamatazz. He didn't want to do – he wasn't a showbiz-y kind of person. He wasn't interested in that. He was interested in playing music. He didn't give a shit about showing off. It wasn't his scene. I thought, *right – let's just be natural.* So I just said, "Just put your hands on your hips – and stand there." And he did. And I think I got one of the best shots of him *ever.*

AP: I know exactly the one you're talking about.

BF: When you blow that up and have a large print on the wall, it blows your mind. I'm really thrilled with that one. I really am. So that was the second session. And it worked. Track liked it, and they ran it as the cover. The one they chose, I'd shot from about waist-level. But what I wanted them to do was choose the one I'd shot from floor-level, which was much more dramatic. But they didn't do it – they chose the one they wanted. I thought the lower ones were more dramatic.

AP: Was there much joking around between Jimi, Noel and Mitch?

BF: Oh yeah, all the time.

AP: Was there anything specific that sticks out?

BF: Not really, no – just a lot of fun. We tried all kinds of things – different clothes they'd brought with them. We were shooting publicity stuff then, for Chas – and then the one for Track records. We just had a good time – we had a lot of fun. And then we'd go down the pub and have a smoke and a drink and enjoy each other's company.

AP: On that – when you're enjoying a smoke and a drink with Jimi – other than perhaps science fiction – what do you talk about, what's the vibe?

BF: Oh, everything. All kinds of stuff. Sometimes it was serious – we'd talk about Vietnam, which we were all against. We thought it was ridiculous, and awful, and we were totally against it. I think Jimi illustrated that best when he played at Woodstock, and he played the American National Anthem. That was one of the best things I've ever seen. It was fantastic.

We'd just – there was a lot of clowning around and chatting, you know? I remember there were some girls nearby and one or two of them were really pretty. Jimi looked over and said to me, "They look useful." So we got chatting to them. That sort of thing, you know?

I do remember something that did wake me up a little bit. He had an afro, and what he'd done is, he'd got some stuff you use on your moustache, some sort of wax – and he'd made little pointy bits over his head, like antennae.

I said, "What are they for?"

And he said, "That's for music, man. 'Cos it's all out there – I'm tuning in to what's out there."

We laughed, but I think he was kinda serious as well, you know?

Another time, there was a kid – when musicians get together they really do get into music together. You know what I mean? They're totally into their sounds. This kid was playing the guitar and Jimi said, "No, no – give me the guitar." He didn't have his guitar with him, so he took this guy's guitar – who was a right-handed player – turned it upside down and played it upside down, to show the guy what he meant. We were like, *what?! How do you do that?* And that's Jimi. He played it upside down.

He had very long fingers. He used to use his thumb – it would come right around the fret. Quite incredible. When I watched him play – it was almost as if the guitar was part of him.

AP: On that note – is there anything else that might illustrate his humor?

BF: Yeah. I never smoked or drank when I was shooting pictures. Ever. But one day, I was in the studio with him and the boys, and there was a break. Jimi rolled a huge joint and gave it to me, and I had a couple of puffs and that was it. I couldn't remember what the fuck to do with the camera. So I'm sitting there – buzzed – and he came over and put his arms around me and said, "You know what? White boys can't smoke." We howled with laughter.

AP: The fact that you were in there shooting, in the studio – Chas was producing, then there was Jimi, Noel, Mitch –

BF: Only in the rehearsals. Because obviously the camera noise or flashed going off would disturb them. So I'd sit in sometimes for recording, but be very quiet. But I'd shoot Jimi in rehearsals. I'd got some pictures of Chas – the only pictures – when he was with Jimi and the boys in the studio. Funnily enough, I've still got some, like the hairdressing ones, that don't get seen very much.

I saw Mitch a few years ago – we had an exhibition at Audi in Piccadilly, opposite the Ritz. They gave Mitch an Audi car if he would come along and speak at this exhibition. They had about six of my pictures in there, and I crept up behind him and put my hands over his eyes and said, "Guess who?"

And he turned around and said, "Brucey!" And we had a big hug and all.

But sadly, he died. Noel lived in Ireland for a while. I didn't see much of him. But the shock of Jimi dying was terrible. We were all stunned. It was terribly sad. Terribly sad. I think – personally, I think he was exhausted. I think they kept him working, hard. He never had any money, by the way. He would just go to his managers and say, "Can I have some money?" And they've give him a thousand pounds, and he'd go and spend that and he'd go back for some more. We weren't really terribly interested in money, believe it or not.

I can't explain that very well, but in the sixties we were more interested in people and the direction the world was going in. the hippie revolution was fantastic, and I was very much a part of that. We did a lot of marches against apartheid, and against the problems that black people were having in America, in Georgia and Alabama. Jimi and I talked about that quite a lot. What he loved was the fact that when he came to England, he didn't know what to expect as a black person in a white society. He was very happy that he was accepted. The musicians, of course – they accept everybody. If you're a musician, it doesn't matter what color you are – you could be *green* and they'd love you, because you're a musician. But he was thrilled that the *people* loved him. People in England took to him. Not all of them – some of the older people said *funny bloke with funny hair and weird clothes* – you know, that sort of thing. But we were all weird. I had my hair down to my shoulders, and a bloody great moustache. And personally, I didn't give a fuck. If you don't like that, then you're square. There were the *squares* – and then *us*. We were the new generation, and we didn't give a monkey's. We wanted to get rid of the old stuff and find new things.

AP: I can relate to that. Can we talk about Jimi painting his guitar – to witness that, backstage at Monterey – could you tell me about that?

BF: None of us had any idea what he was going to do. What was happening was that – the Who were on, and they were known to do big destructive things – smash things up. He had to do something similar, but we didn't know what he was going to do, and we didn't tell anybody. I went into the dressing room – it wasn't a dressing room, really, it was more like a tent. It was all very made-up. It was the first *big* rock festival, really. And it was wonderful. It was absolutely terrific. Yeah, you had to be charged to go in, but the people who ran the thing decided that there were so many people that didn't have any money – *sod it*, let 'em in anyway. So I've got photographs of him there as well.

I think it was early '67, he said, "I'm playing at Monterey in California – are you coming over?"

I was married to an American, so we said, "Yeah, we'll come over and we'll come to the event and shoot you." And when I went backstage, he was just sitting on the floor, and he had a pot of paint and a guitar. He was writing swirly things on it. I thought *that's pretty*. I thought he was just doing it up to make it more interesting. I had no idea that he was going to set fire to it. He didn't tell anybody.

So at the end of his set, which was late at night, he finished and I was standing on a chair in front of the bandstand, 'cos I'd got permission to get up there and be close to him. A guy that I knew tugged my trousers and said, "Your wife is being molested." So I looked back in the crowd, and there's my wife, a very beautiful blonde American girl with flowers in her hair and all that. And there's a hippie – he's not doing anything terrible, but he was about six foot seven and he's got his arms around her. *Oh shit.* So I got off my chair and went back and said *oi you, hop it – go away*. And as I turned around, bits of the guitar flew through the air. Because what he'd done – he'd set fire to the bloody thing while I was remonstrating with this hippie. And then smashed it up and threw it into the audience. So I missed the whole damn thing.

aP: What was the general vibe of Monterey?

BF: Oh, it was great. I was just standing around, talking to a few people. And Brian Jones was wearing a crocheted dress, almost. And I'm standing next to him, and Janis Joplin is standing there, and she looked at me and said, "Gimme a cigarette, honey." So I gave her a cigarette. She had a brown paper bag, and in it was a bottle of drink. So I had a swig of that. So that was my experience with Janis Joplin. I gave her a cigarette and lit it, and that was it.

There was a movement – part of it was drugs, but the drugs just assisted. I can't explain it. There was a fervor. We wanted to change the world. We'd had enough of society as it was. Basically – I think it still happens – you're born, you go to the right school, you pass the exams, you get the GCE's, you marry a girl, you have two children, you get a mortgage and then you fucking well die. We didn't want to do that. We didn't want to know about that; we wanted to do something different. So there were kids living up in the forests of Canada and America, living in tents, starting communities; communes. Trying to do something in a different way. A lot of it didn't work, but they tried. They *tried*. And we tried to stop the politicians – Nixon and the ghastly things they were doing in Vietnam. We knew we had to change the world, and we were hell-bent on doing it.

We didn't succeed. Things went wrong. It faded away. But I was in Haight-Ashbury. It just got out of hand. The drug dealers moved in; there was a lot of venereal disease around because everybody was free-loving everywhere. It just got out of hand. But the ethic, the idea, was there. And that's what we wanted to try to promote. No more racial tension. No more wars. Stop the wars. We didn't want to know. Why should we go to war? What for? What would it achieve? That was it.

aP: Is there one moment with Jimi that sticks with you more than any other?

BF: I think the excitement of his music – when you're talking to Jimi, you had a great time with him because he was a very lovely guy. A very quiet guy, in a lot of ways. But I always felt that there was about ten to fifteen percent of his mind *elsewhere*. It wasn't always with you. He was hearing music all the time. And Chas said that when he brought him over from America, even when he went to take a dump in the morning, he'd take the guitar with him and play. Without an amp – but just *play*. He had the thing round his neck all the time.

I think it was the music. I was late for a recording session one day, and the red light was on, so I couldn't go in. But when the light went out, I went in and Jimi was in the back room with the glass boxes and all the controls. And he waved at me; *come on in, come on in.* As soon as I got in there, he literally pulled me across the room and put me between two speakers. And he played one of the tracks from the first album, *Are You Experienced?*. What he'd done – I'd never heard before, and I don't think many people had heard. He was playing music backwards, and then tracking that and playing over it.

And he was so excited – he said, "I just want to do something *new*. I've been playing in bands and having to behave. I just want to do something new. What do you think?"

I said, "I love it – I think it's amazing."

You could see the excitement. He was always looking for something new. And apparently he'd worked for Little Richard. They called it the Chitlin' Circuit, 'cos they used to do all the black towns. He said that he took off one day and started playing the stuff he wanted to play, and Little Richard really didn't like it at all, because he was supposed to just be keeping time and playing the guitar along with the band. He was so anxious to get out and do something new. That was him.

AP: There's footage floating around of Jimi playing a 12-string acoustic guitar – it turns out that was in your studio?

BF: Yes. We had a session booked, and I got a call from a guy called Peter Neill. Lovely guy. He said, "I've got a

Dutch film crew – can I come and film you photographing the boys?"

And I said, "Yeah, sure." So he came down. I don't know where Jimi got it, but he had a beautiful 12-string guitar with him. He was sitting on a long, tall kitchen chair, like a stool. And he sat on that and played, and we did some photography and the guys filmed him playing. He played one number that's become quite iconic – 'Hear My Train A Comin'. He started, and he didn't like what he'd done and he said, "Can we start again?" So we started again. But he kind of played blues – and then you heard where the music came from. It just came right out.

AP: Did he say anything about the fact that it was acoustic? I think it's the only professional filming of him playing an acoustic instrument.

BF: Not being a musician myself, I was always slightly in awe of when people go together and talked. They would ignore you – they'd be into music. So I just saw it was a 12-string. He played it beautifully. He played it just as he would any other guitar. I think he'd strung it the right way.

AP: There was another moment I read about where you and Jimi were ushered into a back room where there was a platter full of drugs.

BF: I think it was a recording session and about five of us piled into a taxi because there was a party going on. And I didn't have a camera with me, funnily enough. I just was out on the razz that night. I dumped my stuff and joined Jimi and some other friends. I can't remember who the hell they were. That was the trouble. There's a saying *if you remember the sixties, you weren't really there*. A lot of what we did – you can't remember it all. So we piled into this thing. It was in a part of London called Maida Vale, which is a very nice area. We arrived quite late in the evening, and the building was literally going up and down. All floors was music; everybody was dancing. It was fantastic. It was a *party*.

So we banged on the door. The door opened – they said, "Hey, Jimi!" And we were ushered into a side room. We went in, and – you know your granny would have one of those big old chests with drawers in it, where she kept her cutlery? There was one of these huge sort of dressers with a lamp on it. And then on top was all the booze and all the drugs. And we just stood there in front of it. Jimi whispered to me. He said, "You see what I mean? I can't go anywhere without it being all there for me." Which to me was quite interesting, because – who would invite Jimi to a party and have *fuck all* there? You're going to invite the greatest rock star going, and you've got nothing going on? What are you, a square? You're not very hip, are you? You're not having much fun.

So he said, "What do you think?"

I said, "Well, let's get to it."

So we did. I lost him after that. I don't remember the night. Joe Walsh, that great guitarist, wrote a song called 'Life's Been Good'. One of the stanzas goes, *I go to parties sometimes until four, It's hard to leave when you can't find the door.* And that's more or less the way it was. I don't remember that night. I do remember waking up under somebody's raincoat with a girl. That's all I can tell you. And I didn't have any clothes on. So there you go. That was the party.

aP: Which brings me to Chas Chandler. Do you recall any particular moment with him that might tell us something about his character?

BF: I loved him. He had a fantastic sense of humor. He was a real Northern bloke. People who come from the north have one sort of sense of humor, and a different sort of dialect. We have very definite traits from different parts of the country. He was from Newcastle.

I'll give you a for-instance: If you said to a girl, "Where are you going, love?" Their language was, "Whereya gangin' hinny?" They had this boat; they called it the *buwt*. A bloody great ship, and it was moored – full of bars and a restaurant and you'd go down there and dance. It's a crazy place, Newcastle. A rough place. Tough guys. And Chas was a tough kid. He'd see people off – he knew what he was doing. He was a tough guy. But a very nice guy. And he was very funny – he had a wicked sense of humor. I liked him a lot. A nice guy.

aP: What about Mike Jeffery? Did you come across him?

BF: No. I met him once, but it was a *hello* and that was it. I met another guy called John Hillman, who apparently had a contract with Jimi that he could buy all his masters. He's dead now as well. I met several people. The funny thing is, suddenly, loads of people were coming out of the woodwork saying they owned Jimi, or they owned part of him. There was all kinds of shenanigans – lawyers would suddenly appear, speaking for people saying he wrote Jimi's record. There was loads of this going on – a lot of nonsense, really. And even I have been told by much younger people than me, all about Jimi – and they weren't even born then. Kinda makes you wonder a little bit.

aP: Did you ever get a sense of Jimi's philosophy?

BF: Music. It was his life. It was his entire life, in my opinion. He was kind of following his nose, in a way. He'd been discovered by Chas in New York. My life was photography, and he *knew* that I was serious, and I *knew* that he was serious. That's why we got on. I knew he was an artist. I also used to hang out with a lot of jazz men and photograph them. Dexter Gordon, Stan Getz, Zoot Sims. We were good friends and I loved them to bits. I was born in music. My father was a jazz musician in the thirties. Played in all the big bands. He was a Trombone player called Jock Fleming. So I could feel what Jimi was about. It wasn't difficult.

The thing was, he was very quiet. A lot of the pop stars were throwing people out of windows and wrecking hotels and misbehaving. Keith Moon apparently drove over his own chauffeur with his Rolls Royce. Crazy goings on. And Jimi was quiet. In his quiet moments, he'd sit and chat quietly. He wasn't a noisy person. He didn't go around showing off and making a hell of a fuss. He was quite laid back. That was also impressive, if you know what I mean. At a time when everybody had their massive egos at work, all trying to outdo each other. He wasn't like that at all. He was just very laid-back – and *music* was everything.

• • •

There was a part of Jimi that was always centered on music. He was able to focus on other things, to engage in conversation, but part of him was *always somewhere else*. Was he connecting the dots in his mind – getting to the next chord, establishing its tonal relationship to the piece? Was he seeing an endless stream of colors? Was he piecing lyrics together? Certainly, Jimi was always getting his ideas down on the nearest piece of paper – or the nearest napkin.

Bruce's experiences paint Jimi as a softly spoken friend, fond of a laugh. Humble, shy, needing a genuine human connection. Happy to give away his own jewelry and adornments to make sure his mates are properly attired for a given occasion. And giving, musically. Sitting Bruce down between two speakers to experience the backwards recording in stereo... *Listen to this.*

By Christmas 1967, six months after its initial release, *Are You Experienced?* had sold over a million copies world-wide. Jimi had barely turned 25 and had already earned his first Platinum Record. Many more hits would follow – and everyone involved with the Experience knew it. *Axis: Bold as Love* was released in the UK in December 1967; two months later it hit shelves in the US.

Mike Jeffery set the band up with an extensive run of headlining concert dates around the USA. The Experience was mid-tour upon the US release of *Axis*. This time around, the tour had a more direct effect on album publicity. *Axis* was another massive hit.

Janis Ian
New York '68

THE RECORDING SESSIONS for *Axis: Bold as Love* overflowed with creativity. The number of tracks recorded couldn't possibly fit on the album. Jimi decided to save parts of these sessions for the next album, *Electric Ladyland*. Jimi decided to work on the new album at the Record Plant studio near Times Square, and got himself an apartment in Greenwich Village. It was at this time that he also started trying to figure out the finer details of how he might himself own a nightclub. With studio time now running his highest bills, Mike Jeffery suggested that they build their own New York club to rehearse in. That club never got off the ground – instead, it morphed into one of the most iconic recording facilities in history: Electric Lady Studios. While in New York, Jimi enjoyed revisiting his old Greenwich Village haunts like the Café Wha?, the Café Au Go Go, the Gaslight and the Cheetah. Amid this happening scene in 1967, Jimi's friend Carol Hunter introduced him to a young singer-songwriter called Janis Ian.

Janis Ian had her first major hit with 'Society's Child' in the summer of 1966. At that time, America wasn't ready for it. The song caused nation-wide controversy over its depiction of an interracial teenage romance. It was blacklisted by many radio stations; in one extreme case, a radio station in Atlanta was burnt down after playing it. In the middle of all this, the songwriter was receiving death threats. The songwriter – Janis Ian – was fifteen years old.

Nationwide controversy helped to keep 'Society's Child' in the public eye, but it is Ian's songwriting craft and her haunting, poignant vocal, that lends the song its timeless quality. 'Society's Child' was inducted into the Grammy Hall of Fame in 2001 in recognition of its importance to music history. Janis Ian, of course, went on to enjoy phenomenal success in the music industry with 22 studio albums and two Grammy awards among a collection of ten Grammy nominations so far.

Carol Hunter was one of the great bassists of the era. As a trio, Jimi, Carol and Janis jammed at the clubs and inside Electric Lady Studios while it was still under construction. Together they experienced some poignant moments as well as moments of levity and humor. Jimi took Janis under his wing – and Jimi was a good teacher.

janis ian: I guess I knew Jimi from the time I was fifteen or sixteen. Whenever 'Society's Child' came out, and he came back from England and was living in the Village. So right through the Electric Lady days, when he first bought it. And then when it was in process, he and Carol Hunter, a friend of ours and I would go and we would jam. Carol would play incredible bass guitar, and Jimi would play incredible guitar, and I would play really horrendous organ – just trying to vaguely keep up. But yeah – it's strange now, because you don't think when you're young that the people you're hanging out with are going to become legendary. So you certainly don't think they're going to die.

aidan prewett: Was there a moment, in all the time that

you spent with Jimi, was there a particular moment that's really stuck with you over the years?

JI: Well, the night Martin Luther King died, yeah.

aP: Oh, my goodness.

JI: We were at – I can't remember the club. It might have been the Au Go Go; we spent a lot of time there. It might have been the Village Gate. Wherever it was, B.B. King was playing. And Jimi and I were standing at the back, watching. 'Cos we'd go into places after everybody was seated, to kind of stay under the radar. It was April. So it was just before my birthday. Which was April seventh. Dr. King died on the fourth. And B.B. King was playing at the club. We were there because it was B.B. King and he wasn't world-famous like he is today. He was well known to the blues community, and he was known of course to the guitar community, but as far as I remember, it wasn't packed out with people freaking out that it was B.B. King. It was just B.B. King working really hard, as he always did. We were standing at the back and somebody came on stage in between songs and handed him a note or whispered something in his ear. And I just remember that he spoke into the microphone.

He said that Dr. King had been shot and was dead. And I just remember Jimi and I both kind of slumping against the wall, in a daze. *How could that have happened?* You don't think about that. You don't think that that's going to happen. Dr. King was shot earlier that evening, and the world was just hearing about it. So it would have been the first set. I just remember B.B. King playing after that, and the tears running down his face. I don't even remember what we did after that. I remember I walked around for a long time. Presumably Jimi did, or went somewhere. I didn't see him much after that. I can't remember when he bought Electric Lady, but in my memory, I didn't see him a lot after that. In my memory, everything in the country really started to fragment after that. That's a very defining moment. I think the Kennedy assassination was certainly a defining moment. Men landing on the moon was a defining moment, but Dr. King being shot – and them not finding the shooter, on top of it – and them not caring – was really indicative of how far the powers-that-be would go to stop the onward momentum. That they couldn't stop in the end. They've certainly halted it, lately. Certainly pushed back. You know – if people like me and Jimi are guilty of anything, it's that we underestimated how far those people would go in order to maintain their power. And I think in general, people of good heart still underestimate that. It's unfortunate because that's how the despots take control.

So the two huge moments I had with Jimi, I suppose, for somebody who is looking from the outside, would be that moment, and the moment when I was trying to do coke, and be an adult. And turned out to be horrendously allergic to it.

aP: How did that come about?

JI: We were both in LA at the same time. It was kind of this nice time – again, it was a different time in the music industry. It was still a very small industry. It was a business, not an industry. You always ran into each other at airports and hotels, because there were a limited amount of flights, because only businesspeople and people like us could afford them. Nobody took flights for vacation. And there were a limited amount of hotels that would take artists. So we were always running into one another – we would meet up at airports all the time.

I met Jimi through Carol Hunter, who was probably one of the greatest unsung musicians of that era. She died a couple of years ago. She developed Multiple Sclerosis in the '80's, and couldn't play anymore. But at the time, she was the fiercest 12-string player, and Fender bass player in the Village. Certainly on the Fender. And she wound up, I guess in 1971 or '73 – Neil Diamond actually hired her to head up his band, which was pretty unusual for a woman in those days. Carol, introduced me to Jimi 'cos they knew each other from the guitar world.

There's a quote that I came across recently where Jimi had said – I'm paraphrasing – *if you hear somebody playing the bass like it's a twelve-string guitar, that's Carol.* She was an amazing player and singer, and arranger, and writer – you name it. Brilliant woman. Born out of time. She was about three or four years older than me, and she kind of adopted me. There were a number of people who made it their business to try to make sure I didn't get too banged up. Emotionally, or however. And Jimi and she were two of them. I was always invited along to just jam, and fool around. We used to do that a lot at clubs. Places like the Au Go Go or the Village Gate would stay open after hours so the musicians can come in and jam while the staff were cleaning up. One of the clubs got a big Hammond B3. Almost nobody I knew had a B3 that they owned. So you could go in there and fool around on the Hammond organ, after hours – if you were known to the club owner and the staff. They would just clean up around you. It was great. In retrospect it was very magical, but back then it was just *wow, this is fantastic – let's do this.*

So I guess he had bought Electric Lady at some point,

and the studio was still under construction and being remodeled. I remember there were large sheets of – not balsa, but really thin plywood everywhere, stacked. And there were guitars everywhere; there was a B3 with a Leslie speaker; basses – you name it. The instruments were there. It was great. We could just jam – and Eddie Kramer was there, and he would roll tape now and then – and fool around. It was great. It was educational. 'Cos he was so fucking good. Jesus – he was so good. People like me just couldn't even come close to playing like that. Carol was that good, but I certainly wasn't. I was already more concerned with being a songwriter than being a musician.

AP: What kind of songs did you jam with?

JI: In those days – I don't know how it is now – but in those days if you were a young musician, you always started with the blues. You always started with a simple 1-4-5 in D or in E. Usually E. Some people struggled with the B chord. But almost everybody could play in that key, and everybody knew the blues routine – 16 bars, 32 bars – pretty straight-forward. That's what you would do with bands when you were going on stage to warm up. That's what you would do when you were trying to warm up in the studio – somebody would start a slow or a fast blues, and you'd warm up to it. It was really something everybody did. I'm trying to remember, John Sebastian's group did it, the Moody Blues – everybody that I knew then. I mean, even people like Eric Burdon, when I met him, that's how they warmed up when he was with the Animals – at least, to my memory.

AP: In terms of that – did you sing with Jimi? I mean, he probably would have admired your voice, I'm sure.

JI: I don't know – my voice wasn't as good as it is now. I was pretty young. You know, I honestly don't remember. I doubt it, because I was busy trying to navigate the B3 and had no idea what I was doing. So I was probably totally occupied with that. In my experience with musicians – with most things I would say *with my limited experience*, but I've known an awful lot of musicians. And in my experience, great musicians – like a Jimi; like a Chick Corea – great musicians are always humble about their work, and they're always generous. So you would see an Earl Scruggs on the banjo, seriously listening to a ten-year-old struggling through Foggy Mountain Breakdown. Or an Eric Weissberg, on the banjo as well, and watch them give pointers to people. You'd see somebody like Jimi showing me a guitar lick. Musicians tend to be, in my experience, a very generous bunch. Songwriters, as well. Performers maybe a little less so, just because some are more competitive. But again, great performers – people like a Joplin or a Bette Midler or Tina Turner in my experience are always really generous. And Jimi was always, to me, very kind, very generous, very funny.

AP: What was his sense of humor? Was there something that he found really funny?

JI: Oh gosh. You know, I don't remember. It's so long ago. The thing that always struck me about him was his hands. How beautiful his hands were. He had just the most beautiful hands. Long fingers, extremely expressive. Almost like – you know, it's hard because I'm not sure how much is my memory and how much is *my memory of my memory*, if that makes sense. But in my memory, he used his hands almost like he was using sign language. Somewhere, somebody gave me a picture, just of Jimi's hands. I've got it in my files somewhere. I just think that it was one of the most beautiful things I've ever seen. His hands were gorgeous. Watch him when he's talking – not playing – next time. I guess on *The Cavett Show* or something. When he uses his hands, they're gorgeous.

aP: I can picture that in my head right now.

JI: They're beautiful. And that's what I always think of. And again, there's that weird disconnect when you know somebody who was at the time you knew them, famous-but-not-a-God. There was always the Clapton Is God thing. I don't think there was ever a Hendrix Is God. And who is now a God...? It's weird to talk about this, first of all because you miss them. I found out Jimi died just as I was recovering from a fairly serious illness and some craziness of my own, and Jimi dying was one of those things that reminded me that I needed not to do that. It was, in a lot of ways an object lesson, I think. And a lot of people died around that time. Joplin died, Jimi died, Brian Jones died. So there were always a lot of rumors as well, conspiracy rumors. *How is it possible that Brian Jones was dead for so long before anybody figured it out? Who were the hidden people and who were the drug pushers who were supplying them? What was in it for anyone?* There's a lot of that that people like me went *you know what? I'm not even going to go there, because my friend is dead. They're gone, and I'll never see them again.*

aP: Wow... Do you remember your very first meeting with Jimi?

JI: No. But Jimi was just unassuming. Carol introduced us because Carol knew everybody, and Jimi and she were close friends. They may even have slept together at some point. But then again, that was pretty normal too. I mean, Jimi going to the Plaster Casters was not considered unusual, you know? He shouldn't have got quite so stoned.

aP: Speaking of which – if you're sitting backstage somewhere and sharing a joint with Jimi – what kind of stuff would you talk about? What was on his mind during those moments?

JI: You know, I'm sorry – I don't remember. First of all, I wouldn't have been smoking a joint backstage. Well, I might have if it was somebody else's show, now that I think of it. I'd only smoked a couple of tokes once before one show in my teens, and it was such a horrible show that I realized if you were going to be stoned on stage, you were really only going to be communicating with people who were stoned, 'cos that was about it. So I never did it again. But I think for somebody like Jimi, who was older and a lot bigger, physically, even though we were both pretty skinny at the time, I think that for somebody like Jimi, when he was stoned he was just in a natural state if that makes any sense. I mean, dope then wasn't like it is now. Being stoned didn't completely cut you off, and it didn't completely waste you. You could smoke two or three joints in a day and just kind of keep your buzz going.

He was really quiet – he was not an aggressive person – I guess is how I would put it. I've heard of other people who had different experiences with him when he drank, but I was never around him when he drank, so I don't know. But whenever I was with him – I don't know, there was a period when we were all hanging out quite a bit, and a period where we only saw each other when we were passing in airports. But whenever I saw Jimi, or whenever I was with him, he was soft spoken. He was expressive. If I'd been a few years older, I might have called him tender.

AP: What do you think drew Jimi to you?

JI: I don't mean this to sound at all arrogant – but I think talent speaks to talent. And I think that one of the reasons that people like Jimi, or Chick Corea, or Tommy Emmanuel – one of the reasons I think that every great artist I've ever met is humble, is because they know that their talent is a gift. And I think that someone like Jimi who was so *consumed* – consumed would be the other word I would use, *tender* and *consumed* – with music, not with being famous, but with *music*. One of the hallmarks of that is a generous spirit and a desire to be around other people who – again I don't mean this to sound arrogant – but who can keep up. Who understand what you're talking about, who can have a philosophical conversation about music. People who don't judge your talent are drawn to it.

AP: Speaking of philosophy of music – did you ever talk to Jimi about that?

JI: No, I think he would have laughed at me if I'd asked him that. I mean, it was the sixties. People who sat around and talked about the philosophy of music were more like, going to classical places like the old Juilliard ethic or the old Eastman ethic. It's a pity Odetta's not alive, because she knew him and she could probably comment on that. I don't remember ever talking about that. I remember hanging, and I remember talking about politics a little bit. Talking about who was playing where and why – who'd backed up who. There are people that I assume we talked about, like Ike and Tina. I didn't meet Tina until a few years later. I know there were things that we stayed away from. Like, I remember that Jimi had toured with the Monkees, right? And that had been just a really horrendous experience.

That was not something that anybody was going to bring up, because it was just rude.

But it really didn't – I don't know how to explain it, but it was such a different time. Musicians getting together didn't talk about – you'd talk about music, but you wouldn't talk about any philosophy of music, that I remember. You talked about either the hard facts of *yeah, this club owner's a bastard.* Or *this club's great, they'll let you do your laundry.* Or *this venue's great, because the seats are good and the fans like it.* Or *watch out for such-and-such because they've been drinking a lot and they're really pissy when they're drunk.* You'd talk about stuff like that. Plane flights and managers and stuff. Or you would talk about an act that you were listening to, or that you had just seen. There were some albums, like *Dr. John the Night Tripper* that everybody in New York somehow magically – somehow every musician in New York knew about. That was the kind of information you shared. I don't remember getting into philosophical conversations with people. I mean, we were all being very *deep*. It's that age, too. I mean, Jimi was... I can't remember when Jimi was born, or how much older than me he was, but I guess he was about six or seven years older than me. But then, everybody was. So it wasn't that unusual. I think one of the nice things, for me – and maybe for somebody like Jimi, I don't know – is that there was no question of any kind of sexual component, because I was so young. And even though there were girls my age – 15, 16 – who were sleeping around, I definitely was not one of them, and I definitely didn't put out that vibe. I think I probably put out a very non-sexual, not-interested-in-that vibe. Because I wasn't. I would have been interested in the music part. I wouldn't have been interested in that part of Jimi, or Janis, or Richie

Havens or anybody else. So maybe in a sense it was also a relief – like having a mascot around.

aP: You mention politics just now, in terms of something that might have come up in a conversation with another musician. I do wonder whether or not Jimi said anything, or if you remember any kind of comment or conversation to do with when 'Society's Child' was released – because that was such an amazing piece.

JI: No. The song, obviously, was what initially interested most of the – well, a lot of the artists I knew. Van Ronk, or Odetta, or Jimi. And the fact that it had become a hit and that the backlash was so horrendous – I think gave us something in common. Because obviously I wasn't black, but I was certainly being subjected to a lot of death threats, and threats of violence and violent actions.

aP: It's awful.

JI: I think Jimi was much more – he was a black man growing up in America, he went to England to be taken seriously – to be treated like a human, I would imagine. And when he came back to America initially, he really got shat on during that Monkees tour, and then turned it all around and became an icon. But at the time, he was also an icon the way Richie became an icon – through Woodstock. Representing peace. Representing love.

• • •

Jimi was *tender*, and he was *consumed*. Jimi cared about his friends, and he cared about music. And he cared about everybody's music, not just his own. He wanted to hang out with other musicians; he enjoyed a warm connection with people, and he was happy to share his musical knowledge.

And he enjoyed platonic relationships. Jimi was something of a mentor to Janis Ian, as he had been to Bob Kulick at the Café Wha?. Janis and Carol Hunter were friends, supporters, and champions of Jimi and his music. It is clear that Janis remains a supporter and champion.

In February 1968, Jimi started out on a tour that wound its way haphazardly across North America. February started in San Francisco: two shows at the Fillmore West; six at Winterland. Then on to Arizona, back to colleges in California, then Seattle, back to LA, Colorado, Texas, Philadelphia, Detroit, Toronto, Chicago, Wisconsin… March and April were scheduled similarly. Where possible, Jimi escaped back to New York to continue working on *Electric Ladyland*.

It was around this time that Devon Wilson entered Jimi's life. Devon was an experienced groupie, and soon became a self-appointed minder/girlfriend for Jimi while he was in New York. Devon was known for spiking the drinks of her competition, and she was reportedly intrusive during studio recording. But Jimi respected her – she was one of the few people who would tell him when his playing wasn't up to scratch. They stayed in touch over the coming years.

By April 1968, recording for *Electric Ladyland* was finishing up at the Record Plant. Jimi wanted more control over production and was spending more and more time in the studio. Chas was being ignored and he was getting frustrated. The *Axis* mixes going missing had been one of the biggest steps in the wrong direction. Now Jimi wanted to bring in additional musicians and rehearse there as well. And Jimi wanted a double album. That was it for Chas. He told Jimi he was resigning as manager, and he walked out. Jimi was left with Mike Jeffery in charge.

Jack Casady
Electric Ladyland

JIMI REVELED IN HIS NEW ROLE as sole producer of his new
double album. Without Chas' guiding influence, Jimi was
able to record take after take until he was sure he was satis-
fied. He and Mitch recorded more than 50 takes of 'Gypsy
Eyes' across three sessions. Noel was frequently absent,
only contributing bass parts to five pieces – including his
own composition, 'Little Miss Strange'. Jimi didn't seem to
mind – he played many of the bass parts himself. He also
called in some new musician friends to accompany him in
various roles – Jack Casady, Al Kooper, Steve Winwood,
Dave Mason, Brian Jones, Mike Finnegan, and Buddy
Miles all helped out on different tracks. The studio became
an ongoing party, with sessions starting late at night and
ending sometime the following morning.

Jack Casady had jammed with Jimi at clubs and came to
the Record Plant to hang out and take part in a recorded
jam. That jam became 'Voodoo Chile'; an entire side of the
double album *Electric Ladyland*. Casady was well-known
to Jimi – he had provided the unique bass sound of Jefferson Airplane. Jack was an early proponent of a new school
of bass guitar, whereby melodic lines could be carried by
the bass to propel a track and enhance its texture and feel.
And Jack's band was huge. The sound of Jefferson Airplane

helped to define the late sixties through a series of hit singles, classic albums, tours, and performances – including Monterey Pop and Woodstock. They were a major part of the San Francisco sound.

In 1969, Jack and Jefferson Airplane guitarist Jorma Kaukonen formed Hot Tuna, originally a side project. Hot Tuna is now celebrating its 51st anniversary and is still touring regularly. Jack has been recognized for his services to music with his induction to the Rock 'n' Roll Hall of Fame and production of the Jack Casady Signature Epiphone bass guitar.

Jack has also lent his bass chops to many other bands – from his fellow San Francisco groups, The Grateful Dead and Country Joe & the Fish, as well as to David Crosby and Warren Zevon – and of course, to Jimi Hendrix.

JACK CASADY: When Jimi Hendrix came to Monterey Pop, we played that as well – as Jefferson Airplane. And that's where I got to first meet him backstage and say a few things. Musicians like to meet each other, you know. I don't know about rock stars, but *musicians* love to meet each other. People who can play – we always look forward to hanging. And in that environment – I must say, the Monterey Pop Festival was really the first one where it brought musicians of so many different variants, all under one roof, all in about three days. You had Otis Redding; Ravi Shankar; the groups that came out of San Francisco; the groups that came out of Los Angeles. You had The Who coming over from England – so it was all pretty much at the beginning of our careers. It was an exciting time that way, to meet one another. And right away, Mitch Mitchell and I got along very well. I loved his drumming; I loved the way he approached it.

Bill Graham became our manager about a year later – he

ran the Fillmore Auditorium. As manager, as such – and us
hanging out there and having rehearsal studios in an aban-
doned synagogue next door to the Fillmore – Jimi Hendrix
and Mitch Mitchell and I became a little closer because
he would play there. We shared bills together – on one of
the early bills, we headlined over Jimi Hendrix, as Jefferson
Airplane. And as he came back and returned to the Fillmore Auditorium and later Winterland, our paths crossed.
In those days, we weren't working constantly out on the
road. And actually, we didn't want to work constantly out
on the road as Jefferson Airplane.

Jimi and I and Jorma had a chance to chat and talk
under normal circumstances – setting up your stuff; doing
sound checks; waiting around to play. So in that context,
often the conversation is not exactly intimate. But then
again you share a space, because that's the nature of it.
Everything wasn't so isolated back in those days. Particularly when you're on bills with other people and you've got
a fairly small roof, you know? The Fillmore Auditorium
was 1500 people. The so-called dressing rooms were just
little rooms that everybody hung out in. So conversation
came easily and in a pretty relaxed manner.

I think I got to know Jimi a little better that night we
did a recording, a year-and-a-half or so later, for *Electric
Ladyland* in '68. Jefferson Airplane was in New York City,
doing a TV show – I think it was *The Dick Cavett Show*.
The band Traffic had just come over to do their first state-
side tour from England and was playing at a small club
called Steve Paul's Scene in New York, which fleshed out a
lot of up-and-coming groups. So after our taping earlier in
the evening of the *Cavett Show*, we went over there to hear
them. 'Cos you'd go check out the other guys.

Jimi Hendrix had come in that night at the end of the

evening, and he was recording around the corner, so we all saw each other again. After Traffic had finished their set; he invited a bunch of us over – Jorma and myself and a bunch of guys from Traffic – over to the recording studio where *Electric Ladyland* was being recorded. We watched for part of the night – this is around two in the morning or so. We watched him do some overdubs and work on some material for a while. This was under a slight party atmosphere, I might point out – 'cos there were probably fifteen people all there. So there was conversation and it came easy.

I found him to be a gentleman at all times. Soft-spoken – and looked you straight in the eyes. He asked me, "Do you want to play? Let's play a blues..." This is about six thirty in the morning. So he put the changes together; showed us how it goes – and we just ran it and recorded it. Eddie Kramer, of course, would have liked to have – probably – more pristine preparation for this, but it was in the very nature of a jam, so to speak. But the material – Jimi knew what he wanted to do in the song, and the chord changes – we went over that a couple of times. We played the song about halfway through and he broke a string. He replaced the string, we noodled around some, then we did a full take – and that was the take that went on the album.

But I have to say, during that period of time and as we talked, even though there was a number of people around – when I played with the man – we were all trying to do well. Some people have asked if it was intimidating, or anything like that. The idea when you don't know each other very well, everybody will do their best if you set your personality off to the side and just get down to the business and open yourself up – allow yourself to see and sense each one of us. And that's what he did. We looked into his eyes; nothing intimidating. The idea was to make music and see what we could come up with in this unique combination. He had played with Noel Redding – Noel Redding wasn't playing that night. So it was Jimi Hendrix and me. I'd always wanted to play with him; I'd jammed with him before back in the Fillmore days. And of course, Mitch Mitchell and I were grinning ear-to-ear because we got a chance to play together.

The best thing I can say about the quiet moments of Jimi Hendrix that you're talking about, is from my experience, and a short one at that. He was always a gentle man, around me. In the terms of the phrase *a true gentleman* – he was a gentle man. He wasn't aggressive or anything like that. He was all about the music. And he was curious; he'd ask questions – he'd want to know about things. Like we all were. Don't forget, we're all young, here – you know? We're all young and starting out in our careers. Even though I guess I was 24 to 25 years old; he was about the same age. We're all starting out in our careers and we're all anxious to play, anytime we could. Jorma and I carried our guitars – I carried my bass, he carried his guitar – after every Airplane show, we'd go to clubs and whatnot, sit in and jam and do whatever. We played all night long as much as we possibly could – trying to improve our craft and learn new things.

AIDAN PREWETT: I wonder – you mentioned the Fillmore dressing room – it sounds like that in itself was kind of a scene.

JC: Well every dressing room's a scene. You gotta understand – this is what we do: You go in, you do a sound check in the afternoon. Whatever dressing room they've got is the dressing room that you hang out 'til you play at eight o'clock at night. So the nature of being a musician on the road is a lot of hanging out and waiting to play. That doesn't mean you're *partying* hanging out all the time. It just means that that's really your world. That's the world that the audience doesn't get to see. They see you at eight o'clock. And the nuts and bolts of everything that you do – the driving 500 miles a day, getting into cheap hotels, getting up, getting a little bit of rest, driving the next day to the next gig, to do the same thing over again. The nature of it, when you *share* a bill, is kinda nice because then you get to meet people that you admire. You get to say, "Say, man – I really admire the way you play. It's great to meet you." And all that kind of stuff. It's really pretty easygoing. Like I said before, musicians love to meet other musicians; they love to meet other players.

ap: And you performed onstage with Jimi at Winterland, is that right?

JC: Yes – a little later on, after *Electric Ladyland* was recorded. The great thing about that is – I'll say it from a musician's point of view. People ask you to sit in, and back in the day, Jefferson Airplane asked people to sit in with them, the Grateful Dead did; Jimi had people.

So when it came to Winterland, he said, "Jack, you wanna play something?"

"Yeah, we can play 'Voodoo Chile'?"

But we did 'Killing Floor' and another thing and I came up and played. There's a nice picture of that floating around somewhere. It shows all four of us on stage, with Noel on his Gibson ES-335, and I'm joining Jimi for a couple of songs on stage. Which was great. I mean, I'm not trying to downplay anything, but when you're amongst great musicians – and don't forget, these are my contemporaries – a lot of people forget that. But you want to be enthused by other people's drive to create well and to create something unique. When you see other people do it, it makes you want to work really hard on your own stuff.

aP: So when you were on stage with those guys, what was the dynamic like?

JC: The dynamic is to try to play well. There's Jimi Hendrix here, there's Noel Redding and there's Mitch Mitchell. We're looking at each other and we start the song. You try to play the song really well. You listen really well to each other. You know – feeding off each other; excited to be up there playing together. Jimi's playing with me and he doesn't know how I'm gonna necessarily approach things, 'cos we haven't – the numbers are blue space numbers. There's plenty of room to move around there, amongst the arrangement. So he's feeding off of me – I'm a new adrenaline for him; he's new for me. Mitch Mitchell was pulling it all together and playing off of all of us. Noel Redding's up there playing. It was a great time; a great time to do that.

aP: Was there a difference in the dynamic to the studio? Did you step out onto the stage at Winterland and it was discernably a different dynamic in the group?

JC: Well, I wasn't making a record with Jimi. We did a blues-based jam and played that song, then I left. So the dynamic wasn't that changed. In the studio he had more control of the atmosphere – that's why he overdubbed crowd noise and all that. He wanted that atmosphere, of a live song that happened to be in the studio. And now we had the real thing in Winterland. And live is *live*. In the studio you don't have those 5,000 people in front of you, or whatever the crowd was.

We finished that recording at seven-thirty in the morning. Then Jorma and I jumped in our station wagon with all our equipment and drove down to Washington D.C. 'cos we had a gig that night. The mode of choice in those days – the late '60's, was the LTD station wagon. You'd pile all your stuff into it – the English call it an estate car.

ap: I have in my notes here that you received a phone call from Jimi – he actually asked permission to use 'Voodoo Chile'.

JC: Yeah, after we did our recording, we went on our tour. He continued recording and I believe he went on tour and did some stuff. Then I was back in San Francisco in the office at Fulton Street; a big mansion that we owned that we used for our offices. I was in the office, and a phone call came in from Jimi and we talked for a while. He said, "Listen, man – I really liked that song we did together. Do you mind if I put it on the album?"

I said, "What, are you crazy? It's fifteen minutes long!" And we laughed. I said, "Of course – I'd be honored. It'd be great." So that's how it happened.

ap: There's a rumor floating around, given that this was close to when Noel left the band, that Jimi perhaps asked you to join. Is there any truth to that?

JC: Well, he never put that forth to me as a question, as such. I mean, obviously there was synergy going on when we recorded and we had an easygoing relationship. But I *had* a band. One of the things that I find most paramount – I'm a loyal kind of guy. I don't jump ship easily. I stay with the crew that I like. The Airplane was evolving into a really creative group at that point, plus we were starting Hot Tuna at the same time – my plate was full.

Jorma and I have our friendship and our dynamic and all of that. So that question was never put to me, as such. I think it's mentioned more now in retrospect, just because of the dynamics of the way things fell in Jimi's life. But then a year later he had his old buddy from the army playing bass, Billy Cox. So I imagine that that's the direction that Jimi wanted to go. It's hard to say, because everything stopped so soon afterwards for him.

aP: Do you recall seeing Jimi at a time where he was really enjoying himself?

JC: Recording 'Voodoo Chile' was a benchmark moment in what little time I had with Jimi, in what short life he had. I think I saw Jimi at his happiest when he was recording *Electric Ladyland*. He'd just gotten control of his own stuff. That's what we all were trying to do. You start out wherever you go – all your control is held by the record companies. After we recorded *Surrealistic Pillow*, with 'Somebody to Love' and 'White Rabbit' on it, and that was a success – it came time to renegotiate our contract. That renegotiation was, "Hey – we want control in the studio." It's not that we didn't do our own thing up until that point, but we wanted more control and more time to experiment in the studio. And of course, the Beatles were doing it – they started doing more interesting things inside the studio and the studio atmosphere. And other bands started to do that as well. So when I saw Jimi and went out and recorded with him – a side of what became a double album; unusual then. The mere fact that he put a fifteen-minute blues improvisational piece on the album was unheard of then.

In any case, I saw him at his creative happiest because even though he had just parted ways with his producer Chas Chandler, he was doing it himself and I'm sure he was worried about it – there was pressure and all that stuff going on – at the same time, he could open himself up.

And I saw him right in the midst of that. It was an incredibly creative album. I think his most creative album. So I would have to say that I saw him at his happiest then. At least from my perspective. And don't forget – I'm not in the band with him. Jorma and I have a joke – people have asked me, "How come you guys still get along?" I just turned 75; he just turned 79. Jorma comes in with a short answer – he says, "'Cos we've never had a band meeting."

The Jefferson Airplane was notorious for these band meetings that would just leave your stomach wrenched and churning away – people battling for this and that. Jorma and I didn't do any of that. Jorma and I knew each other when we were kids. His father was in the State Department, my father was a dentist – my uncle was a doctor, my other uncle was a lawyer, all professionals. Then there was us making music. Well, when we did that, we were expected to go to college and get a real profession, and music was just part of the sideline. So we had memory points in our relationship that had nothing to do with building as business as a band. And so we can draw upon that in matters of respect for each other. Which is really the essential element for people to get along over a long period of time. You don't have to agree with everything they say, but you have to respect what they say.

AP: I wonder if you might have had a particular moment with Mitch Mitchell that could sum up his character.

JC: I actually had more moments with him than I did with Jimi. Mitch and I just seemed to hit it off really well together. He had a great wry sense of humor; a bit mischievous – and you can tell that through his playing. His jazz influences are really underrated within the context of what you hear him play in the Jimi Hendrix Experience.

Throughout all the albums he played on with Jimi, he has a pretty light touch. But it's a *heavy* sound you think of, coming out of the Jimi Hendrix Experience. At the same time, when you're watching Mitch playing, he's not really bashing the drums. He's got those jazz sensibilities and the timing, and the way he used the cymbals and the snare. I thought he was a really creative drummer.

We shared a lot of our jazz influences together – Roland Kirk and Miles Davis; all the early players of the '60's – a host of players. Those influences were part of my fabric and part of his fabric. So we talked about that stuff a lot. But then again, we were now coming into our own in creating music and putting it down on record as a statement. I'm much more influenced by Charlie Mingus than I was by any electric bass guitar player, 'cos when I started playing bass guitar in 1960, the Fender Jazz bass had just come out. I started playing that. There were hardly any electric bass guitar players out there. So a lot of my influences came from the jazz world about what to do on the bass instrument – as well as the guitar world and even the cello world. So Mitch and I got along just fine with that kind of stuff.

And he was a real thrill to play with. I mean, here I am, a bass player working with Mitch Mitchell, the drummer. So he's got a different take on things. But the drummer Spencer Dryden had the same influences that we all did. Spencer's work with Jefferson Airplane is really brilliant. He's got that wide listening palate of people that influenced him on the drums. And Spencer was a little older than us – he's from all those West Coast drummer guys. They played up all the West Coast in the jazz scene. Spencer had all those influences. I had more of the East Coast stuff going on – Ornette Coleman and Roland Kirk. A little more aggressive kind of stuff.

But as far as Mitch Mitchell goes, that really made him an interesting drummer. And personally, I like that period of time that Jimi recorded as the Jimi Hendrix Experience, with Mitch Mitchell. I think that's really some of the best work.

AP: I spoke to Eddie Kramer the other day, and he was talking about the studio dynamic with Jimi, and particularly Mitch. I was thrilled to hear about that. I wonder if you could speak to what it was like working with Eddie.

JC: Oh, Eddie's the greatest. I have great, great respect for him and his role in recording all those years, up to today. Eddie was great in the studio, from my perspective. Always respectful, always trying to do the best he could. I know a little more about recording now and I know how disjointed the physical reality was at the time, in dealing with strangers in the studio in a somewhat party atmosphere. But that doesn't mean the whole record was made that way. From my perspective of seeing him that night and him recording – he was the greatest. He was great. An easy guy to talk to – I've talked to him since. A dear, sweet man and I have nothing but respect for the man.

AP: Lastly, Woodstock… watching that movie as a teenager was one of those defining moments for me – is there a moment from Woodstock for *you*, that has really stuck with you?

JC: That's a hard one – there are so many moments. I think just the fact that we were – a lot of bands were on stage. The stage was fairly large; there was no other place – there was no real backstage, so to speak. You got a chance to see so many other performers. But of course, one of the big stars at Woodstock was the people themselves. You looked around, and particularly when *we* went on – which was daylight, we were supposed to go on the night before – and saw a somewhat bedraggled but enthusiastic happy people – and around 400,000 of them. All out there in front of you. That was a moment that was just awesome. And humbling at the same time. And then you kinda thought, gee – there's really 400,000 of us out there.

• • •

Musicians love to meet each other. Jimi wasn't out there just for the paying gigs. He knew he'd have a better time finding a club in whatever city he was in and just sitting in with a local act. The spontaneity and excitement of playing with other musicians seems to have been the impetus for inclusion of so many varied players on *Electric Ladyland* and in the later lineups of his band. Jimi craved variety. He never wanted to perform songs the same way he'd played them before. Playing the hits quickly grew tiresome. The audience expectation of onstage destruction was even more draining. So the inclusion of Jack Casady onstage – and with so many others in the studio – was a welcome change for Jimi.

Jimi's career was burgeoning. He had two hit albums out, with a third on the way. He was playing live shows all over the country. America was welcoming Jimi back with open arms. England was sliding into the rear-view mirror. Kathy Etchingham was still in London, growing impatient. And Jimi's schedule wasn't going to let up anytime soon. Mike Jeffery was sending Jimi wherever the money was. In May 1968, the money was at the Miami Pop Festival.

Miami Pop was the first festival organized by Michael Lang. He caught the bug and quickly started planning for another festival in Upstate New York the following year. Jimi's performances in Miami on May 18 and 19 gave Lang

all the confidence he needed to think bigger – and Woodstock was conceived.

Jimi's first set at Miami Pop is now held up as one of his
great concerts. Two helicopters delivered the band directly
to the backstage area – instruments and cables in hand,
tuned and ready-to-go. They leapt from the helicopter and
raced onto the stage. The crowd of 25,000 was in hysterics.

The second show, however, was almost completely
washed out. Only a handful of stragglers braved the wet to
see Jimi struggle with waterlogged equipment. Eventually
Jimi grew frustrated and gave up; he threw a parting gift
into the crowd – a previously-burnt sunburst Fender Stratocaster. The guitar was retrieved by a roadie and given to
Frank Zappa, who was also on the bill. Was this the same
guitar that had first been torched at the Astoria in March
1967, at Keith Altham's suggestion? It is likely. Jimi only
burnt three guitars that we know of. Or maybe four. It is
contentious.

In any case, Jimi poured his exasperation from the gig
into a new song, one of the last to be recorded for *Electric
Ladyland*: 'Rainy Day, Dream Away'.

Meanwhile, Mike Jeffery's handling of the money was
completely opaque to his artists, which also included Eire
Apparent and Soft Machine. While Jeffery continued to
buy up property in the US, the UK and Spain, Jimi and the
band were still living in apartments. But their needs were
provided for: when Jimi asked for something, he usually
got it. Guitars and other equipment were a given – and
Jimi could usually sign for other purchases like cars, clothing and an increasing variety of pharmaceutical products.

Noel Redding, meanwhile, had started his own band
called Fat Mattress. Noel began pushing Jimi and Mike to
include the band as a support act for the Experience. It was
that – or he was going to quit.

Neil Landon
Majorca '68

IN EARLY 1968, Mike Jeffery and Chas Chandler jointly purchased a nightclub in Majorca, Spain. They called it the Sgt. Pepper's Club. After Chas quit the Experience in June, Jimi, Noel, and Mitch travelled to Majorca to spend a week in one of Mike Jeffery's mansions. A holiday, Mike? Nope. Here they would rehearse new material and perform at the opening of the Sgt. Pepper's Club. Keith Altham joined the group, along with Neil Landon of Fat Mattress.

Noel Redding had been playing bass with the Experience for more than eighteen months and was itching to play lead guitar again. Fat Mattress became his outlet. The band featured Noel on guitar and vocals, Neil Landon on lead vocals, Jim Leverton on bass, and Eric Dillon on drums. Fat Mattress quickly secured a management deal with Mike Jeffery and went on to record two studio albums, alongside their touring support of the Jimi Hendrix Experience.

Fat Mattress vocalist Neil Landon had been connected to the Jimi Hendrix Experience as soon as Noel Redding was recruited as bass player. Redding and Landon were mates; they had played together in an English combo called the Burnettes from 1962 to 1965. Landon joined the Flower Pot Men in 1967 and scored a top-ten hit with 'Let's Go To San Francisco'. He then re-joined Noel in Fat Mattress in

1968. Neil Landon went on to enjoy a storied solo career and continues to tour regularly in Germany and the UK.

Neil had a car in early days of the Experience. Jimi and Noel Redding did not. So Neil often found himself driving them around London. Neil had spent time in the Merchant Navy and spoke with Jimi about his army days. In the US, Neil was privy to a brief moment between Jimi and members of the Black Panther Party. But Neil's strongest memories of Jimi are of their time in Majorca. The mansion, the substances, and the endless party.

neil landon: There was lots of mischief in Majorca – lots of girls. We had a really big house with all marble floors, and a big grand piano in the big room downstairs. There were loads of rooms there, so there were always girls around. Jimi always had plenty of girlfriends. We shared one girl – she came over to see me, I think – and she ended up with him, or the other way around. I'll never forget – she had a broken leg. She had her leg in plaster up to her thigh. But it didn't stop anything from going on, you know.

aidan prewett: I'm just visualizing this house in Majorca, and these shenanigans happening – was there a moment that happened during that time that sort of summed up the atmosphere?

nl: Well, what happened was – I don't know if you've heard of amyl nitrate? These things that you pop. And in those days, the end of the sixties, they were quite *in vogue* with musicians. I was in bed, and Noel was in bed – we were both in bed in one room. Some of the rooms had more than one bed. And then Gerry Stickells came in – he and Mitch Mitchell had just come from America. And they came up to both of us at once and popped these things under our noses. And that was very weird. That was their way of saying *hello*.

aP: What a time!

nL: There were all sorts of things that happened, like Mike Jeffery used to have a thing about flights – he used to book a flight and then not take it. He'd take the next one because he was worried he was going to be in a plane crash. And of course, in the end he died in a plane crash. We were all supposed to be in Majorca at a certain time, and he got there later and he told us why.

aP: Could you tell me about the best you ever saw Jimi perform?

nL: I think it might have been in Majorca – 'cos it wasn't a proper gig, it was a session. But I went on stage with him, which was amazing. He was always good. The Experience's first gig was amazing as well – that was in the Bag O'Nails. I was with them the first gig they did – as the Experience – in England. I remember people floating in in caftans. The folk singer Donovan floated in, in a floor-length caftan. It was all of a moment. There are certain things you remember, and that was an amazing gig – although it was one of the first ones. Very raw.

aP: Did Jimi do anything flamboyant, even then? Or was it more subdued?

nL: I think it was a bit more subdued, then. More concentrated on what they were doing. As I said, I used to take them to gigs. These sort of things gradually came out – like playing with his teeth. I mean, he always did that anyway.
But it was great to tour with him. I met him when he

came to England, and we got to know each other. He was a very quiet sort of unassuming bloke. And he couldn't really believe what was going on, I don't think. I used to take him to gigs, at the beginning. They didn't have a car – and it was quite funny, sometimes you'd be going along and he'd start screaming – sort of like shouting – using his voice. And he reckoned I was a better singer than him, he used to say, and things like that.

ap: Speaking of that time – Noel and Jimi must have been quite close friends, especially in the early part of that.

nl: Yeah, they were – yeah. It never really became that they had terrible rows or anything. I mean, Noel used to get frustrated because Jimi – with his type of guitar playing, he didn't need much bass. He just needed a simple bass line, you know? And Noel got frustrated towards the end, but also he was drinking a lot – which didn't help. And Jimi was obviously taking what he took. But there was never any big animosity, I mean – you know, not that I felt – between them. Obviously there was some. But not really like, sort of, punching each other or anything like that.

ap: Did you ever see them having a really good laugh over something?

nl: Yeah, we used to laugh a lot. Like, over these things with amyl nitrate. And Noel used to call Jimi *Jimi Jangles*. Yeah, we had some laughs. We were in Tuscaloosa, I think – when we were on tour with Jimi in the southern states we couldn't stay in the town. We only ever stayed in one town – that was Memphis – but apart from that we always stayed outside in a motel. And Jimi – at this place there wasn't much going on, but the girls that were there were all around Jimi's room, so Mitch decided to try and pull a really big American cowgirl. She was really big, you know. I mean, she had a good figure, but she was big like an American footballer. And I remember him trying to sort of chat her up, and I'm not sure what happened, but she picked him up and threw him in the swimming pool.

Then there was the other side of it, when we were in Memphis, and I always used to go and have a chat with Jimi in the evening. But in Memphis, because they were smoking in the room, and the roadies put stuff around the door, so it didn't come out – the smell. I went to see Jimi, and I went in – he just shook his head and said, "Not now," and there were all these Black Panther people sitting around him, talking to him. I suppose they were trying to get money out of him. So I just walked out, you know – and left them. I never heard anything more about that, but they were always after him for money, I think – at that time. Especially when he was in the southern states. Probably trying to get him to support their cause, or whatever it was. The Black Panthers weren't really – I mean, Martin Luther King was something different.

AP: Was Jimi a political person?

NL: Not really. I never noticed anything that political, really. I mean, he did 'The Star-Spangled Banner', didn't he? That was taking the piss a bit, I think. But no – with us, we always mostly talked lightly about things. Never too deep. It was always – you were a bit high on something, you know – when you talked. In one ear and out the other.

AP: So you're sitting in a hotel room, and it's just you and Jimi Hendrix – what kinds of stuff do you chat about?

NL: It all depends where we were, I suppose. We used to talk about his time in the army, I suppose, and my time in the Merchant Navy. It wasn't easy for Jimi in the army, in those days – being black. You've got to remember that it's not all that long after black-only regiments and white-only regiments. I mean, it's quite a while before that, but still.

And general things that were going on – like *who's going with who*? I don't know – it's so long ago. Noel would have been good to talk to because he kept a diary. But I never kept a diary. I haven't even got a photo with Jimi. There must be some somewhere, but I haven't got any.

ap: Would you say that Jimi was a charming person?

nl: Yes, I think he was. He had something about him. He had a charisma. As I said, he didn't really talk too much. When we weren't on tour and I'd go around to see him, and he'd be sitting on a cushion in the room with his girlfriend, Kathy. It didn't matter what he was doing, he'd never say "I haven't got time now." Just that one time with the Black Panthers. But that wasn't him, that was them. And he'd always invite you in and say "Howya doin'," "What's happening?" and all that sort of stuff. But you know what it's like – over the years you forget all the little things that you talked about. He was always friendly. I'd never seen him get really annoyed about anything. He was probably too nice, maybe. To the managers, anyway. The way he got – he did get a bit fiddled with his money and things. The way it went through the Bahamas, and suddenly money ended up in Panama. That couldn't have been easy for him.

ap: Was there a conversation that you might have had with Jimi that stands out?

nl: The last time I saw him, we did a big festival in Germany, the Isle of Fehmarn. It was his last gig, I think. And we talked about – he was going to take my flat. I had a studio flat in London, and I'd bought a house in the country and was in the process of moving from the flat to the house. And he wanted the flat. And of course, it never happened. So that would be the last conversation we'd had. And I don't think he was too happy about the fact that the band had broken up, and that Noel wasn't there anymore.

• • •

Neil Landon witnessed Jimi's excitement at the formation of the Experience, and he was there for Jimi's anguished final tour. He was there for some the most heightened experiences, as well as some that were decidedly less pleasant. And for the sense of loss – of what might have been – when Jimi died.

The Experience's later US tours were often visited by members of the Black Panther Party. Jimi was a major figure in the music world. He was a black man with a prominent voice, and he was encouraged to use it for political means. Jimi's audience was largely white, and he wanted to open himself up to the black community. In 1969, Jimi helped organize a free outdoor show in Harlem, called the United Block Association Benefit Concert. But Jimi was reluctant to align himself directly with any political party.

Electric Ladyland was released in October 1968. Its success eclipsed both *Are You Experienced?* and *Axis: Bold as Love*, spending two weeks at number one in the US charts. Inside the Experience, however, tension was building and relationships were fragmenting. In just two years they had released three albums and played nearly 500 gigs. From a management perspective, that was standard operating procedure. The given wisdom was that the shelf life of a pop group was about two years. Mike Jeffery's approach was clear: Run an act into the ground before their popularity ran dry. It was only in later years later that managers like Peter Grant of Led Zeppelin realized that hiatus from touring often incrcases demand. A well-earned rest wasn't available for rock stars until about 1973.

Lennart Wretlind
Stockholm '69

WITH THE BENEFIT OF HINDSIGHT, it's clear that the Experience started to fall apart as soon as Chas left. Noel and Mitch started openly questioning Mike's financial arrangements and things were becoming unpleasant. In January 1969, the press got hold of the formation of Fat Mattress as a headline – *The End of the Experience*. They weren't wrong, but Mike Jeffery didn't want the world to know. It might hurt album sales.

Jimi was now 26. He'd spent two years on the road and was about to embark on another major tour – three months across Europe. But he was glad to have a home base in London, where Kathy had rented the flat at 25 Brook Street. Here they enjoyed brief moments of stability in between tour dates. On January 8, 1969, the Experience set off for Sweden. Chas Chandler was in the audience and met up with Jimi backstage. Jimi asked Chas to return to management – he knew he was in Mike Jeffery's stranglehold. Legal documentation shows that Jimi had already been trying to ditch Mike, to no avail.

While in Stockholm, Jimi was interviewed by a young Swedish Radio journalist called Lennart Wretlind. Wretlind had followed blues music to the US in the mid-'60s and returned to his home country a wealth of musical knowledge. Wretlind's interviews with Jimi, Janis Joplin, Jim Morrison, Frank Zappa, and Patti Smith have been noted for their laid-back style, and they continue to be used regularly in documentaries. Wretlind's work in broadcasting continues to this day. His Spotify program *Wretlind's Värld* is sponsored by Sony Music and Parlophone, in the interest of furthering exposure for the world music genre. Wretlind is a three-time winner of the Swedish Radio Academy's Grand Radio Prize.

A transcript of Lennart Wretlind's full interview with Jimi Hendrix follows this chapter. Backstage, Jimi only had a few minutes to spare. But it's clear that Jimi sensed Lennart's sincerity. Lennart's own soft-spoken nature almost mirrored Jimi's. Lennart wanted to discuss and understand Jimi's career and the *music*, and that's all. In the space of a few minutes, the connection between Lennart and Jimi is clear. Jimi loved to talk about music with people who were passionate – and curious.

LENNART WRETLIND: I was sort of prepared for the interview because I was at the Monterey Pop festival in June of 1967. And I was sitting so close – just in the sixth row or something like that. The Who had just been on, and they had wrecked all their equipment. It was really scary. And then Jimi Hendrix came on about half an hour later – they had actually done some bidding to see who would follow who. You probably know that story. But for him, it was fantastic. And sitting so close, and never having experienced anything like that before, I'm sure I was scared. I was a correspondent for Swedish Radio at the time, and I had an obligation to stay in my seat. But otherwise, I felt like I should really get out of there – it felt dangerous, seeing him smash the guitar, and throw out burning pieces of his guitar towards us.

AIDAN PREWETT: It's a pity you didn't grab one of those pieces.

LW: It didn't land next to me – but it was like being in a war zone, kind of. And in connection with that festival, which was so peaceful, and so different from Woodstock. Monterey was just a cute little festival. Someone is quoted as saying that the bands liked Monterey so much more than Woodstock because at Monterey they met nice people, but at Woodstock it was like helicopters and mud and insanity. There was nothing like that at all at Monterey. It was completely sane. Not insanity – except for the Who and Jimi Hendrix. That was really frightening, but so exciting at the same time.

So I didn't know what to expect when I met him two years later, in Stockholm in '69. He had a concert at the Concert House in Stockholm. And this was just after the sound check, so he didn't have much time – he only had about five or ten minutes. But he was so calm. He was like a teddy bear. Nothing of the intensity that I'd seen at Monterey. He said he wanted to have something he could talk about, because he felt like he hadn't – he'd just been so involved with the music. He needed to be with the people, so to speak. I was so surprised that he was so warm and human, and non-stressed.

I also did a similar interview with Janis Joplin that same year. She recorded a TV show for Swedish TV and we just had five minutes, but I think there's a lot in that interview. Probably just because I was just really interested in *her*. I didn't ask her or Jimi Hendrix about drugs or any of that. We just talked about the music, and it made them relaxed and open. Especially with Janis Joplin. She's really relaxed. So those interviews have been used a lot.

But you know, another day at work… It's interesting; the

BBC called me maybe 30 years later and wanted to use it. It was surprising because you'd think that the BBC would have so much good stuff. But apparently they wanted to use my interview.

aP: It's wonderful when you do catch someone in a really comfortable place.

LW: Yes, it really makes a difference, I think.

aP: In Stockholm, did Jimi seem as though he knew he was performing for a Swedish audience – did he note that in any way?

LW: Oh yeah – he was so aware of it because, as you'll hear in the interview, he had been out to a small club in Stockholm, and met some Swedish musicians called Hansson & Karlsson. And he then recorded one of their songs. So they jammed together.

aP: When you met him – was there anything that struck you as being quite different to his image – the celebrity image of Jimi Hendrix?

LW: Oh definitely. Of course, he was dressed up like the image, but he really was like a huge, cute teddy bear. He was so warm and open – like he wanted to give. Even though we had only a few minutes – absolutely. Yeah, that was the thing.

aP: That's beautiful. I'm really thrilled to hear that – because it paints a different picture to that wild man image.

LW: It was the same thing – I interviewed the Doors twice. Especially the first time, they were just four very polite boys. And then seeing Oliver Stone's film, which was just madness and insanity. It's like – those images sort of *win* and stay with us. But they're ordinary people, and they're under a lot of pressure, and sometimes they do weird things.

AP: How did it come about that you were sent to Monterey?

LW: That was all my own initiative. I was a freelancer; they didn't send me. I really wanted to come to America – I wanted to get close to the soul and blues music, and it was just sort of good luck that I ended up in San Francisco. So I was working in a record store in 1967 for the whole year. And I called up the people who were in charge of the Monterey Pop Festival. It was a young guy called Derek Taylor, who was a press agent for the Beatles. He was running the Monterey Pop Festival, together with some other people. He was so open – I called him up and said, "Hello, I'm from Sweden." He didn't even ask me for my credentials, he said, "Well, I'm sure that you'll want one of those tickets for your girlfriend as well, won't you?" So I got two press passes for the three days of the festival.

AP: How perfect.

LW: And the tickets were in the first few rows. The wonderful thing about that festival was that it was so mixed. When Otis Redding was on stage, Janis Joplin just happened to sit right in front of me. It was just as exciting to watch *her* dancing as it was to see Otis Redding's performance. She was so wild – she was just jumping in her seat. And of course, it was the first time Otis Redding had appeared in front of a largely white audience. And so many of those artists – that was how they broke for the American audience, at the same time. I mean, Jimi Hendrix – nobody had really seen him in America at that time. And the reason that he appeared there was that Paul McCartney insisted.

Paul McCartney was also a member of the board for the Monterey Pop Festival. So that was important. And he also insisted that Ravi Shankar should be there. So Ravi Shankar had the whole Sunday afternoon of the festival.

For me, that was a really important time of my life. It planted a huge seed for my radio work – the fact that you could mix brilliant music like that. The span from Jimi Hendrix to Ravi Shankar and everything in between. And also the atmosphere – they had people there like Brian Jones of the Rolling Stones walking around the fairgrounds. And nobody really bothered anybody. The atmosphere was sort of *oh, there's Brian Jones, but we shouldn't bug him. He's one of us.*

aP: That's beautiful. How many times did you see him perform?

LW: Three times – I saw him at Monterey, Stockholm and the Isle of Wight in 1970.

aP: That's another great concert film. So of the three times – does anything stick out as being particularly honest about his performances?

LW: Definitely Monterey, absolutely. For most of the performance in Monterey, he was – especially if you think about it afterwards, you realize that he was putting on a show. He was really friendly there, and honest. And the venue was quite small. Maybe only a couple of thousand people in the arena. Everything was very close – not like seeing a small dot. Even at the Isle of Wight, he was so far away. And of course, Stockholm was a very surreal concert. But Monterey was really the right place. And he reached his audience – a really open audience.

Lennart Wretlind Interview with Jimi Hendrix
January 9, 1969
Backstage at the Stockholm Konserthuset

JIMI HENDRIX: Hello, this is Jimi Hendrix – and here's something for your head.

LENNART WRETLIND: Do you think you'll make fewer personal appearances?

JH: Well, we're gonna have to, because like – we haven't had a rest since we've been together, you know. And like, we're gonna have to take a rest sometime or another, or else our music's going to come out really, really…bad. Or it's not going to come out proper – the way we want it to. So you have to have proper rest. And mental rest, too – before you can really create nice sounds and music.

LW: Do you plan to record any jamming – things with any English musicians?

JH: Oh yes – yeah, definitely. We like to record some jamming things with a lot of people. Especially Hansson & Karlsson – remember them? Hansson & Karlsson, and like, Stevie Winwood, and – you know – whoever.

LW: Your new album *Electric Ladyland* – this is the first time you've produced anything yourself.

JH: Yeah well actually, we were getting our things together the other two times, you know with *Axis* and with, uh, *Are You Experienced?* But most of those were, like, predominantly handled by Chas and all that. But this was the first time I did it by myself, completely.

LW: It's said to have been very expensive – seventy thousand dollars – is that right?

JH: Yeah it was about – I guess about sixty thousand dollars, I guess. Well yeah, it was like, really expensive because with, uh, recording and playing at the same time – which is very – you know. There's a whole lot of strain on your soul. So therefore, we have to always go back in the studio again and re-do what we might have done two nights ago, you know.

LW: For the future, you still see the experience keeping together, then?

JH: Oh, probably – yeah. But there's no definite breakup thing, like that. We might work a little less, but our records will be better, you know. Because we'll have better piece of mind, you know. 'Cos I get very bored, regardless of how good anybody else is – and I'm sure other people might get bored, too. It's like – I get bored with myself. I can't play guitar anymore, the way I want to. You know, I get very frustrated sometimes, on stage, when we play. I think it's 'cos there's only three pieces. I like to work with other things, too. And I'm sure they would too, you know. But that doesn't necessarily mean we have to break the group up, you know?

LW: Tell me about this one track – 'Crosstown Traffic' – is that just the three of you?

JH: Yeah, and I was playing piano on it. And then, uh, we sang the background. You can always sing about love, and different situations of love. But now we're trying to give solutions to all the protests. And the arguments that they're having about the world today. So we'll try to give our own little opinions about that – in very simple words.

Anybody can protest, but not too many people can offer a decent answer. So we're gonna try to do that. Every time we come into town, everybody's always looking towards us for some kind of answer in what's happening to them, you know. Which is a good feeling, but it's very hard. So therefore, I have to live the life – I have to witness all these bad scenes and all these good scenes, so then I can say, well – what *I* found out, instead of just reading books and all that. So therefore I'm going to get all these words together in nice, heavy songs – very straightforward songs – and just sock it to 'em. Properly.

• • •

Lennart Wretlind was in the audience in the front rows of Monterey Pop. It felt *dangerous*. But meeting Jimi in person, he was like a teddy bear. *He was so warm and open; he needed to be with the people.* And Jimi spoke of his own need to connect with people, on a musical level and on an intellectual level. People were looking to Jimi for answers, and he was starting to think of ways that he could help to provide them. When Jimi stepped onto the Woodstock stage eight months later, he presented the world with his findings.

Before that, in February of 1969, the Jimi Hendrix Experience returned to London for two shows at the Royal Albert Hall. It was here that Fat Mattress made their debut as support act. The Experience returned to the States in mid-March for more recording sessions at the Record Plant. These sessions included contributions from some of Miles Davis' band, guitarist John McLaughlin and bassist

Dave Holland. Jimi was looking to experiment more and push aural boundaries with spontaneity in the way Davis had with the recent release *Bitches Brew*.

The next US tour started in Raleigh, North Carolina on April 11, also with Fat Mattress, but Jimi had hit a wall. With no let-up in the schedule, he was exhausted and creatively drained. He'd also lost his patience for Noel's preoccupation with his side project and the pair were arguing frequently. Jimi invited his old Chitlin' Circuit bass player and army buddy Billy Cox to the show in Memphis on April 18. Jimi told Billy that the Experience was going to split. Billy was put on stand-by.

The tour continued until June 1, 1969, during which time the most notable event was a drug bust while entering Canada in May. Jimi was later acquitted, but the possession charges loomed over him until December. There was some time off in LA in June, where Jimi was finally able to regain some energy. On June 20, the Experience played the Newport Pop festival outside LA, and Jimi jammed with Buddy Miles for the first time, as well as members of Eric Burdon's new band, War.

Denver Pop followed on June 29, where Jimi announced: "This is the last gig we'll ever be playing together". This was a surprise to everyone, including Noel. Noel took his cue to leave the band, and he flew back to London. Jimi called Billy Cox. They had another festival to prepare for.

The following week, Mike Jeffery rented Jimi a large property in Shokan, upstate New York, where he could recuperate and rehearse with Billy and the new band. Jimi decided to augment the three-piece with 'earthier' percussion and an extra guitar. He had toyed with this idea earlier, but Mike Jeffery had vetoed it. Now Jimi was pushing back. He called the band Gypsy Sun and Rainbows. They were in-and-out of Shokan for the next six weeks, as they prepared for the nearby Woodstock Music and Art Fair.

Jerry Velez
Gypsy Sun & Rainbows

GYPSY SUN & RAINBOWS was expanded to include percussionists Gerardo 'Jerry' Velez and Juma Sultan, as well as rhythm guitarist Larry Lee. These musicians joined Mitch Mitchell and Billy Cox. Together they all moved into the rented house in Shokan and began rehearsals. There was a feeling of anticipation: the idea of 'Woodstock' had started a real buzz in the counterculture. Rumor had it that this concert would be big. Nobody could know just how big, yet. Jimi spent this rehearsal period enjoying a semi-isolated existence in the country. Two horses lived at the property and he was able to take morning rides down to a nearby lake. This was the break Jimi sorely needed. It was one of the last periods of time that he ever really got to himself.

Jerry Velez was recruited by Jimi to play congas. His Latin style was the counterpoint to Juma Sultan's African rhythms. The musicians played off each other, and the new rhythms provided the impetus for several new instrumental works. These pieces paved the way for Jimi's move from the pop scene toward jazz fusion. Some of them – 'Jam Back at the House', 'Woodstock Improvisation', and 'Villanova Junction' would premiere at the Woodstock festival. The Band of Gypsys was exploring new sounds; Jimi was experimenting. Larry Lee provided vocals for two songs,

'Mastermind' and a cover of the Temptations' 'Gypsy Woman'. These tracks are not included on official Woodstock releases but they can be found online. They provide evidence of a more relaxed, inclusive Woodstock finale. Jimi wanted musical space to bounce off other players and to form a unit that would support experimentation.

Mike Jeffery stayed at the Shokan house on-and-off. It was clear that Jimi was fed up with their deal. Jerry Velez was privy to a number of arguments between Jimi and Mike. Jimi wanted out. It has been reported that Jimi was kidnapped from the house by Mike's underworld contacts and kept in isolation for several hours before Mike 'arranged' for his release. The theory is that Mike staged it all to intimidate Jimi. Mike was in charge and he wanted it to stay that way. He wanted Jimi in a money-making three-piece band.

Woodstock was the first professional gig for Gerardo 'Jerry' Velez. After his time with Jimi, Gerardo – who now goes by his proper name – became one of the founding members of jazz fusion group Spyro Gyra and went on to contribute percussion to myriad albums and touring bands; David Bowie, Elton John, Nile Rodgers, Duran Duran, and Slash are just a few luminaries that he worked with along the way. Gerardo now runs the entertainment company Gerardo Velez Productions.

But back in 1968, Gerardo Velez was a twenty-year-old regular around the New York nightclubs. He'd grown up with Latin dance and rhythmic grooves, and had found a way to sit in with established musicians on the club stages. Gerardo's congas contributed a novel element to the touring bands in their New York gigs. The grooves were magic.

GERARDO VELEZ: I met Jimi at a venue called Steve Paul's Scene. Steve Paul was the manager of Johnny Winter and

Edgar Winter. He brought them from Texas up to New York and introduced them to us and to our community. That night, Rick Derringer was playing, Jeff Beck was playing, and I was playing. I came with my group of people; Jimi had his group of people. He sat behind me, and when I was done playing with Jeff and Rick, I went back to my seat and he tapped me on the shoulder and said, "Hey man, I love the way you play…let's get together and play – do you wanna come up when I'm playing?"

I said, "Sure."

I never perceived Jimi as the right vehicle for me at that time. Don't forget, we're all thinking we're going to be somebody, and there I am in the mix with everybody. Okay – these guys are too loud. Where the hell am I going to fit in?

So we jammed, and it went great. And then after that we went to the studio and recorded and all that. And then I said, "What are you looking to do, man?"

He said, "Well, here's what I'm looking to do. I'm looking to do some other stuff. I'm going to bring in Billy and my old buddy from the army, Larry Lee. I want to do something different, I want to add some African rhythms, and Latin rhythms."

I said, "Okay, that sounds pretty cool. I'm in. That sounds like something that can happen. You're way too loud as a trio – I get it; I understand."

He said, "Great. Let's do this."

And that's how the relationship started. We were two young guys talking about music, about politics, about culture. He came from Seattle. And in New York, the big city, he wasn't prepared for a lot of things. He was more of an observer than an implementer. I was the implementing guy. I would get the parties together – the girls, the drugs, the cars – all that stuff that we needed to get around New York. I'd get a private space for us, or whatever. So that's how our relationship started, as friends. Going out, chasing girls. He really didn't get high that much. I got high much more than he did, and most of us did. He dabbled. I always looked at him as a dabbler than an actual hard-core guy in anything other than playing music.

We were like the odd men out. I'm Latino, he's a black guy. Our mutual experience, growing up, was that we always felt like we were the odd person out in the groupings. And we always kinda were. And we learnt how to deal with that and accept our position and be the best we can with who we are. We used to laugh about that. He'd hit me up when he'd come to New York and we'd hang out. Because, you know – I had different things already in motion. Different players; different things, a different scene. I was into the scene, and he plugged in right away, as soon as he got there.

AIDAN PREWETT: Making music with Jimi – how did that play out?

GV: Jimi had two trunks filled with records – steamer trunks; those big steamer trunks. And in those steamer trunks he had all kinds of music in there. We had turntables, we had all the gear. We would just put on anything. We'd reach in, we'd close our eyes, pull out an album, we'd play it. It could be classical. And we'd go, *oooh boy, let's go.* We'd put on the piece and we'd be playing along with it. That's how we started making music together in Gypsy Sun and Rainbows, A Band of Gypsys.

We would go to this trunk and just pop out records. He introduced me to all these black comedians who later became famous, like Redd Foxx and Moms Mabley – all these black comedians who were hysterical. But they didn't cross over from the Chitlin' Circuit at that time. Don't forget, it was 1968 I met Jimi. So we're still in civil war. We're still trying to make our own, and I'm involved with a lot of activity in that area in New York City.

When Juma came into the picture a little later on, Juma took him downtown to listen to the Aboriginal Society that he was involved in – which were African rhythms. If you listen to the Woodstock concert, there are instrumental songs that Jimi never did before of that nature. Why? Because we were more of an instrumental band, which later became fusion. A band I'm very proud of that I'm one of the original members of – Spyro Gyra – we're the best-selling contemporary jazz group of all time. That's what I was doing with Jimi. We were breaking new ground.

Listen to 'Jam Back at the House'. That Mozambique beat. *Da da Ba da da Ba da da dada Dum.* I brought that to the table. And he brought the *wah – dada dum dada dum*, which was more his thing. We just blended it – that's why we called it 'Jam Back at the House'. At the house, that's how we used to jam. We put on some music and then oh shit, let's get that idea. And he had a quarter-inch back then, to record things.

We spent a lot of time in that room, the downstairs room of the house, coming up with sounds, making music. He showed me a little bit of stuff on guitar, which I should have followed up on. Unfortunately, I didn't. And he would bang away on some congas that I had. So we helped each other come up with different rhythms and grooves. That's how a lot of those songs worked, like 'Machine Gun' that he came up with later on with Buddy, 'cos Buddy was really creative. Working in the studio, Buddy was like the best musician out of all of us. What I mean by that – he was the most versatile. He played the shit out of the drums, he played organ like nobody, and could kick the pedals. Buddy could kick pedals and play organ and sing in perfect pitch.

Jimi said, "Oh listen, man – let's let Buddy do the singing."

Michael Jeffery, his manager, said, "No fuckin' way is he doing the singing on your fuckin' record, alright? I draw the line there."

He said, "Well, okay – I guess."

But then when they went out on the road, did you see how Buddy sang 'Changes' and 'We Gotta Live Together'? 'Cos Jimi was getting out of his deal with Michael Jeffery.

aP: Is there a moment from the house at Shokan that has really stuck with you?

GV: It was six o'clock in the morning – we had been playing all night and partying. I always liked to go for a ride. There was a lake, I'd go for a swim. I'd take the horses sometimes. And then go to sleep. And then get up in the late afternoon and start all over again. Sex, drugs, and rock 'n' roll, baby. We were hanging out one morning and I said let's go riding. There were two horses on the estate that he had up near Woodstock. I'm a good rider – I was excellent back then. I'd just throw reins and I'd just do it bareback. I said, "Come on."

Jimi said, "I'm not doing it bareback!" So I said *okay*.

So I went to the horse and I put on a saddle. We'd been partying like maniacs, so I'm not really paying attention. When you put a cinch on a saddle, which is the underside of a saddle on a horse, you've got to pull it up tight. Horses are smart in the sense that they expand their stomach when you're doing that. If you don't realise it, when they loosen their stomach there's all this give in the cinch.

So I helped Jimi up – I boosted him onto the saddle. He had the reins in his hands and he was clicking along, clicking along.

"Oh, you're doing great man. Come on, let's get out of the barn area – you're doing great."

He's holding onto the rein and he goes, "Alright, well – wait a minute, hold it…hold it-" and the whole saddle started going over to the side. He fell in horse shit. I could not stop laughing. And he got up – he wasn't a curser. We're New Yorkers, we curse like truck drivers. *Fuck this,* and *get the fuck outta here* and *God damn it.* Suddenly Jimi was *really* cursing.

"Dude, I'm really sorry, man."

"What happened, man? Look at this, I got horse shit on me, man. This is your fault, man."

I said, "No – I believe it's the horse's fault."

He was covered in shit, so he immediately ran into the house. He was a little pissed off. I didn't go into the house right away 'cos I couldn't stop laughing. The expression on his face – the violation on his face said everything. The look of *traitor.* It was priceless. It was like *you set me up,* almost. *You punk'd me.*

AP: Is there a particular conversation with Jimi that comes back to you?

GV: Yeah – this is one of the lessons I've learned. Because up until then – Woodstock was my first gig. Playing with Jimi and other people was a lot of fun. Like I said, I wasn't a professional, but I was in a band that never got anywhere – and then I met Jimi when I was 20. So that kind of took off from there – you just would like your career to go sideways from there. Mine didn't – I felt like I fell off a cliff. But I learned how to be a musician and learned some of the things that Jimi showed me by example. For instance, I came to the studio with half a dozen girls, all kinds of great drugs, champagne, everything. Okay, we're gonna have this incredible party with all these beautiful girls. So I said, "Okay – come into Studio B." And he came into Studio B and there we all were.

He said, "What's going on, man?" You know, "We're here to work." We're here to work. And I'm like, "Yeah, I know that, man – but let's have some fun too." He said, "No – we can do that later, Jerry. We'll do that later. Take your friends, take them all, and please go." But he did it so cool that I felt like – whoa – that really was not a right thing to do. Then as I became a professional in the industry, I became more adamant than even he was – into spirituality and the stage and recording. And the process is as important – or more important – than the creation itself. And I messed with the process of the way he was thinking and focusing and all those things that you do in the studio. Having a bunch of party animals come in is not what you do. But I had thought, *hey, we're rock 'n' roll, this is just gonna be a big party.*

AP: I heard that Mike Jeffery was at the house in Shokan, and there were thin walls – so you heard some discussion between Jimi and Mike. I'd love to hear something about what you heard.

GV: I'll tell you exactly what I know about that. Jimi would always say Michael Jeffery owed him three-and-a-half million dollars. He would say, "Oh yeah, it was a fucked up deal – excuse my French." That's what he said. "My deal sucks, but I'm getting out of it – I have control of my life, don't worry, Jerry."

The incident was: Michael Jeffery was in the other room. He said, "Come here, Jimi." And they went in.

Michael said, "Who's this fuckin' kid, Jerry Velez? No-one knows him."

Jimi said, "Yeah, but I love the way he plays and he's making really great music…and I've got my army buddies."

Michael was pissed. Jimi said he was in charge of his own life. He said he'd do this tour to make the money… Basically *and then you're outta my life.*

Michael Jeffery was certainly a dark individual. Mood-wise, energy-wise – he vibrated on the negative frequency, that's for sure. And it was evident by his tactics with Jimi. It was intimidation; it was control.

But he did make Jimi's career. And he was sensible – you know, looking back as a musician and a band leader with a career of my own.

Michael was saying, "It's about *you*, man. Forget about Buddy singing and all this other stuff. What are you doing, man? You're splitting up the trio which is making you all the money, that everybody wants to hear."

"But I'm tired of doing the same music. I don't want to do this 'Purple Haze' for the rest of my life. I'm doing something different with these guys – I'm having a great time. Let me explore what I want to explore."

"Okay. Do your exploration. Do this fuckin' gig and then let's do this tour." And that was it. It happened more than once – the arguing happened on several occasions.

aP: It's been reported in a few places that Jimi was somehow kidnapped from the house in Shokan. Was that – do you know anything about that?

GV: I don't know anything about that. I really don't. Someone else mentioned that – I said, "Kidnapped? What are you talking about?" You know, if that happened I think I would have known. But maybe not. Maybe it was such a thing that: "I'm not telling anyone." And then, of course – for his own safety – why would he tell me? I was a friend, I'm not his lawyer. We all had loose lips back then. *Did you hear what happened to Jimi?*

So I don't know anything about that. I don't know the legitimacy of that at all. But stranger things have been said. About Jimi and other artists. Folklore and urban legend.

aP: So – the big one: In terms of Woodstock, is there a moment for you that would sum up what that experience was?

GV: When we got there, they gave us a house and they just kept postponing our gig. Jimi was staying in the back in a room, just practicing and playing. He'd come out and he'd talk, but we were all just partying and hanging out. People said *we'll get some girls, get some drugs, whatever you guys want, just enjoy.* So I was running around like, *hey man, this is fantastic – we're so happy to be a part of this.*

We heard things in dribs and drabs, because all that was available to you was radio at that time. And the roads were closed – you couldn't get near the festival, so they had to bring us in through a back road. And I would keep going down to meet people and bring them up and have a good time. And then when it came time to go on stage we were like, *okay, let's do this.* And then we got to the stage and then there was more delay. It wasn't like we got backstage, *let's do a sound check real quick and then jump on it.* That took some time backstage. Jimi was like a stallion wanting to get out of the chute, and the chute hadn't been opened and he'd been waiting for ten hours.

And then he was introducing a new band, which was us.

We didn't know how it was going to be received when he was doing instrumentals. But he was tired of just playing the same old songs. So he felt that the reason we lived in that house off of Woodstock was to do this new concept. When we did the concept, the sound sucked. Jimi was having problems. I couldn't be heard. The bass player was way too far on the other side – Billy. They didn't have enough bass on Jimi's side of the stage. I was right next to Jimi – I couldn't hear shit but guitars. So it was very chaotic. When you looked at Jimi in some of the photos and saw he was – he would look down and try to let things kind of work out – move on and pick up the next song, kind of thing. But there were many moments when I looked at him... I overplayed. It was my first gig and we were all crazy. I wish I'd had the opportunity to play with Jimi into the future but when I look back at the whole ensemble, there was a lot of overplaying. Juma, myself, Mitch... Mitch didn't give us any space to really do it – he never wanted to; he didn't like the whole concept. And he was more a jazz drummer, where Buddy was a funk and pocket drummer and we fit in perfectly. Buddy and I jammed forever, until his death.

But Jimi took a big risk having me involved with the band, because Woodstock was my first professional gig – and my birthday. My birthday is August 15th. We played on the 18th, but I was partying for my birthday a week before my birthday, until after that event. There was a lot of partying going on. Jimi was always concerned about the music. He was a true musician. I learned a lot about being a musician with him. Staying with the music focus. "You can party, man, but it's not about the party. It's about getting the creations out." It's like, oh man. Good lesson.

aP: A few weeks later you were in Harlem for another

concert – could you talk me through a moment from that concert?

GV: Yeah – he wanted to play for his people; he wanted to touch base with Harlem and people down there. The day of Woodstock was the Harlem version of Woodstock – James Brown, the Temptations – all the best black acts in the world. But Woodstock overshadowed that festival.

So after that Jimi said, "Man – I wanna do something, man… This festival didn't get any recognition – look at the talent they had…" I said *yeah man*. I left it at that. Being a New Yorker I knew that things happen in different areas and you've just got to bear with it. They give everybody a chance, so to speak, in New York. So he said, "The hell with it, let's play in Harlem." They put up a makeshift tent, and unfortunately it was September – it was 104 degrees under the tent. And the sound sucked, and Jimi wasn't happy. He had a lot to say, and the sound sucked. It was the early days of production and sound – little speakers. And Jimi needed what we have now, with a lot of balls and presence to the sound system. They didn't have that. He created that with his feedback and all that. There was a lot missing there that he would have loved to use.

AP: Did you get a sense of Jimi's philosophy toward life – or music?

GV: He'd sit there with his book of notes, and I'd have my book with my ideas. That was part of the experience back then. Writing the ledger – that was the way before we had computers. So especially entertainers and creative people, as you know – you have your book, you put in your notes and so on. So we did a lot of that, sitting around, coming up with ideas and listening to different stuff. I introduced him to a lot of the Latin stuff that he didn't know about. And some of the New York guys that he was wondering about, who I knew because my good friend owned that club Slugs' and knew all the jazz greats.

After the Woodstock festival, Jimi had a certain number of gigs he had to undertake as a trio, because he had already booked those shows. And that's when he said *I don't want to do it with Mitch and Noel anymore – I want to do it with Buddy and Billy*. And that's how that kind of merged. When he was coming back to New York, we were all going to get back and do something, which after that became known as fusion. 'Cos Miles Davis was doing Bitches Brew; Miles was doing stuff in the studio.

I knew Miles 'cos he lived a few houses down from my girlfriend. So I knew Miles pretty well, hanging out with him. I brought them together once to hang. We never talked about it again – Miles was doing hard drugs at the time. Jimi never did any hard drugs. I did hard drugs, but he didn't do *real* hard drugs.

But Jimi felt kinda helpless. And he felt that the only way we can get to what's going on in the world today is by opening up and bringing in these other elements of world music. We heard groups like Osibisa and all these other cool groups that came to play and he was like *wow – look at these guys.* They were killing it. He would be beaming from it. He wanted to go write about it.

For instance – 'The Star-Spangled Banner'. He wanted to do that. I said, "Why should we do that – we're the counterculture. Let's do something else."

He said, "No, I want to do a version of that." So *hey, it's your band, let's go…* And of course that's the iconic moment of Woodstock, when he did that. In that sense he was a visionary: *I think this is going to do more justice.*

So with us it was about getting out there and experiencing. Like I said, I was the forward guy and I'd go get the girls and I'd meet the people. And the after-hours. He loved the after-hours. I took him to hang out with all the guys at the Cotton Club… a gazillion after-hours. They close the doors, everybody starts playing music, and that's it. A lot of that stuff wasn't recorded because not everybody had a recorder. We weren't worrying about posterity. It was about the moment.

• • •

Gerardo Velez knew Jimi as a bandmate and personal friend. In the six weeks they spent at the house at Shokan they were able to create new sounds and work with a new group of players – Mitch Mitchell was no longer the sole percussionist in the group. It was a fertile time for Jimi to explore the world of fusion, to improvise, to compose new pieces, and to relax a little. Gerardo provides us some great insight into Jimi's creative process at the time; how he was magpieing from so many diverse records in a steamer trunk, and working with new grooves from the percussionists. Still, their preparations could never have readied them for the ultimate chaos of the first gig they were to play as a band.

Woodstock opened officially on August 15, 1969 – Gerardo's 22nd birthday. Gerardo made sure he was there in person. Meanwhile the other members of Gypsy Sun & Rainbows listened to the radio in awe as descriptions came in of the festival that they were about to play.

Woodstock
An Aquarian Exposition

JIMI WAS THE HEADLINE ACT FOR WOODSTOCK. By that time – August 1969 – he was the highest-paid performer in the world. Only the Beatles, if they were still touring, could have commanded $100,000 USD for a major show – $700,000 in today's money. For Woodstock, however, Jimi took a significant pay cut, as Mike Jeffery saw the potential of this 'prestige gig'. Everybody was excited about the festival; nobody knew just how big it would be. Michael Lang, who had also organized Miami Pop '68, arranged facilities for about 75,000 people. He had a permit for an attendance of 50,000. But when 456,000 people showed up, Lang and his partners were forced to declare it a free concert. Army medical units were sent in and Max Yasgur's farm in upstate New York became its own city for three-and-a-half days. Perhaps most remarkably, amid the rain, mud, and chaos, this city really was a celebration of peace. Almost no violence occurred.

The documentary film *Woodstock*, directed by Michael Wadleigh, survives as a testament to the astonishing event. For the documentary *A Venue for the End of the World,* I caught up with some of the film crew as well as the festival's Head of Production John Morris and Lighting Designer/ Announcer Chip Monck.

AIDAN PREWETT: The first time I heard your voice, it was, "Ladies and Gentlemen, the Jimi Hendrix Experience" – I was like, "Who is this guy with this voice..."

CHIP MONCK: Who said the wrong name of the act! It wasn't the Experience.

AP: True...Well, at least you got the Jimi Hendrix part right.

CM: Somebody brings it up every time.

AP: 'The Star-Spangled Banner'. Do you remember that happening?

CM: Absolutely. It was over, it was finished, it was done with. It was just something – you stood there with your mouth open. In his white leather – better than Daltrey fringe, with the beadwork. It's a stunning shot that will always remain in my mind.

AP: What was the feeling?

CM: Well, unfortunately there were only about 25 or 30 thousand people left. But it was... they were absolutely awestruck. What a wonderful way to begin a week. *Here's Monday morning.* Some people saluted.

JOHN MORRIS (ARTIST LIAISON): I kept Jimi driving around in circles for three days. He was supposed to play two different sets. And his manager, Michael Jeffery, who I knew – and Mike would keep calling up and saying 'alright, when do you want him to come in and play?' I said not yet Mike. When do you want us to come play? Not yet Mike. Literally we did this for a couple of days, because he was not necessarily the one who was going to close the show. And in the end, we just ran out of time. And it was like, "okay, now bring him in.' And it was late in the night on Sunday night, and it was totally accidental. The whole thing. I got him up on stage, and I lay down, and I passed out and went to sleep, because I was exhausted. The next thing I knew, I heard 'The Star-Spangled Banner'. He played his set with the Band of Gypsies, and he went into that. Which we had no clue was going to happen. And I sat bolt upright and went, "Oh my God." And then went back down and went to sleep. And about the time he played, there were only about 25 or 30 thousand people left.

Toward the end of the Sunday night we wanted to have, if we could, keep going and keep playing, so people wouldn't leave an be on the roads in the dark – 'cos we thought it was dangerous. People paid no attention and went home – a lot of them – 'cos they had to go to work the next day. But I got Jimi on stage after literally three days of him riding around in circles, with Mike Jeffery – his manager – saying, 'Can we come in now?' *No.* And they were great about it. But I finally got them on stage – and I went straight up to my trailer and lay down, straight out like a light. And I was out until I heard the first chords of 'The Star-Spangled Banner'. And I sat bolt upright on one elbow, listened to it and went: *It's over. It's done. That's good. This is the perfect way to end it.* And lay right back down and went to sleep. And probably woke up about four or five hours later and looked out the window.

The whole area where the show had been, 90% of the people had all gone. They'd left sleeping bags and cooking pots and pans and all sorts of other stuff. And it was a muddy mess. And it looked exactly like the civil war photographs of Matthew Brady's, of different battle fields, after the battles had happened. With no artillery or anything, but it was just totally desolate, totally done. So I dragged myself up and I went for a walk – all over the site. And it sticks in my mind as one of the most amazing parts of Woodstock. I thought somebody might be dead somewhere, somebody might be hurt somewhere. I didn't find anybody, which was wonderful. But it's a shot that wasn't in the film – that would be – the helicopter going up shot… but it really was, for me – *okay, it's over. Nobody's been harmed.*

JEANNE FIELD (CAMERA ASSISTANT): I thought that he was supposed to end the show. I mean, I thought that was all planned. And I thought, *how perfect.* Sha-Na-Na had been on – such a crazy little act, and then here comes Jimi Hendrix, who was like a God in our world, really. And I figured he was either exhausted from staying up all night, or disconcerted that there were so few people he was playing to.

JOHN BINDER (LOCATION SUPERVISOR): Just conceivable stoned…

JOHN MORRIS: Possibly.

JEANNE FIELD: And so he was kind of noodling. His act had no real center to it, it wasn't like he was really putting it out there, and I think he did say – didn't he say?

JOHN BINDER: 'You can all go home now; I'm just looking for something.'

JEANNE FIELD: And he was. I mean, he was just noodling. And then all of a sudden – you know. He *got* it. The first chords. And literally, was electric. It was electrifying to us. I was at his feet, which was pretty amazing. Michael Wadleigh literally was under his microphone with his camera.

Dick Pearce, who I was working with, was off to the right a little bit, but we were right there. And it was such a great ending to that. And as John said, there were probably maybe 25 or 30 thousand people which, at that point could have been a great crowd, but comparatively was not. And then he shifted down into 'Purple Haze', and it was just perfect.

JOHN BINDER: But I think bringing the politics and our sense of antagonism with America at that time, because of the war, for me it was the culmination of that whole decade. I thought, in an artistic sense. Just that moment.

DALE BELL (ASSOCIATE PRODUCER): It was funny, because he was working with a new band, and they had not practiced or rehearsed very much, And he was saying at some point in there, something like, 'I'm just noodling, I'm just trying to find a tune, and we're just going to play slowly, and maybe it's going to be a little bit off-tune as we're trying to search to really synchronize our harmony', if you will. And then he explodes into this most disharmonious – if you will – musical explosion of sound. And you really wonder what it was that Jimi was looking at, or what did he see when he was playing that. What was going through his mind as he cascaded these chords, these riffs, and exploded.

JOHN BINDER: Well Jimi had been in the 101st Airborne.

JOHN MORRIS: Yeah, he was a paratrooper.

JOHN BINDER: I'm sure that was part of his comment.

JEANNE FIELD: It was combat.

DALE BELL: Yeah. And he visualized it musically, or it

almost wasn't music, it was a sound effect, or a series of sound effects, I think, that culminated what was going on in the '60's and I think maybe even was looking forward. To what he saw – the disharmony of the '60's – had actually represented to him, and to the people he represented.

AIDAN PREWETT: Did any of you get a sense of how the audience reacted?

JOHN MORRIS: I was asleep.

JOHN BINDER: The audience was very sparse, and they were scattered. The group that was within our purview, we were on a shelf in front of the stage, and the fence behind that, the crowd had – it was quite sparse. And it was more, to those of us who were still standing, it was a little bit in the direction he was saying, that it was the visual end. These were the stragglers of the war. And what he said eloquently about the battlefield and its decimation, was all of a piece. And Jimi had – hitting that song, and those opening notes, I think, was part of the whole denouement of all those days.

JEANNE FIELD: Everybody was so wasted, by this morning. Not necessarily on drugs but just by the experience, and filthy, and there are some shots of the audience in the film and it shows how people were not at their best. But that's as it should be.

DALE BELL: Jimi, I think, he did this – *'scuse me while I kiss the sky.* That to me was like, *I'm not singing only to those who are left, the stragglers on the Matthew Brady landscape – I'm really going for the world.* "'Scuse me while I kiss the sky." That was his sort of homily to all that *was,* all that had been before, and all that was to come afterwards. It was an incredible moment – he defied Michael Wadleigh to continue filming. You know, when he put his foot down on the foot pedal and he stared straight in to the lens. It was like, *You're never going to believe what I'm gonna do next.* It was that sort of arrogance, pride, humility – marvelous. Marvelous.

aIDan PREWETT: John, you were talking earlier about Jimi Hendrix, something with a camera? I'd love to hear that.

JOHn MORRIS: I met Jimi the beginning of the week after the Monterey Pop festival, which I didn't go to. But I was standing outside the Fillmore West with Bill Graham. And Jimi was coming down because he was going to play a concert on the back of a truck in Golden Gate Park. And he got out of the back of the van he was in and handed me a Polaroid camera, and said, 'Somebody gave me this, can you show me how to make it work?' So that was my initial meeting, initial interaction with Jimi. It was one of the first Polaroid cameras. And it was just, somebody had given it to him. It mystified me too. Four of us ended up getting together, trying to figure out how to make it work.

JOHn BINDeR: You should have handed him your guitar and said, 'Can you show me how this works?'

• • •

In the weeks following the festival, Jimi continued to frequent the house in Shokan. But people had figured out where he was living and he started getting hassled – by fans, by members of the Black Panthers, and by some of Mike Jeffery's shady business partners. Mike was turning up the pressure for Jimi to return to a three-piece band.

Jimi was about to turn 27 years old. He briefly moved to

the Hotel Navarro on Central Park South and assembled his musicians. Jimi told them that the Gypsy Sun & Rainbows trip was over. The band was now Jimi, Billy Cox, and Buddy Miles: The Band of Gypsys.

Legal issues relating to contracts Jimi had signed in the Chitlin' Circuit days meant that Jimi had to deliver an album of largely original material to Ed Chalpin of PPX Enterprises. Mike Jeffery was livid, but figured that the cheapest and easiest route would be to record a live album. So over New Year's Eve and the first day of 1970, four concerts at the Fillmore East were recorded with Jimi, Billy, and Buddy. These were the only four shows that the Band of Gypsys played together. One further occasion, a benefit concert for the Vietnam Moratorium Committee, happened at Madison Square Garden on January 28. They only made it through two songs. Jimi's drink had been spiked with bad acid.

John Storyk

Electric Lady Studios

WITHIN WEEKS OF THEIR FORMATION, Mike Jeffery had already arranged for the dissolution of the Band of Gypsys. He called Noel immediately following the Fillmore East gigs. The legal obligations to PPX Enterprises had been fulfilled and he felt that the time had come to re-form the original Experience. Fat Mattress were also starting to dissolve, and Noel was feeling ready to come back. Mitch had always understood the Band of Gypsys to be a temporary arrangement. As consolation, Buddy Miles was able to bring his band on the next tour as one of the support acts.

Jimi spent most of February 1970 at New York's Record Plant, racking up further bills for Mike Jeffery and pushing him to get Electric Lady Studios up and running. Then in early March, Jimi learned that in the eleven months he had spent away from England, Kathy Etchingham had married someone else. He flew to London to try to convince her to leave, to no avail. Exhaustion was mounting and, after the drink spiking incident in January, his health was declining, and glandular fever had taken hold. Nonetheless, he returned to New York and the Record Plant to prepare for the next tour in April.

Noel had a change of heart and didn't return to the band. Billy and Mitch accompanied Jimi for more heavy touring across America through late April, May, June, and July 1970. Three concerts were cancelled in May due to Jimi's health. In mid-June, Electric Lady became operational and Jimi would spend most of the time between tour dates in his brand-new studio.

Architect and acoustician John Storyk graduated from Princeton University in 1968 and designed a New York nightclub called Cerebrum. Jimi loved the club's layered, flowing design and quickly recruited Storyk to plan out his own club, Electric Lady. When Eddie Kramer walked through the building site and noted its acoustic possibilities, Jimi and Mike Jeffery were quickly persuaded to change tack, and Electric Lady Studios was born.

John Storyk had to scrap his nightclub plans and completely redesign the space for recording. Studio A was ready for use in June 1970, and Jimi spent several weeks recording tracks for what eventually became *First Rays of the New Rising Sun*. Electric Lady went on to become one of the world's most iconic studios; a base of recording operations for David Bowie, Led Zeppelin, Kiss, the Rolling Stones, Blondie, Alice Cooper, Patti Smith, Guns n' Roses, and more recently Daft Punk, Taylor Swift, and Lana Del Ray, among many others.

John Storyk quickly established himself as *the* premier recording studio architect and acoustician, designing private studios for Bruce Springsteen, Bob Marley, Alicia Keys, Whitney Houston, Aerosmith, Green Day, and Jay-Z. Other acoustic-focused buildings have also featured his designs, including the Swiss Parliament and the Zurich Airport.

As an architect, John had a chance to see Jimi in a light that few people did – walking around a construction site on a sunny Greenwich Village afternoon. Jimi would chat with the workers and communicate more in terms of shapes and ideas than through architectural plans. John became close with Eddie Kramer and spent a lot of time with Eddie at Woodstock. As an architect, John knew Jimi as a client.

JOHN STORYK: Jimi was more-or-less my *first* client. Which is unusual – quite unusual for a 22-year-old, more or less only out of school for a short amount of time, to get a call from him. Actually it was from his manager. "We'd like you to do a club." The original call was to build a club for Jimi. A blues club. Actually, to convert a club that I used to go to and listen to music in – the Generation. He had seen a club that I had designed – really, the very first commission that I did. And he liked the club because of the nature of it, and he said, "Well, we'll get the person who did that club to do my club." This was in the Village – Greenwich Village, early 1969. So that was the call.

I met with him, I think actually really only twice, to be honest. In preparation of that design I did – I have a drawing dated February '69. My recollection of Jimi, first of all – he was extremely quiet. Almost shy. Now, the Jimi I saw was always sort of in the late afternoon. Not at two o'clock in the morning with whatever he was doing at two in the morning. Not the backstage performing Jimi. Although I was once backstage. Actually, I was backstage at Woodstock.

AIDAN PREWETT: Woah!

JS: Yeah, because a lot changed in that year, of meeting him – and August of '69. Which is another story. So, you know – he was very polite. Almost shy. Didn't read drawings very well, but knew what he wanted. What he liked about this club was that this club was all white, and you changed into a gown and you would enter the club and the club had lots of lighting changes and image changes. It was sort of like an experience or a sensorium for three hours. It was a little ahead of its time, I think. And rather primitive. But it became one of the go-to places in New York in the winter of 68-69. And he went there one night – that's why he called. And he wanted some of those ideas in his club. He wanted everything to be able to be changed; he wanted a lot of flexibility with the lighting. He didn't really want to have very many straight lines, he wanted everything to be curves. Those were the images that he expressed to me. And then kind of left me alone. It was very unusual.

Now, you have to realize – I'm 22 years old and I really had no idea what this was supposed to look like. I'm out of school, I'm working in the day. I was actually still in a band. And here comes the first sort of client, who happens to be a celebrity. Although I'm not a guitar player – I'm a keyboard player – obviously I knew who Jimi Hendrix was. Like everybody else, I loved the music. So this was quite – I didn't really know how you were supposed to behave. So I said, "Okay, let me do some sketches and I'll come back." Which I did. And he liked the drawings which had this kind of curved stage, and the back of the club curved up and over into the ceiling, which also had a kind of propeller shape to it, with lighting tucked in. So this was all very exciting. I don't know whether it was ahead of its time or behind its time, but it was *at the time*. So imagine the winter of '68-'69 in New York City. These were exciting times. These were incredible times. And of course my life had changed very quickly. The Cerebrum club became very famous. It was on the cover of *Life* magazine. All kinds of things were happening all of a sudden.

But, at the last minute, the club idea got scrapped.

Because his engineer, whose name is Eddie Kramer, who you might have heard of, of course – producer/engineer Eddie, had convinced him to not do the club. Eddie didn't have any interest in the club. Now there's another idea that I have to tell you: One of the ideas that Jimi had – either he or his manager, to be honest, I can't even remember. But it was an idea that was imparted, was that in the back of the club there would be a small control room, and they would record everything that was in the club. So it was almost like it was going to be his private club. And this was going to take place in the basement of a building on Eighth Street, in the club that was called the Generation – which was *the* blues club to go to. Where he used to go all the time. I always thought that this was because his bar bill was so big, it was easier to just buy the club. Which is what they did. They didn't buy the building; they bought the lease. Just took over the club.

Now, Eddie had no interest in the club. Eddie had just come over from the UK and he wanted a studio. And Jimi was racking up huge studio bills because he was independently producing, and he was rehearsing in studios, which of course is wrong. He was sort of in the forefront of what is now the new model – that artists make their own music, and then you give it to the record company when you're done. But at the time, Jimi was one of the few people doing that because he *could*. The record company had no choice but to sort of wait 'til he was done. They knew they would get a very valuable property. So Eddie talks him out of the club, and of course I watched my first major commission disappear about as fast as it arrived. And that was a terrible moment. I remember when that happened. I remember getting the call. But somehow, they allowed me to stay on and do the studio. Even after I reminded them that I had never actually been *in* a recording studio. And so life changed again, right on a dime. A whole bunch of events happened. I left my job; I created an internship with another acoustician who knew a lot about radio station design. I did some reading, went back to graduate school for a few months to try to learn some stuff, and lo and behold – a year or so later, Electric Lady was born. Even before Electric Lady was done, I had two other studios to do. So, make your first project famous, I guess is the bottom line there.

So during that time, I did have some contact with Jimi. He would come down to the construction now and then. That was always an interesting moment. And it was always late in the day – I always assumed he wasn't getting up at eight in the morning. He would love to walk through the construction – again, extremely quiet. Very quiet, very polite. Always very nice to everybody. But he'd make changes. All the doors had these kind of rectangular windows in them so that you could see through. They were the standard studio doors that you could buy at that time, in the limited market that we had. One day he walked in and he just said, "Can we make these windows round?" He didn't want them squared. So all of a sudden eight doors disappeared. Eight new round ones appeared. Those doors ended up in other studios in New York. Hysterical. I remember that, very vividly. Everybody looked at him. *Okay – it's your money.*

But he would come down, he loved to talk to the workers. He's always walk through. He couldn't read drawings; he never looked at the drawings. He just always looked at shapes. And he organized a big mural that got painted in the lobby, which went all the way down the side of the long corridor – a sort of space-type mural. Pieces of that are now in the studio itself. That's one of the very direct contributions of Jimi's. There was some color in the studio – most of it was white; still is white. But he did have some input on some of the colors. Purple was one of the colors, no surprise.

And of course, he always looked exactly like what you would expect him to look like. Very well dressed – a scarf and all that stuff. But I guess it's his quietness and politeness that I remember more than anything else. He basically let me do what I wanted. Three thousand clients later – it probably is that kind of number, years later – I would have to put him as one of the top ten clients. Not because he's famous, and not because the studio launched my career – but because *he was just really nice*. He hired me, and never really – he basically let me do what I wanted. I, of course, just assumed that that's the way it's supposed to be. Of course, it didn't take long to learn that that is, in fact, *not* exactly what happens. In fact, it's rather rare that that happens. So I guess that's… being so quiet and patient. I guess he saw something in this club and then he saw something in the sketch for his club, and he just let me go.

Of course, Eddie had a lot to do with the studio. Not so much the architecture, but the vibe and some of the systems and whatnot. I didn't know anything about recording – all the equipment specs and everything. That all came from Eddie. And then Eddie has gone on to be a lifelong friend. Years later he's still a close friend. I see him and talk to him with frequency. He now lives in Canada.

So that's my Jimi story. He wasn't someone I hung out with every night, but I was fortunate enough to have – maybe I saw a side of Jimi that a lot of other people didn't see. Four o'clock in the afternoon walking through a construction site.

aP: A very unique perspective, definitely.

JS: Yeah, it's a little different to some of the other experiences, I would imagine. Everything else is just legend
or stories to me. Of course, I remember the day that he
passed. Actually, it was Eddie who called me. You know – it
was horrible. All this time and energy, and he never really
got to use it very much. A sad moment. But his legacy to
me is as one of the pioneers of the project studio. That's
what he built. He basically built a personal project studio
with commercial specifications. To this day it's one of the
top commercial studios in the world. And certainly an
iconic one. But what he was building was a private project
studio, in the basement of a rather intriguing building that
I knew about even in college, 'cos it was done by one of my
favorite architects – Kiesler.

I didn't realize that I was in that building – the old Film
Guild building – until after I got started. I knew it was in
New York, but I had no idea that every time I went to this
club in college, and even when I started in the demolition
phase, I didn't know I was under the theatre. I knew it was
a theatre, but I didn't know it was *that* theatre. So it was a
very strange moment when I found that out. Life had a lot
of twists and turns for me in those few years.

Of course, by the time the summer of '69 came around,
the studio is about to open and by then I'm doing several
other studios, including studios for Albert Grossman in
Bearsville. I got introduced to Albert by a college room-
mate who was the road manager for the Band, and the next
thing you know, I'm doing that studio. And, in fact, I went
to Woodstock *with* Albert and the Band. And of course,
Jimi– now that I think about it, that is the last time I saw
Jimi. No, no – that's not true. I saw him once or twice
during construction. 'Cos that's '69. The studio opens in

the summer of '70; he died in September. Yeah – once or twice more. But that's one of the few times I saw him play live. I didn't go to Monterey, but I was at Woodstock.

aP: I mean, of all the gigs to have been present at – ever…

JS: That was another one that you might want to time travel back to. To tell you the truth – the story of it and the legend of it, the idea of it – the reality was actually better. It was exciting. The moment was exciting. Every attempt to reproduce it going forward has been a failure because it was only meant to happen once. It was a complete freak event. I mean, on many levels it was a failure. It was a financial failure. But it was just one of those moments. A little bit like Live Aid. There are those moments where you can't duplicate them. They just happen. There was a lot of energy there.

aP: You were on the side of the stage? Could you sort of paint that image?

JS: Yeah – I never went out in the mud. I basically arrived backstage, helped out a little bit picking up some stuff. I remember something got stuck in the mud back there and everybody – including Albert – went back and picked this thing up. It was very funny. I spent most of my time in the truck, actually – with Eddie. By then of course, Eddie and I were working together all the time. So I just hung out in the truck. I was never in the mud outside, so I didn't get the full experience.

aP: So Jimi walks on stage – where are you? What does it all look like? What does it sound like?

JS: It didn't sound that great, I'll be honest with you. I was a fan, but I'm not a guitar player. But I don't know what it sounded like out front, 'cos I wasn't out front. You know – I never thought 'The Star-Spangled Banner' was the best representation of his music. I guess you have to kind of – I understand why he did it, and I understand what it did, and of course the times. Try to imagine August '69 and what was going on in the United States, with Vietnam and all that stuff. But I'm a B.B. King, James Cotton guy. I played in a blues band for three years in college. So I was much more of an R&B person. I liked the album work. I never really thought the Woodstock performance was something that was that interesting to me. But I understand why he did it, and I respect that.

AP: So standing on that stage – did you look out, did you get a sense of what the audience was?

JS: Yes! 400,000 people out there. It was incredible. I'd never seen anything like that in my life. No one had. I don't think there was a crowd that big until then. It was like a sea of people. It was incredible. Extraordinary. But when Jimi came out it had gotten very thin. It was the morning. But I was there the day before when it was a full crowd. It was incredible. It was amazing to look out at. But I've consequently spoken to people who were out in the mud. It was funky. It was messy. So now we're in an era with pretty pasteurized concerts and festivals. They're all quite organized and whatnot. And they're all very expensive, of course. I think the magic of Woodstock is essentially how it evolved. It started as this small thing. So the whole way that the Woodstock festival evolved, both physically and even musically was pretty organic. Not really planned. I mean, in retrospect the promoters got the credit for it. But essentially, they failed, financially. But I think that's the beauty of it. At the end of the day, the *name* remained. The name is everything. But I don't think Jimi's performance was the best performance, to be honest.

aP: But in terms of an iconic performance…

JS: Oh, in terms of an iconic performance, obviously.

aP: Do you have a favorite memory from Woodstock?

JS: Yeah, I do – soon after we arrived backstage. I was just standing around with Albert Grossman 'cos I had gone with Albert. Albert and I became pretty close friends. He almost was kind of a mentor to me, and I ended up living on his property for twelve years and designing. Albert built a lot of buildings. Almost every building in Bearsville, he built. Three restaurants, a recording studio, a theatre, a video studio that's now a radio station. Numerous other houses. And I either designed or renovated almost all of them. I sorta was his in-house architect for a while. And he gave me a place to live, he gave me an office in New York, and really helped me a lot as I was getting started in the early seventies.

So we arrived at Woodstock together. Now, Albert always wore the same thing. Dungarees and a Mexican shirt. I don't think he owned any other clothes. So we're standing around out the back. I think actually some of the guys from The Band were there. Some other artists and people. And something got stuck – a big road case or something. Because even backstage it was muddy. And just all of a sudden, everybody – including Albert – somebody said, "Hey, we've got to pick this up." And so everybody was in the mud, getting dirty – just picked this thing up and moved it five feet to get it back onto a sturdy platform. I'll never forget that. It's not what I expected from Albert or any of these – I forget which musicians were there. To this day I can re-imagine that scene. I'd only just arrived. I didn't even know, really, what I was arriving into. I had no idea really. I was perhaps not even planning on going. They said *okay let's go.* So, alright – let's go. We came in the back way, through the artists' entrance. I'll always remember that.

AP: I would love to hear – in terms of Jimi's personality – you mentioned that he was quiet. Was there something that he said – maybe at the construction site. I'm picturing a hard hat, but I bet he didn't wear a hard hat.

JS: No, no, no – nobody wore hard hats. I wish I could give you that – but my answer is basically going to be what he didn't say. What Jimi said to me – is that he didn't tell me what to do. He just told me his original idea for the club, soft, white, curved lines. And he just let me do what somehow came out. I don't know where it came from. The big live room at Electric Lady is more or less unchanged in fifty years. And he – I guess it's what he didn't say. It's the fact that he just threw out an initial image, and just let me start a career. For that I'm going to be indebted.

• • •

John Storyk was given free rein with the drafts and construction of Electric Lady. Jimi recognized John's talent and was laid-back enough to trust John to faithfully execute his ideas; Jimi's interest in creative collaboration bled through from the stage and studio environments into his other endeavors too. Jimi wanted to see what other artists could bring to the table, and he wanted everybody involved to feel comfortable and work at a peak creative level.

From June 1970 onward, Electric Lady Studio A was

opened for Jimi to use whenever he was in New York, which was not often enough for Jimi. Recording time was squeezed into two-day blocks between tour dates. The early part of the tour crossed from California to Wisconsin, Minnesota to Oklahoma, and Texas to Pennsylvania. In June, the Experience played Tennessee, Indiana, Maryland, New Mexico, California, Colorado, and Massachusetts. July was similarly packed.

Meanwhile, Mike Jeffery was hatching another scheme. Jimi's track 'If Six Was Nine' had been used in the hit counterculture film *Easy Rider*, and amid the success of *Monterey Pop!, Dont Look Back,* and *Woodstock,* Jeffery wanted a piece of the celluloid action for himself. His idea became *Rainbow Bridge,* eventually released in 1971. It was a haphazard production, following the journey of a New York model as he meets a variety of counterculture 'drop-outs' in Hawaii. Filming was scheduled to coincide with Jimi's tour dates in Honolulu. The film concludes with a performance from Jimi, Mitch, and Billy on the side of the Haleakala volcanic crater. It was directed by Chuck Wein, who had worked with Andy Warhol on several Factory films. The entire production turned into an acid-addled mess, notable only for its inclusion of the last footage of an American concert by Jimi Hendrix. Here, Jimi could have been enjoying some Hawaiian rest and relaxation. Instead, two days were spent on set for this chaotic, incoherent film.

The US tour officially concluded in Honolulu the day after filming. It was the first day of August 1970. Jimi spent most of that month at Electric Lady Studios. Here, he was able to work on what became his final recordings, which included 'Straight Ahead', 'Freedom', 'Dolly Dagger', 'Drifting', and 'Angel'. These recordings now form the basis of the posthumous album *First Rays of the New Rising Sun.*

Jimi's last recording session was on August 22. The official opening of Electric Lady was held a few days later. The party got messy and Jimi wasn't in the mood. He left early; he had a plane to catch the next day. The Isle of Wight Festival was calling.

Lee Oskar
The Final Performance, '70

1970 WAS THE BIGGEST YEAR YET for the Isle of Wight Festival. The previous two years had seen Bob Dylan, the Who, and Jefferson Airplane, but this time Jimi Hendrix was the headliner. It was a major three-day bill featuring Miles Davis, the Doors, Joan Baez, Joni Mitchell, Jethro Tull, Leonard Cohen, and Sly & the Family Stone, among many others. It was also a major year for biker violence, echoing the Rolling Stones' trouble at Altamont the previous December. Impromptu bonfires erupted, several cars were torched, and crowd beatings occurred around the outskirts of yet another festival city of bigger-than-Woodstock proportions.

It was a shaky start for Jimi, Billy, and Mitch, but they steeled themselves and went on to present some gems of the Hendrix live catalogue. They took the stage after Jethro Tull in the early hours of Monday, August 31, performing again for a small fraction of the festival populace. Like at Woodstock, much of the audience had to go to work in the morning. The concert was filmed by award-winning documentary filmmaker Murray Lerner, but due to financial problems the footage was not released until the 1990's. The result is the concert film *Blue Wild Angel: Jimi Hendrix at the Isle of Wight* – Jimi's last official concert in the UK.

Jimi wanted to get back to Electric Lady Studios as soon as possible, but Mike Jeffery booked six other festival dates in Sweden, Denmark, and Germany in the first week of September. Jimi's final concert was at the Love and Peace Festival on the Isle of Fehmarn, a little German island in the Baltic sea, just a short ferry crossing from the islands of Denmark.

This concert was an unpleasant one. Bad weather delayed Jimi's appearance until the morning after he was originally scheduled. Biker violence and general chaos had again erupted throughout the festival. When the band finally appeared, the audience took a while to warm up, some even booing in the early numbers. To top it all off, Billy Cox had been suffering from serious attacks of acid paranoia. This time it was Billy's drink that had been spiked.

They flew back to London to prepare for yet *more* concerts that Mike Jeffery had scheduled elsewhere in Europe, but Billy's acid problems were getting worse. He was near catatonic. The concerts were cancelled, and Billy flew home to the States. Jimi suddenly found himself in London with nothing-in-particular to do.

And then Monika Dannemann called. She had met Jimi on tour in Germany the previous year. They didn't know each other particularly well, but Jimi agreed to hang out with her now – he was at a loose end. Dannemann's stories have often been dismissed as unreliable, as details would tend to change on each telling. One such story was that Jimi had professed his undying love to her when he returned to London. After years of erratic behavior, Monika Dannemann took her own life in 1996.

What is clear is that they spent a few days together before Jimi died. On Tuesday, September 15, they went to see Eric Burdon's new band War at Ronnie Scott's Jazz

Club. Eric invited Jimi to come back and play with them the following night.

Lee Oskar was the first person that Eric Burdon recruited for War. This band became the last group ever to jam with Jimi Hendrix. Jimi joined them on stage on Wednesday, September 16, playing through War's hit 'Tobacco Road' and the Memphis Slim blues 'Mother Earth', followed by an instrumental jam. Jimi promised to return the next night. When he didn't show up, the band knew something was wrong. Toward the end of the final set, one of the War roadies took a phone call from Monika Dannemann. Jimi was sick.

Lee Oskar provided soaring harmonica riffs and solos for War at its inception and still plays regularly with original members Howard E. Scott, B.B. Dickerson, and Harold Brown. The band was originally put together by Eric Burdon of the Animals, so it was only natural for War to become tight with Jimi. Lee was just 19 when he joined in 1969. That same year, Jimi invited him onto the stage to jam at the Newport Pop Festival in Devonshire Downs, California.

During the 1970's, Lee grew dissatisfied with the small range of high-quality harmonicas on the market and decided to set up his own company. Lee Oskar Harmonica began production in 1983 and opened up a new world of high-quality instruments, alternate tunings, and replacement parts to harmonica players worldwide. Next time you're at a blues gig, ask the harp player what brand they use. It'll be a Lee Oskar.

Lee Oskar: The last time we saw Jimi was the last time he ever played. He came to *Ronnie Scott's Jazz Club*, where Eric Burdon & War was playing. We were the first contemporary band that *Ronnie Scott's* had. It's is a hardcore jazz club. They had Zoot Sims and John Coltrane, Roland Kirke, Stanley Turrentine – you name it. Great, great players. But we were playing this place for three days and it was sold out. And I remember the *Melody Maker* magazine in London, they had a front page: *Best Live Band I've Ever Heard.*

But Jimi Hendrix – I mean, I was in awe that I was around him. He came in the second day to sit in with us. He got on stage and we were playing 'Mother Earth', and he actually knew my name. I mean, I was flattered. He leaned against the wall – he was not in good shape. He literally looked at me: "Lee, am I sounding okay?" I was the kid who was just in awe, and just soaking it all in. I don't know how to put it in words. It was pretty amazing for him to actually acknowledge or recognize me. But he played, and to me he played *amazingly*.

There was a guy literally in front of me, while I was playing – a little to my right, almost in front of me. Between me and where Hendrix was. He was recording on a reel-to-reel tape. So it was recorded live, and it was confiscated. And that's why you may hear cassettes floating around, with very bad sound quality. I finally got hold of it myself.

But if I can give any insight about any of this, it really was all the *yin & yang* of the sensationalism. The negative and the positive. It was always something more than the music was about. Whether it was the struggle of being in sync with your art; or being bigger than life and nobody gives a shit about anything except your fame. That had a very big effect on me.

ᴀɪᴅᴀɴ ᴘʀᴇᴡᴇᴛᴛ: I would love to know what it felt like to be on stage with Jimi.

ʟᴏ: At Newport Pop, when I was invited up, my mic was

having issues. But I felt really honored because Hendrix himself asked me to come up. So everybody's treating you really nicely. But my playing was terrible, if I remember – I couldn't hear myself. I have seen some videos. You have to look really hard for it, it's a long video that was shot back then. But that was quite an experience. I was impressed with the fact that *my dream is coming true – I'm being associated with all these famous people* – almost like I'm a groupie myself. But my dream was to make it in the music business, and so that was an amazing opportunity just to be with Eric Burdon, and then to have a chance to play with Jimi.

I saw Jimi Hendrix around that time at Eric's house in Laurel Canyon. Jimi was talking to Eric. I don't want to put my foot in my mouth, 'cos I hate to say it, but it was almost like he was talking about suicide. He was talking about, "It's up to you now, Eric." Like he wanted to give up, or he was just tired of the bullshit. That's the feeling I got. And then they'd talk about bouncing music off the satellites and the moon. That kind of stuff. "It's up to you, Eric, to continue the journey..." But I didn't sit there and have a conversation with him. I was there, and I was listening.

Then the next time was when we came to London to play and Jimi came to see us. He was staying with his girlfriend Monika, a German girl. And then the next day he came and sat in. And he asked me, "How do I sound?" So it was like, *wow – unbelievable. He's asking me...* to me it was amazing. You know what I mean? The way he plays, it was like raindrops – just the way he *flew* it. The way his guitar sounded. Even though he probably wasn't in his best shape.

The next day he was supposed to come back. Toward the end of the show, we saw Terry McVay, our roadie – Eric's roadie since the Animals. Terry was a shipyard kind of a guy from Newcastle, and he was very sharp and very practical.

Terry had got a phone call, apparently it was Monika. She said that Jimi is unconscious, he puked or choked or something. Terry said, "Well, call an ambulance – immediately, and get him to the hospital." Eric jumped off the stage and they split. They went to the hospital. Me and my friend Judy went out and walked around London. It's very eerie so early in the morning. We were just – in *shock*, because we had found out he had died.

Then, all I can tell you is, we were told – we were *told* – that we cannot talk about the possibility he committed suicide. We were told not to even talk about that, because it had something to do with the insurance. In other words – whoever was going to collect the money – there's no way that it was suicide. So we were warned to shut up. To keep out mouths shut. There was talk about a letter, although I've never seen it. But Eric claimed there was a letter stating that he intentionally chose to do what he did.

Then we came to the Fillmore West in San Francisco. Eric would say, "I'm the captain, you're going to be the co-pilot and we're going to be flying together." He would just start off something and rap some words, whatever. And we started playing music behind it. That's how we used to jam. This particular night – it's the only time he ever did it – that night he said he was going to read the letter that Hendrix left for him. I don't have a recording of it, I don't remember what the words were, but he read this thing while we were putting music behind it.

So the question is, *did he commit suicide?* Did he give up intentionally, or was it just an accident? That whole thing is just a conversation. But we were told never to talk about it.

Later, we came to Seattle – it's funny, it's where I live now. We came to do a gig, and the phone rings in my room. And this voice says, "Is this one of the War members?" And

I said, "Yeah." He says, "Well I'm Jimi Hendrix's father, and I'm wondering if while you guys are in town, you would do a benefit show." And it really – I was young, so the way he asked me, it threw a curve. It was like *who in the fuck? Your father's going to call for a benefit when his son has just died?* You know – that's how I took it. And of course, later I put it together. It was probably he was struggling to try to get the estate. He had to figure out how to raise the money. Me being very young and naïve, maybe the way he asked it – as a youngster it was like *that's just wrong.* I didn't get it. I may not have realized he was trying to raise money. Although it turned out, his father was right on. Surviving, trying to get the estate back from the people that might have been plundering it. I understand it better now than back then.

aP: I'm wondering – what would it be like, the first time that you meet Jimi. Could you paint some kind of a – what was the feeling? That very first moment when you met him.

LO: I was just in awe of all of it. I was in awe, first of all, just to be in company with such amazing stars and musicians and energy. I was a youngster; it made my dream come true. If I was as mature as I am today, I would have perceived it very differently. But I really picked up on the uncertainties of being famous. And the sensationalism. That hits you really hard when you're just in awe, and then you see this insecurity and uncertainty. It's very human – *that* I can understand today.

aP: Was it a party, at Eric's house?

LO: There were a few people; there were some crazy people…I'm not going to go into what they brought with them and all that. It wasn't a big party; it wasn't a huge crowd of people. Those conversations probably wouldn't even happen then.

aP: Was is kind of a situation of Eric saying, "Hey Lee – this is Jimi. Jimi – Lee." Was it that kind of little introduction?

LO: With Eric, I don't remember hearing him saying, "Hey Jimi, this is Lee Oskar." People there knew Eric; they were hanging with Eric and comparing notes – peers to each other. Somehow, they knew that I was part of Eric's new band. I was staying at Eric's house, on the couch – otherwise I would have been on the streets.

Basically, I was a fly-on-the-wall. It was more that I was around with Eric Burdon, and where Hendrix would be at different times. I would be there with Eric and I would hear conversations, you know. Jimi was – in my opinion, from observing him talking and everything – he was very frustrated with a lot of things. He wanted to be embraced by the jazz scene and the African Americans, rather than just the white pop scene. I know that he was challenged with the fact that he had to go out and play every night, with the expectation of the sensational burning of the guitar.

What they had in common was that Mike Jeffrey had ripped them off. That's what all the guys felt, that they were being ripped off by Mike. And then the people that were around Jimi Hendrix always had a hand out – everybody was partying, but Jimi – he felt pretty alone. So I was around these people when Eric was the center of the attention, and I was right there in the middle of it. Not outside. So I was a fly-on-the-wall. The things that I got out of that were very compelling.

aP: I would love to hear – that experience that you had is quite unique, really. I mean, to be a fly-on-the-wall in amongst all of these incredible happenings… So is there a moment *as* a fly-on-the-wall that has resonated most with you?

LO: Yeah – I don't know if it haunts me, or if it's a life lesson thing: people like Jimi Hendrix were bigger than life. But he was a human being, like any of us. We eat, we shit, we like to feel acknowledged and all that. But he seemed like a very quiet, very shy person. And I was a pretty shy person, so for me to even see that – he wasn't a rock god personality like a Jim Morrison, he was very soft spoken. But you could feel he was troubled. The expectation that was on him; he was tormented. He didn't want to go burn a guitar ever night. He wanted to be embraced by people like Miles Davis in the music scene.

It's like Prince, and Jim Morrison. The expectation of life – the expectation of what they are, and what they really are to themselves is a very lonely, very bad situation. Everybody knows them, but they don't know anybody. And the people that he's supposed to be trusting, he has a very ill feeling about – like Mike Jeffery. And so, if you're alone and you feel like that, you've got to be really strong.

The only person I've ever seen in the industry who has survived that, was Bob Dylan. When everybody was the folkies and they wanted the acoustic guitar, electric guitar was like the devil and the enemy. What I've seen and observed, it felt like *this guy took the other way than Jimi Hendrix.* I mean, he coped with it by saying, *I'm going out and playing electric guitar.* And even The Band, I understand, said you know, *it's suicide.* He said, "I don't give a fuck – I'm going out there." And they got booed. But he broke the ice, and he survived. And he could be constantly creative.

A guy like Jimi Hendrix, he was very – I mean, I'm not

a psychiatrist, but he was very insecure and very confused. Very unhappy and frustrated and felt very alone. I remember the people around him – the same friends Eric had, everybody in New York – it was limousines, partying and all that. But it was all advances. It's *all* advances. Nothing is earned.

AP: At this time – what were you, nineteen? Something like that?

LO: Yeah, I was nineteen – going to be twenty. Yeah – nineteen.

AP: This is such a fascinating journey for me – I mean, how do you go from growing up in Denmark, and then... it seems like you must have been in the country less than a year, and suddenly you're *huge* in the American music scene.

LO: Well, I wasn't *huge*. Yes, my dream was to make it in the music business, and I was very ambitious. I was on the streets, and I met Eric at a club. There were a couple of clubs that let me in for free. One was called The Experience, and the owner was Marshall Brevitz. That was a place quite far away from the scene of the Sunset Strip. It was a jam place. It was way out of the radar of what was *in*. I mean, the in place was the west edge to the east edge of Sunset Strip. On certain nights the Coliseum, where the famous bands would play – it was Jimi Hendrix, it was Jethro Tull – or Led Zeppelin. Whoever was playing there, it was known that people from the band that played there, would come and jam at The Experience. So it was quite a place, always packed with people.

There was a band called Blues Image. And their lead guitar player was Mike Pinera. Blues Image came in from

Florida, and they were friends with the owner, Marshall Brevitz. So they would come in and jam, and Eric would come in and jam. So Eric and I became regulars. Every week, we would end up in the club, and I would be sitting in with Blues Image and Eric Burdon. That's how I connected with Eric, and then Eric wanted to form a band. So I went to see Phil Spector with Eric – Phil Spector wanted to make a record deal with him. Then we went to see Steve Gold and Jerry Goldstein, who became partners with Eric, and the management for War.

And that's how one thing led to the other. And next thing I know, I'm sitting around a swimming pool with Eric and the nucleus of this band that we went down to see, that was called the Night Shifts. And we decided that day, sitting around the swimming pool, to call it War. Eric Burdon and War. I mean, I was on the streets, knocking on doors and trying to do whatever I could – and when it happens, it happens. It's just one of those things.

AP: When you say you were on the streets – did you come over from Denmark, with no connections, no money to get you started – but just this talent and self-belief?

LO: Yeah. Not really much connection – there were some people in New York that I originally associated with. I got really concerned, because I didn't know – I didn't want to sign. I didn't understand English enough, I didn't know what to sign. So I split. When I was in New York, they set me up in a hotel. I didn't even know you could sign for room service. So I was there for two days without food. And then I convinced some people to go to California. I went to San Francisco first, the Bay Area – you could find a good place to sleep. You know – hippies, man. I thought, I'll hitchhike from there down to Los Angeles. And that's a whole story in itself, but finally when I got to L.A., that's when this all started happening.

aP: In terms of performing on stage with Jimi, was there a particular song that stands out as being...*this is the song to jam with Jimi Hendrix.*

LO: I mean, the jam at Devonshire Downs was such a freakin' mess. I mean, I couldn't hear myself and everything. It's embarrassing if you ever hear – I saw on the film, the volume of my microphone suddenly came out *way* loud. It was terrible. But it was more about the sensationalism than the music. But at Ronnie Scott's, I would say that was music. Those tunes that we played, 'Mother Earth' – which I always loved playing, and that night I played the horn lines. I love the horn lines; I would play the harmonica with the saxophone. But I didn't do a solo – Jimi Hendrix did a solo, and Howard Scott did a solo. And the other tune we did that night was 'Tobacco Road'. I always liked playing that back then.

Just in a nutshell, he was an amazing player. He seemed very shy. He was the opposite of a Jim Morrison. Jim Morrison would just make a party and be loud and whatever. Hendrix wasn't like that. I just felt his insecurity about dealing with all the wannabes; that everybody that wanted something from him.

aP: Is there anything I've missed? Is there anything else that we haven't spoken about that you think people should know about Jimi Hendrix?

LO: Here's what I can say. This is important to me to really say. The lesson is that as an artist – true to your art – you want to have a fan base, which is the ultimate reward of your art – to be acknowledged. But the danger within that is that you have to keep the momentum in sync as you develop. And the management – if they don't make that connection with the fans on a regular basis, it's very quick – all of a sudden what you're doing artistically has roamed to a place that is so removed from what they expect you to do. And it's so detrimental.

When you get famous, people hold onto that. And it's easiest to influence your fans when you have the proper setup with your machine – the promotion, the PR, the people to communicate on a regular basis. With social media today, it's much easier than it was back then. But just because it's easier, there's still that danger of not keeping the fans right there with you. If Jimi had had a good PR connection, he could have gone in and played whatever he wanted to do, and people wouldn't be booing, and he wouldn't be burning his guitar, right? So that's really the lesson in it all.

I mean, a guy like Prince, I didn't know him. But it felt to me like that. He was bigger than life – *he's a genius* and all that. It's the sensationalism. He had a lot to keep up with, with expectations. That's a lot to keep up with if all of a sudden your heart is singing a different song, and you wanted to do something else that could be amazing – but nobody gives a shit because they want to you to do the same thing, just like a circus. There's a lesson in that.

• • •

Lee could sense that Jimi was troubled. Jimi was trying to please too many people, while struggling to have his own needs met. He wanted to be accepted and embraced by the jazz scene, but he was hounded by the pressures of his management, the pressures of his now varied relationships, the pressures of his existing audience, and the pressures of his waning health. He desperately needed some time off. But Lee Oskar also saw the side of Jimi that we have encountered through the eyes of other musicians: Jimi wanted to work creatively within so many varied styles and forms of instrumentation. And Jimi wanted to foster the young players, to invite them on-stage, offer encouragement, collaborate, and build on their exposure. Jimi gave so much of himself to others.

There are so many theories floating around regarding Jimi's cause of death, but no definitive answer has ever been provided. Scotland Yard reopened the coroner's inquest in 1992, but the investigation was dropped by the Attorney General the following year. The public was left with the original finding from 1970: 'Inconclusive'.

In the weeks before Jimi's death, he found himself surrounded by people from his past. He saw his family in Seattle, and he caught up with old friends on the tours in America and Europe. He bumped into Kathy when he got back to London with Billy. Devon Wilson and some of the old coterie from New York had swung into town. Jimi even briefly caught up with Ed Chalpin, who had signed him in the early days and held him accountable for *Band of Gypsys*. Eric Clapton had bought Jimi a guitar and was hoping to see him at a gig that week. It seemed *everybody* was in London, to see Jimi off on his next adventure.

Leon Hendrix
Coda

As Jimi's younger brother, Leon Hendrix holds insight into Jimi that nobody else on the planet can offer. Leon was born in 1948 when Jimi was five. The two brothers shared a difficult upbringing – Leon himself was fostered out on a several occasions, while Jimi stayed on with their father, Al. Leon is a recording artist in his own right, and I was able to catch him in the wake of a European tour cancellation due to the early outbreak of Covid-19 in Italy.

Leon's book *Jimi Hendrix: A Brother's Story* provides a portrait of his time with Jimi in a way that only an irreverent little brother could. One brilliant moment has Leon clutching bare electric wires, holding them in place so Jimi could hear his guitar through an old radio/stereo speaker. The teenage Jimi had pulled the speaker apart and rigged it to allow for the accommodation of an instrument cable. Leon held on for dear life just so his brother could hear himself play. Leon's story of his time with Jimi is quite moving, and I was keen to see whether I could glean some other details.

aidan prewett: Your book has so many fantastic moments. I mean, you getting electrocuted by the radio being pulled apart was amazing.

LEON HENDRIX: Well I got used to it. You see, linemen that work on electricity on the lines and stuff like that, they develop this kind of immunity to being shocked. The shock off the record player to the speakers, it wasn't that bad. I got used to it. When we were kids, we both stuck our fingers in the socket, just to see.

AP: Oh my God.

LH: You didn't do that?

AP: No, I've always been terrified of that.

LH: Oh. You know – stick your finger in there. It's okay.

AP: The thing with Australia is that we work on 240 volts rather than 110, so it's a bit more of a shock.

LH: Oh, that's right! Oh my God, you're right.

AP: Leon, I wonder if you could tell me – is there a moment with Jimi where you remember him at his absolute happiest?

LH: Yes, I can. He was living in New York City. He played at the Café Wha?; he made a hundred dollars a week. He had a car and a girlfriend. That's when he was the happiest.

AP: That's fantastic. Did he tell you about this over the phone?

LH: Oh yeah, he always called me. He always called me and told me what he was doing. He said he bought a Plymouth car, which he had to really steer fifteen times to get the car to turn right. In other words: he was happy. Girlfriend; hundred dollars a week; Café Wha?; He was in ecstasy. It started to go downhill the more he got famous.

AP: It's amazing how that happens. It happens with so many people. It seems they get gobbled up by the sharks and the industry.

LH: Exactly. People are taking advantage of him, and he can't fight back because he wanted to play music. He didn't know about the legal stuff involved with his music and stuff like that. He trusted his management. And when you trust your management and the management knows you trust them, they're going to take advantage.

AP: Definitely.

LH: That's the seed of Cain. Do you know why God didn't kill Cain for killing Abel?

AP: I don't. Why?

LH: It seems to be like, *damn, God would really want to fuck him up.* But he didn't. He let him live and he let him proliferate all over the earth. But he said, "You can't create nothing. You can't harvest nothing. But you can be the management of my creative children."

So they're all in management.

AP: That's so right. That's amazing.

LH: You see, if we as musicians can't be exploited, we'll never be out there. It's like a give-and-take thing. They exploit us and we get to play the music all over the earth. Because if we're not exploited, we go nowhere. Nothing happens. So I'm happy now if they want to exploit me. Because I know I'll be out there if they exploit me. 'Cos they want money.

AP: That makes so much sense. It's almost the yin and yang of the world.

LH: You're true. It's yin or yang. You're either on the good seed, or you're on the bad seed. There's no grey in between. And God's people are creative. They created everything that's on the earth today, because God gave them this awesome thing called imagination. We search for the music and we search for the poetry and we search for the arts and the crafts. These things belong to *us*, God's people. The other people, they're trying to take advantage of everything. Which is okay, you know. Just so long as you know which side you're on, you'll be cool.

AP: Is this a philosophy that Jimi shared? Do you know what his thoughts were – were these his thoughts as well?

LH: You don't even know the shit that Jimi taught me. I mean, we're talking about universal-ass cosmic winds and other wireless life. Your cell phone can tell you right now that the wireless world actually exists. We're talking wirelessly from LA to Australia and we're not bumping into nothing. And there's billions of calls passing through our conversation right now. Going in other directions. So the wireless world is actually a real world. Our memories and our dreams – it's so spiritual, it's awesome. I just love it. And Jimi taught me this early.

• • •

Leon and I had our conversation cut short by an incoming call – he was being whisked away to band practice. By this stage America was beginning to feel the impending Covid-19 crisis and Leon and I were unable to reconnect. But maybe it was meant to be that way. This brief encounter with Jimi's brother left me feeling euphoric. These few moments provided a glimpse, not only of the Hendrix family character – but also of the nature of Jimi's outlook on life. It is clear that Jimi experienced genuine happiness within life's more simple pleasures.

Perhaps most interestingly, Jimi knew he was being exploited. Maybe he just didn't care. He just wanted to make music.

Outro

I NEVER HAD THE CHANCE TO MEET JIMI; I was born much too late. But as a guitarist, just *hearing* Jimi was phenomenal. I first heard 'Purple Haze' at age fourteen and that was *it*. I spent weeks practicing that solo until I could finally play some patchy version of it. I have spent the ensuing years trying to master some of Jimi's live tracks, with absolutely no success. But I have Jimi to thank, in part, for where I am today – teaching music, making films about it, and writing about it.

And so the story goes for countless guitarists since 1967. That critical moment, hearing Hendrix for the first time... it's incredible. Sometimes you can catch a glimpse of that feeling again by putting one of those tracks on through headphones and really just *listening*. To consider the thought that somebody had used an instrument to *make those sounds*. The opening notes to 'Purple Haze' take me back to that place – fourteen years old; my first electric guitar. The idea that maybe I could learn to make those sounds, too. Maybe someday that would take me somewhere. Of course, you later learn that you can't *be* the next Jimi Hendrix. If you want to make any kind of impact, you have to carve your own path. You have to break a few rules. More than a few.

But we have the tools available to us. And if you're an artist reading this, you have the tools in front of you, right now, to break some rules. If you practice enough, network enough and develop *your* own voice, you can get to where you want to go. People told Jimi he'd never make it. *Your chances are slim; it's a tough industry; get a real job.* They'll tell anyone who's trying; they've never tried themselves.

For this project, the rule to break was *you must quote only brief selections from interviews.* I'd rather enjoy a real conversation, unfettered by the standard conventions of a biography. After all, we're trying to explore *character* – Jimi's character and that of his friends. That takes a little immersion. How often do we get to sit down and chat with the people who loved Jimi as a human being, as well an artist? We now know a little more about the people for whom Jimi let his guard down – the people Jimi chose to bring with him on his journey. And we have been invited on that journey too. From our new and privileged perspective, we see a side of Jimi that breaks sharply from his image as a psychedelic demigod tearing up the world of popular music. His time spent relaxing with friends was largely contemplative, humorous, and – of course – immersed in music.

Jimi was there for the music. The theatrics served him as a means to reach a wider audience, but he soon tired of on-stage destruction and focused on immersing himself in a world of sound. He started taking music to places it had never ventured, and he continued to push this process further, on-stage and in the studio. His studio work quickly outpaced the technical capabilities of the recording systems, so he built his own. And even Electric Lady Studios, the most advanced studio of its day, bent double under the strain of Jimi's prodigious output. But the sheer number of recordings Jimi made have provided us with a major catalogue of material, some of which is still to be mixed by Eddie Kramer. Much of the Hendrix catalogue released under the Experience Hendrix label is of staggeringly high quality. It is astounding that Jimi was able to achieve these results using recording equipment that is now fifty years old. We are lucky to have Eddie Kramer to masterfully pull all the elements together for us.

This was an intimate project. I was attempting to connect with people to ask them about a friend from long ago. That proposition could be difficult and problematic for any person. But intimacy is what I got. In every instance, people opened up very quickly when they could see that they were speaking with someone who genuinely wanted to get to know Jimi better. I wanted to figure out who Jimi was – and that's all. I wasn't interested in dredging up rumors or trying to unearth some kind of salacious or controversial material. In fact, I was pleased to find that the few unpleasant rumors that do exist about Jimi have been disproven by Kathy Etchingham. And throughout this process there were so many great moments, moments that made the hair on the back of my neck stand on end. Sometimes it felt like maybe Jimi was listening in on another line.

The moment I realized that my approach was really working was in one of the very first interviews – Bob Kulick. Bob experienced that *teenage-guitarist-first-time-Hendrix-moment* with Jimi playing guitar *three feet in front of his face.* When I hung up the phone from that conversation, I knew this book was carving its own path. That was a Hendrix story I had never heard before. It's definitely not just a sound-byte. Janis Ian provided another early moment like that: *These stories shouldn't be interrupted. They need to tell themselves.*

Only two friends of Jimi's close friends declined to be interviewed for this project: Billy Cox and Linda Keith.

Both were polite and very encouraging – but their days of giving interviews are over. The response from both was: *I've already said everything that I can say.* It is unfortunate that neither Billy nor Linda have released an autobiography. I would be first in line to purchase them. The response from Billy and Linda reinforces how lucky we are to have spoken with so many of Jimi's friends and confidants. We have been able to immerse ourselves in Jimi's world through their eyes to get to the heart of the matter – what was Jimi all about? What was it like to hang out with him? Now we know a little more about what that must have felt like.

In my mind, I keep going back to Bob Kulick. His story, as the teenage guitarist at the Café Wha?, is exactly what young guitarists experience when they listen to Hendrix. It's a major frickin' turn-on. Bob Kulick learnt from Jimi like we did – but from Jimi himself, not just by playing the records until they were worn out. Bob experienced Jimi's personality as a teacher, on a two-way street. Bob learnt a lot, and I am sure Jimi took something away too. Nobody will ever experience that again. It is a terrible tragedy that no further guitarists were able to learn directly from Jimi. We are forced to imagine the experience Bob Kulick received first-hand.

But if a guitar lesson from Jimi Hendrix is what you're after, just put on the record. He lives in those notes.

Appendix 1

Harry Shapiro

Mitch & Noel

September 18, 1970, between midnight and 11am – when Monika Dannemann finally (how many hours later?) phoned the ambulance – are hours that have remained open to speculation and rumor for fifty years. But there is one thing I'm sure of: I'd rather remember Jimi for how he lived.

Over the years, a number of Jimi's friends and acquaintances have also passed on. For this book, I was fortunate to speak with some of his closest friends who are still with us and in great health. But of course, I would have loved to interview Mitch Mitchell, Noel Redding, Chas Chandler, and Buddy Miles.

Mitch, Noel, Chas, and Buddy each spoke to Harry Shapiro for his book *Jimi Hendrix: Electric Gypsy*, first published in 1990. I tracked Harry down to see what insight he could lend into their relationships with Jimi. Harry's book is a clear influence on every other Hendrix book I have come across. If you are keen to fill some of the gaps left by this book, Harry's book is the one I can most highly recommend. I have been using it as my 'Hendrix Bible' since 2001. *Jimi Hendrix: Electric Gypsy* features 723 pages of insightful detail about how Jimi lived, put together with

Caesar Glebeek, who founded the Jimi Hendrix Information Centre.

Harry has written similarly detailed books about other
musicians, including Eric Clapton, Jack Bruce, Alexis
Korner, and Graham Bond. He has also written extensively
about drugs and drug abuse, and was head of publishing
for DrugScope, a drug information and policy center in
the UK.

Aidan Prewett: I spoke to Neil Landon last night, talking
about Fat Mattress and their support act and their time in
Majorca. Neil was a really good friend of Noel, and so I was
really interested to hear about Noel and Jimi's relationship
early on. Because everyone knows how it ended – but that's
not my interest. My interest is – in his friendship circle,
what was Jimi like? I had a couple of really nice things
come out of that conversation with Neil.

Harry Shapiro: Were they *friends* though? 'Cos Noel
always seemed to refer to Jimi as *Hendrix*.

AP: Right! Wow…

HS: *Hendrix* rather than Jimi. I got the feeling that they
didn't really socialize. And that's not unusual in bands,
because people don't understand that musicians in that
situation – it's a bit like going to work. It's their job. They
often find they have to be 24/7 with people they're at work
with. It's a bit like being at the office – it's like spending six
months on the road, going to the office. It wouldn't really
work. And you wouldn't really want to spend your *off* time
with the people who you see all the time at the office. And
I think that's often the way with bands. So whether they
were really friends, and whether they really socialized – I
don't know what Neil's take on this was, but I don't get

that impression. He may have been closer to Mitch than to Noel – although I'm not sure they hung out that much either. 'Cos they got famous, they'd have their own entourage anyway. I get the feeling that Noel and Mitch would have been more likely to have hung out with the crew. They were more kind of like that – less in the spotlight. Nothing like the same way that Jimi was.

ap: I need to ask: of the people who are now deceased, specifically the ones who were interviewed by you – could you give me a stand out moment, or something that was really revelatory – from one of these people who I will *never* have the chance to speak to.

HS: I suppose the most significant interview, to be honest, was with Kathy. And the reason is that it took me about two years to get her to agree to talk to me. Because she'd already been ripped off by one author, who came around and took some of her old photos and disappeared and never gave them back to her. And when anybody wanted to interview her, basically all they wanted to know about was *was he good in bed?* and all this tabloid sex stuff. And I think at the time, her husband Nick was a GP, working not far from where I lived. And I kept leaving messages and writing letters – because it was pre-email. *Nothing.* I thought, okay – I'll just have to let that one go.

And I was having a dinner party one day, and the phone rang. I said, "Oh, hi – who's that?" And she said, "It's Kathy." I took a massive double-take, and I said, "Oh – okay – hello!" And she said, "I'd like to do the interview." So I said, "Oh great! When do you want to do it?" And she said, "Now." *Okaay...fine.*

So she jumped in a taxi. It couldn't have been more than about ten miles, at most. She came around, I excused

myself from the dinner party. I sat her in the front room
– I really had no questions at that point. I was completely
unprepared. So I just kind of *winged it*. She wanted to listen
to some music, so I put 'The Wind Cries Mary' on. It was
dedicated to her. She and Jimi had had this major row, and
she'd hit him with a frying pan or something. She's like,
"I hit Jimi Hendrix with a frying pan." And he went out,
he kind of stormed off, and in a quieter moment – we're
talking about quieter moments – he wrote 'The Wind Cries
Mary'. 'Cos her middle name was Mary – Kathy Mary
Etchingham. And she just started crying, listening to this
song. And that sort of started the relationship, and I interviewed her properly. But it was a massive icebreaker. She
could see I wasn't some sleazebag hack who was just going
to ask her all the obvious and awkward questions. But I
think that is probably the stand-out interview. Because, to
be honest – most of the other people I spoke to – Chas,
Mitch, Noel – people like that – first of all they had told
their story to other people.

There was one – an accountant called John Hillman.
John Hillman managed the account in the Bahamas into
which money from the Animals and Jimi Hendrix disappeared into some sort of black hole. And I was very surprised that he even agreed to see me. I mean, it was quite
an interesting interview. He was blaming Mike Jeffery of
course, for everything that went wrong. To be fair, he said,
"Well, Mike can't answer for himself." He was dead by then.
He died in 1973. He's someone I would have really liked to
interview. Whether he would have agreed to see me, I have
absolutely no idea. There was another interesting interview
with a New York lawyer. I came to understand that New
York lawyers shout, even when they're being nice. He spent
the whole interview shouting at me. It was amazing – I

thought I'd upset him. But I hadn't. He was just shouting – it's what New York lawyers do.

I think it was the whole thing of trying to find out what happened to the money. And the whole business of Jimi allegedly trying to get away from Mike Jeffery. He didn't think Mike was taking his best interests to heart. It was generally a very difficult time. We're talking about the quiet life of Jimi Hendrix – well I'm pretty certain there were very few of those moments. But he wasn't a party animal. My understanding is that you could go to a party; Jimi would just be sitting on the couch in the corner. He wasn't trying to be the center of attention. Just *walking down the Street* he was the center of attention. And back in those days of course, he wouldn't have been surrounded by a whole phalanx of bodyguards and minders and stuff. You could just go up to him and get an autograph, or say "you're a great man" and he'd go, "Hey – thanks, man." I know a couple of people who did exactly that. Not me, unfortunately. People were just accessible then, in a way that has disappeared. With the exception of the Beatles or something. Most people were just accessible. Which had its downsides, obviously.

So – interviews that stuck out for different reasons would certainly be Kathy. John Hillman simply because he was an accountant, and accountants and lawyers tend to be very circumspect – client confidentiality and all this. And of course, it's a *get out of jail free* card, because they don't have to tell you stuff they'd rather not tell you.

But for most of the other people – the obvious people kind of had a story to tell. Noel in particular was full of grievance over monies that he felt he was due. Their endings were both extremely sad – they both succumbed to alcohol in one shape or form. The last time I saw Mitch,

I couldn't believe it that he remembered me. It wasn't that long ago. He was in a right old state, I have to say. It was a concert – he was playing with Mick Taylor. The playing was not exactly what I would call playing. But he came of stage – I was backstage with Mick Taylor, and he came over and said "Oh – Harry Shapiro". I thought, bloody hell that's good – I haven't spoken to him for about fifteen years. So I was really quite impressed with that. So we passed a few words, and then a few months later he just died.

And Noel – I think the problem for them was, *what do you do after Jimi Hendrix?* Musically, neither of them did anything. I mean, Mitch was an extremely talented drummer. And he should have gone on to other bands. He didn't have a big ego – I don't think it was like, "He was with Jimi Hendrix, he'll have a head as big as Africa and he's just going to be a pain in the arse." I don't think he ever was that. I never really did understand why he just sort of disappeared. There were a few odd desultory bands that he joined where nothing happened.

AP: Was there a moment, in all your research for *Jimi Hendrix: Electric Gypsy*, that you went: "Right, I have found the very moment that sums up Jimi's character."

HS: Something like – Jimi on his own, sitting in Electric Lady studio, with Eddie Kramer in the control booth. And no one else around. No groupies, dealers, hangers on, etc. Musicians probably not there either, because certainly during the days of Experience, I think Mitch and Noel got a bit cheesed off with Jimi re-recording the solo for that hundredth-and-nineteenth time. They all thought the take was fine, but he obviously didn't. Musicians often say the safest place for them is on the stage. And I think to some extent that was true for Jimi, although as I mention in the book – and others have as well – eventually he got very fed up with being this clown, as he kind of viewed it. You know – guitar between his legs, playing with his teeth. All of that theatrical stuff. Which, I have to say, was a rod he made for his own back. He started doing that, and then it became a thing that people expected.

And often the sound systems back then weren't very good. When he played the Isle of Wight, he had a local taxi firm coming through the speakers while he was trying to play. And you see these banks and banks of Marshall amps that he and other bands used. Part of the reason was that the equipment kept breaking down. You had to have backup equipment so that the roadies could switch things around when the speakers failed. Whereas, when he got into the studio with producers who were sympathetic, and could understand what he was doing, and just let the tape roll – and just let him sit and create. I think that was his sweet spot. That was his safe spot. And that's probably where he felt most relaxed and calm. Because the title of the book says it all. He was an *Electric Gypsy*. He had no permanent residence; he just went from hotel to hotel to odd rented house, to studio, to party, to club. He was constantly on the move. So, a restless spirit, no doubt. But the oasis of calm, I would imagine, was when he could just be in the studio by himself.

aP: Did something surprise you in your research, that you came across and went *what on earth does this mean?*

HS: I don't think anything particularly surprised me. Because I'd read all the other books before I'd even thought of doing this one. I think most of the key elements had come out. And by that time I had already written biographies of Graham Bond and Eric Clapton and one or two others.

But I did realise two things: One, when you do these books, you really have to triangulate a lot of views and opinions. Because, particularly when you're dealing with somebody famous, and who died in tragic and unusual circumstances – I wrote this in 1990, so already you're talking about a twenty-year gap. So memories fade. And those memories were probably befuddled by dope and acid, which one has to bear in mind. And then you really have to triangulate all of this, and try to come to a consensus about events, and how they played out.

And I suppose the other surprise was right at the end – which I was never really able to follow through properly. Subsequently I helped to develop this – I think Tony Brown's book is probably the best one on this, about the last days of Jimi's life – which is the fact that I'd bought the whole story about how he died, because I'd read it so many different times.

When I went and actually spoke to the porter who admitted Jimi when he came in in the ambulance. No one had ever spoken to him before. He had no axe to grind, no agenda. Just an ordinary bloke. He gave me a completely different version from what I was getting from Monika Dannemann, who told the story over and over and over again. And that's when I began to think *no – okay*. It got way more complicated than that afterwards. That sort of set me on a trail. The surprise was that *things were not as they seemed.* And it turned out subsequently that things *definitely* were not as they seemed. Even though what happened in the end and how it happened and who knew what and who did what still remains a mystery.

And it remains a mystery, because – pretty much – all the key people are dead. I spoke to most of them at the time. Talk about triangulating events. That was... I mean,

Jimi can't be in three places at once. He might have been
an electric gypsy, but he couldn't be in three places. *I saw
Jimi…* and at exactly the same time, *yeah, he was over at this
party.* So in the end, you sort of go, *okay…* But anyway –
the best current overview of those last 24-48 hours would
be Tony Brown's book.

One thing that did strike me – from a public point of
view – if you wanted to hone in on the essence of Jimi
Hendrix, it would be that Woodstock performance of 'The
Star-Spangled Banner'. It might be an obvious thing to say.
But just watching that performance again – he was just
totally in his own world. Most people had gone home –
there were only about 20,000 people there on the Monday
morning. Of a total audience of 400,000. But he clearly
didn't care. He just went on there and did it, and I think
it's an astonishing performance, as much for what he did
as for the sense of where his head might have been while
he was doing it. I mean, I'm not sure he was really on that
stage. He went somewhere else, and it's an astonishing performance. Just him there using electricity as an instrument.

AP: Is there anything in your research and interviews
and such, where something clicked for you to distinguish
between Jimi Hendrix the image, and Jimi Hendrix the real
person?

HS: I think it was really talking to Kathy, primarily. Because
I think she was probably the most stable element in an
otherwise pretty chaotic life, of people who just basically
wanted something out of Jimi. Wanted a bit of him in
some way, shape or form. To bathe in his reflected glory.
And I think that – yeah, there was the onstage Jimi. There
was the flamboyant Jimi, with the clothes and all of that.

But we're talking about quiet moments, and Kathy's got

a book. And you do get a sense from that of a Jimi who was quite happy sitting in their flat in London, listening to some music, fiddling about on an acoustic guitar. He just wanted a bit of peace & quiet. There were those moments of opportunity. Some with Kathy, some in the studio. But the pressures on him were enormous, in terms of just trying to be *in the world*. He was just surrounded by people the whole bloody time. This is not to say he was antisocial or anything. If you listen to *Electric Ladyland*, it's got that bit in it where you can hear people kind of shouting and yelling in the background. He was a people person from that point of view. And I don't think I ever saw an interview that he gave where he expressed any kind of – I mean, he must have thought he was the luckiest bloke on the planet. He came out of nowhere. He came to England with just a guitar in a case. Nobody had ever heard of him. Nobody knew who he was – and within about six months he was an international rock star. So from that point of view he had nothing to complain about. But on the other hand, I think he became a hostage in the end. And he wanted to take a break. I think this is what he really needed – he needed a proper break. And he had a bit of it around the time of Woodstock, up at the house in upstate New York. But it wasn't a good environment. Probably a bit too much coke floating around. It wasn't good – he wasn't really writing much.

This was a time when most people thought rock music was ephemeral; it was never going to last. *So we've got to milk this for everything we can.* Album, tour, album, tour, album, tour. Fly here, fly there. Do it all before the bubble bursts. It took someone like Peter Grant, who was the manager of Led Zeppelin and then Bad Company, to realise that you could take a band off the road maybe for a year or more

– and people would not only *not* forget you, but you would come back twice as big as you were before, because you'd been taken off the road. And I think I'm right in thinking he was the first manager to realise that you could do this. And he was absolutely right. And if Jimi had survived, I'm not sure Mike Jeffery would have let that happen. 'Cos Mike Jeffery was an old fashioned pop man. And to be honest, Warner Bros. Records were looking for the next load of hits. So it was all based on hits – you've got to have hit singles, otherwise it doesn't work. So his downtime should have happened. It was the same with Eric Clapton. I always got the feeling that Clapton's heroin addiction was almost an excuse – and I wrote about this in the book. I don't know if he ever saw it, or ever thought about it. But it was a way of saying, *there you go – I'm a heroin addict. Now go away and leave me alone.*

aᴘ: Yeah – right!

ʜs: So he holed himself up in his mansion in the south of England – basically shut his door on the world. And ironically it was booze that almost killed him, rather than the drugs. But he got through it all, and I think part of that was having some decent R&R. Decent time out, when you weren't being badgered by all sorts of people. Jimi could really have done with that – kind of re-coup. Go and live in Hawaii for a year. Interesting, that's where he wanted his studio built. He wanted his studio to be built in Hawaii. But Mike Jeffery wanted it right in the middle of the music business in New York, not stuck out in Hawaii. But if they'd done that, if he hadn't died, that would have been the perfect hideaway for him. So long as he had the people around him who were going to give him the time to do that. He had the wrong manager for that. Jeffery would never have let that happen. He needed someone else. But of course, that's all hypothetical.

• • •

While many books were consulted in the making of this project, *Jimi Hendrix: Electric Gypsy* has been the most useful and the most enjoyable. Harry's book paints a portrait of Jimi as a gentle soul – overworked, sometimes to the point of breakage – but at his core, a genuine, benevolent figure who just wanted to create amazing sounds.

It is clear in Harry's book – and I hope in this one – that Jimi was so *loved* by his friends. And for those with whom his interaction was more casual, his impact was extraordinary. Meeting Jimi was an experience that lives on with the people who were lucky enough to have it.

Appendix 2

Dr. Bob Brown

September 18, 1970

Dr. Bob Brown was the first doctor to attend to Jimi Hendrix at St Mary Abbot's Hospital in London in the morning of September 18, 1970.

It just so happens that Bob Brown is also one of Australia's most respected environmentalists. He was national leader of the Australian Greens from 1996 – 2012, serving in the Senate throughout this period. Bob spearheaded a number of policies to reduce the impact of climate change while working to reduce harm to old-growth forests and endangered animals. In 2003, Bob was suspended from the Senate for 24 hours after he interrupted a speech by visiting US President George W. Bush at the height of the invasion of Iraq.

Bob retired from the Australian Senate to become director of the Sea Shepherd anti-whaling movement, and now oversees the Bob Brown Foundation, for preservation of the ecological integrity of Australia.

AIDAN PREWETT: I read your book *Optimism* last week and thought immediately I must get in touch with you because your chapter on Jimi – it's quite impressionistic.

APPENDIX 2   DR. BOB BROWN

I'd love to get a sense from you – a sort of play-by-play of what happened?

BOB BROWN: It was in the morning – I was just outside the emergency department or casualty section at St Mary Abbot's Hospital and he was brought up from an ambulance on a trolley – a bier. And his lady friend was coming along behind it. But he was dead and had been for some time. He was then taken from – instead of into the casualty department, into the emergency section. It wasn't I, but another Australian doctor who certified that he was dead.

AP: When the bier came in and it was immediately apparent that he was dead, were you the first person to sort of – to come in contact with him?

BB: As a medical person, yes. But I just saw him, checked him – there was nothing to be done. But they kept going; they were moving. I just came along with the trolley, walked with it for a few steps and on it went. But saw that there was nothing to be done. They were going the right way to the emergency department but there was nothing to be done there either. I have spoken with the other medical, the Australian medical doctor. You might be able to contact him. I can't remember his name now, but he was a medical specialist; senior to me. And he issued the certificate.

AP: May I ask what – I mean, he was unresponsive, obviously, on the bier. Was there an immediate giveaway that it had been some kind of overdose?

BB: No. All that was apparent was that he was dead and beyond recovery.

aP: How do you tell someone is beyond recovery – there's obviously no pulse, no breathing…

BB: Yeah, well people – after they've been dead for a while, it's classical medical knowledge; when there's not life. When somebody's not got life in them anymore.

aP: But evident that he had been dead for some hours.

BB: For quite a while, yes.

aP: What are the signs that someone's been dead for a bit?

BB: Well these don't apply to him, because he was effectively my patient at the time. But – the classic symptoms that a person has died. The body is no longer warm, and so on. And the person's not breathing. And that doesn't necessarily mean that you can't resuscitate them. But you look at their vital signs; you look for their pulse, you look at a person's eyes and so on.

aP: When he was wheeled in, was it immediately apparent to you – *oh, that's Jimi Hendrix.*

BB: No – I didn't assume anything. I was in a busy casualty department and it was another person coming up the track. It really wasn't until afterwards… It was clear it was Jimi Hendrix with his girlfriend there, but it wasn't really – that didn't, and doesn't – I'm just a doctor, it doesn't enter into one's head that this is anybody… Anybody coming in in those circumstances deserved to get the best medical treatment available. But there wasn't a medical treatment, and there isn't, for anybody in his circumstances.

But you know – it's one of those things where time is dislocated. And you only wish that you could have been

there some hours earlier. But life's full of that – that situation. That's not how the universe works.

aP: With Jimi – the girl with him, I believe that would
have been Monika Dannemann – were there any other
people specifically that seemed to be of an entourage?

BB: That's all I remember, but of course there were ambulance officers who were moving the trolley and had been
in attendance; the usual medical people coming around. I
mean, this all happened in the space of less than a minute.
Because it was very important to get whoever this was – and
it wasn't known in advance that it was Jimi Hendrix – but
whoever it was, it was very important to get them properly
assessed and if there was anything that could be done, do
it. But that wasn't to be.

aP: My understanding is that he must have taken the overdose of sleeping pills around five or six in the morning.
And then by what time of day was this specifically?

BB: I think it was about seven thirty or eight, as I recollect.

aP: Right – wow, okay. In my reading, certain books and
things have said it was more like eleven am.

BB: Well, it may have been. I was on the morning shift;
I can't remember exactly. It may have been. I can't at this
distance just recall where the clock was sitting.

aP: You've done a brilliant job of recalling what you have
done, given that it's nearly fifty years since it all happened.

BB: I think it's very likely that I came on at about eight
o'clock and it seemed shortly after that.

aP: And this is all at the time of Vietnam, and I read

somewhere that you refused to medically certify people who were being called up – is that right?

BB: No – that was at Canberra Hospital the year before, in 1969. My senior colleagues a year earlier had refused. So they brought all the conscripts back to be seen by the junior doctors. We were under instruction that we had to properly medically examine them. It was clear that they had been called up and they were going to be medically examined, so I and a couple of my colleagues devised a system.

There were people who wanted to go to Vietnam; who wanted to be enrolled. If they had flat feet or whatever which might have excluded them, we could overlook that. And for those who didn't want to go, I'd use that example of saying to them, "You've got a bit of acne there, young fella. You'd better come back in a week's time because that's not good for the tropics. Don't eat chocolate, don't eat cream, don't have hot showers, don't eat citrus fruit, etc.' And they'd come back in a week's time much much worse.

The other standard question was whether or not they were homosexual, because that was an exclusion clause too. So it helped. It didn't in every case work, but it certainly helped legitimately to sort out those people who were opposed to the war and weren't wanting to go, from being sent against their wishes into that war. It was just a simple means of helping out.

aP: That's brilliant – I mean, what a clever approach. Bob – have you got time for one more question – which is completely unrelated to Jimi Hendrix?

BB: Yes… [Laughs]

aP: Could you tell me, what is the feeling when you're standing in Parliament – George W. Bush is delivering a speech and you *know* that you're going to interrupt. What does that feel like?

BB: Well, on that occasion, my heart started pounding – whether I liked it or not. I wasn't in control of this, this was the nervous system in play. I was a bit worried – it was literally pounding in my chest – that I wouldn't be able to get up. So I just forced myself to my feet, just at the time, well into his speech, that he started talking about the Iraq war. That's a case of your intellect overcoming your automatic responses. There was a bit of an internal battle going on there. But it happened, and I'm very pleased it did. In hindsight I'd have been forever kicking myself for not having said it. But you know – there were two hundred and forty or so parliamentarians in there. And except for my other Green colleague, no one was going to say anything. As I said in the book, with Bush there you could hear a pin drop. It was like the second coming. It's incredible how gatherings of people can be mesmerised in a way like that.

But who knows – with Donald Trump now having debauched the office of President, he's actually pulled the rug from under the esteem that that office had. It was the *office* that was enormously respected by Americans, as well as non-Americans. But Donald Trump has put an end to that.

AP: With that in the back of my mind for the last couple of years now – I wonder: Is it possible that for a mainstream kind of right-winger, does it appear as though human life is kind of dispensable?

BB: Well, in wartime it does become dispensable. It's the age-old concern that orders are given by people in safe locations. *The Charge of the Light Brigade* comes to mind:

Theirs not to reason why / Theirs but to do and die. There is a curious situation in the world whereby people who lack empathy very often get to the top, because they're ruthless and self-invested and egoistic. And they're the very wrong people to be put in charge of the lives of thousands of others. But that's the way the world has it, and we've just got to be aware of that. You currently see the dictatorships around the world and how democracy is dealing with them. I'd go for democracy every time, but dictatorships don't care about that. They don't care about your finer feelings. They're on their ruthless way to power. And you've got to *know* that if you're going to survive in that political environment. So it takes very tough-minded people to be in politics if they're going to be successful.

AP: As you were for many years. And I'm so glad that you were there.

BB: Well you know, I was also never minister for anything. Not even Westerly Winds. Because I said what I thought, and it didn't fit the prevailing economic powers and this *growth-mania* that's leading the world into the abyss. It didn't fit with that. It was a very privileged thing to be in Parliament, and I just hope that more people in the future... Here's the trick: On the one hand thick-skinned, on the other hand warm-hearted. And those two things don't come together very readily.

• • •

In this appendix I hope I can be forgiven for including the second part of Bob Brown's interview. It frames something of the context of the world that Jimi missed out on. Most of Jimi's friends got to see this world. But in his own time, Jimi had to be thick-skinned. And he was definitely warm-hearted. Jimi cared about people. It is obvious that he cared about his friends. And his friends still care for him a great deal.

Within an hour of speaking with Bob, I received a text message from Leon Hendrix: He was good to go for a short interview. In the strange kind of way that things just happen – these two interviews came just two days after I finally got to speak with Kathy Etchingham. I had almost given up on all three. But after speaking with Leon and Kathy, I realized that I had the privilege of speaking with them at a time when they're in their 70s, having accumulated so much life and spirit. Sadly, Jimi wasn't able to see them get there.

Further Reading

Of the great many books and articles that were consulted during research for this project, the following is a list of the most helpful, interesting, and entertaining. Of course, many of the people interviewed have published their own books which provided major insights prior to interview. Each has been of major assistance. I have listed these here, along with some others that assisted me greatly.

Altham, Keith. *The PR Strikes Back* (Blake Publishing, 2001)

Binder, John. *Before First Light* (F-Stop Books, 2016)

DeCurtis, Anthony. *Rocking My Life Away: Writing about Music and Other Matters* (Duke University Press, 1999)

Etchingham, Kathy. *Through Gypsy Eyes: My Life, the Sixties and Jimi Hendrix* (Victor Gollancz, 1998)

Field, Jeanne: *F Words: My Life of Film, Food, Feminism, Fun, Family, Friends, Flaws, Fabric, And The Far Out Future* (F-Stop, 2016)

Hendrix, Leon. *Jimi Hendrix: A Brother's Story* (Thomas Dunne, 2012)

Ian, Janis. *Society's Child: My Autobiography* (Lucky Bat Books, 2012)

Kramer, Eddie and McDermott, John. *Hendrix: Setting the Record Straight* (Sphere, 1994)

Shapiro, Harry and Glebeek, Caesar. *Jimi Hendrix: Electric Gypsy* (St Martin's Press, 1992)

Brown, Tony. *Hendrix: The Final Days* (Omnibus, 1997)

Bell, Dale. *Woodstock* (Michael Wiese Productions, 1999)

Cavett, Dick. *Talk Show* (Times Books, 2010)

Clapton, Eric. *Clapton: The Autobiography* (Broadway Books, 2008)

Cross, Charles R. *Room Full of Mirrors*: A Biography of Jimi Hendrix (Sceptre, 2005)

Evans, Mike. *Woodstock: Three Days that Shook the World* (Sterling, 2009)

Lang, Michael. *The Road to Woodstock* (Ecco, 2010)

Lowenstein, Rupert: *A Prince Among Stones* (Bloomsbury, 2013)

Mitchell, Mitch. *Jimi Hendrix: Inside the Experience* (St Martin's Press, 1993)

Mosley, Walter. *RL's Dream* (W.W. Norton, 1995)

Nash, Graham. *Wild Tales: A Rock & Roll Life* (Three Rivers Press, 2014)

Norman, Philip. *Wild Thing: The Short, Spellbinding Life of Jimi Hendrix* (Hachette, 2020)

Prewett, Aidan. *Woodstock at 50: Anatomy of a Revolution* (Political Animal, 2019)

Redding, Noel. *Are You Experienced? The Inside Story of the Jimi Hendrix Experience* (Da Capo, 1996)

Shadwick, Keith. *Jimi Hendrix: Musician* (Backbeat Books, 2012)

Smith, Patti. *Just Kids* (Ecco, 2010)

Tiber, Elliot. *Taking Woodstock* (Square One, 2009)

Townshend, Pete. *Who I Am* (Harper Perennial, 2013)

Wall, Mick. *Two Riders Were Approaching: The Life and Death of Jimi Hendrix* (Trapeze, 2019)

Acknowledgements

To my wife, Schy, and our little ones, Felix, Parker & Quincy, who continue to inspire me every day.

For believing in the book, pushing for it, and working through many hours of edits, Lewis Slawsky and Alex Wall at Political Animal Press, who have rallied around this project to make it as groovy as possible.

Thank you to Debbie Golvan of Golvan Arts Management, who pushes for these books – and more to come!

This book was a major research task – and any mistakes in the text or interviews are solely my own.

In loving memory of D.A. Pennebaker and Bob Kulick, who will live on in rock 'n' roll legend forever.

For their generosity of spirit, Kathy Etchingham, Keith Altham, Roger Mayer, Gered Mankowitz, Eddie Kramer, Chris Hegedus, Al Kooper, Anthony DeCurtis, Bruce Fleming, Janis Ian, Neil Landon, Jack Casady, Lennart Wretlind, Gerardo Velez, Chip Monck, Jeanne Field, John Binder, John Morris, Dale Bell, John Storyk, Lee Oskar, Leon Hendrix, Harry Shapiro and Dr Bob Brown.

For their assistance in liaising with the artists: Cash Edwards, Vanessa Kaukonen, Sri Oskar, Nancy Balik, Judy Somers, Lisa Troland, Brenda Anderson & Bruce Cherry.

For their ongoing support: Durham Prewett, Vicki Prewett, Natasha Prewett, Mitchell Prewett, John Lewis,

Matt Dowling, Timmy Byrne, Anne Leighton, Stuart Coupe, Mick Wall, Belinda Peterson, Rod Peterson, Amelia Peterson, James Hallal, Verity Edris-Peterson, Emran Edris, Emily Prewett, Mal Odam, the Sumner family, all at South Oakleigh College, Chanty & Lynx, Siân Llewellyn, Andrew Massie, and all my students past present & future.

• • •

A Note on the Cover

Cover photograph by Bruce Fleming – an outtake from the *Are You Experienced?* album cover shoot. Jimi is wearing a jacket given to him by Kathy Etchingham.

Lightning Source UK Ltd.
Milton Keynes UK
UKHW020812121220
374971UK00008B/915

9 781895 131536